The Retired Military as Emergent Power Factor in Nigeria

The Retired Military as Emergent Power Factor in Nigeria

J. 'Bayo Adekanye

Heinemann Educational Books (Nigeria) Plc

HEINEMANN EDUCATIONAL BOOKS (NIGERIA) PLC
Head Office: 1 Ighodaro Road, Jericho, P.M.B. 5205, Ibadan
Phone: (02) 2412268, 2410943; *Telex:* 31113 HEBOOKS NG
Fax: (02) 2411089/2413237; *Cable:* HEBOOK Ibadan.

Area Offices and Branches
Abeokuta . Akure. Bauchi . Benin City . Calabar . Enugu . Ibadan
Ikeja . Ilorin . Jos . Kano . Katsina . Maiduguri . Makurdi . Minna
Owerri . Port Harcourt . Sokoto . Uyo . Yola . Zaria

© J. 'Bayo Adekanye 1999
First published 1999

ISBN 978 129 434 5

Printed by Johnmof Printers Limited Ibadan

Dedication

To the memory of my father
James Olaniyi Adekanye (1903 – 1975)
alias James "Akanti" or James "the Accountant"
Who taught me and the three others
That the will to succeed
Can surmount all difficulties.

Foreword

Although treating an art which I never professed may perhaps seem a presumptious undertaking, I cannot help thinking myself more excusable than some other people who have taken its practice upon themselves. For an error in my writings may easily be corrected without harming anybody but an error in their practice may ruin a whole state.

Machiavelli, *The Art of War.*

Preface

The research on which the study is based was completed in 1988, and the manuscript submitted to the publishers in 1989. The first corrected galley proofs were returned in 1991, the contract for the book was signed in April 1993, and the publication was supposed to have been produced and copies out shortly thereafter, that is by late 1993 or latest early 1994. However, due to certain unfortunate circumstances, including the death of the printer originally handling the work, publication of the book got unduly delayed. Otherwise, by now, we should actually be talking of issuing the second edition (with some up-dating of course) of what from all indications, would have been, and still remains, a potentially successful book venture.

Two major interrelated events have taken place since this research study on Nigeria's retired military as emergent power factor was completed a little over ten years ago. First, and the more recent, a retired army general and former head of state, General Olusegun Obasanjo, has come from retirement as well as his subsequent prison sentence to contest for and win the February 27, 1999 presidential elections meant as the last stage in the Abubakar transition from military rule. When retired General Obasanjo is sworn in on May 29, 1999 as scheduled, he becomes the first civilian democratic president of Nigeria's next republic. The presidential elections making this possible, as well as the other preceding election into various state assemblies, state governorships, and National Assembly, were noted for their uniqueness in attracting such a large participation of top retired military generals and their display of sheer influence, new-found wealth, connections with government, "old-boy" networks, organisational skills, and experiences. They are the source of the political power that the top retired generals now command.

The second consideration, not unrelated to the first, is that all previous attempts to restrict the class of retired generals from political participation, including those undertaken by the civilian presidency of Alhaji Shehu Shagari in 1981 and General Babangida's regime in 1987, have proved ineffective in stemming the emergence of the retired military as an elite of power. Recently, in the context of national debates on retired General Obasanjo's qualifications for the presidency, the author has had course to refer the public to the second of the bans, that is contained in the "Participation in Politics and Elections (Prohibition) Decree No.25 of 1987". The author had thought, mistakenly, the ban was still subsisting. Actually, even at the beginning, the particular ban on both the old-breed civilian politicians and the top retired generals placed by the Babangida regime did not look like the kind of restrictive measures that would be easy to enforce or sustain - indefinitely. All the top retired generals as a group and the late Maj.-Gen. Shehu Musa Yar'Adua in particular, were convinced the ban would not last. How could any electoral system prove durable that completely left out a strong and rising new elite such as the retired military? In this, they had been proved right. As it turned out, by December 1991 the ban had been lifted; though when the real transition began in late 1998, the ban's stoutest opponent, retired Maj.-Gen. Yar'Adua, was himself no more around to participate in the process. Much of all this had long been predicted by the author.

Of course, it is impossible for a research study that was completed, and its manuscript submitted for publication, some ten years ago not to be dated as regards some of its basic data, even if the overarching thesis on which it is built still stays solid. For example, some of the retired military business companies, such as the *African Oceans Line* (AOL) established in 1986 in the shipping business as a joint venture originally involving retired Maj.-Gen. Shehu Musa Yar'Adua and Chief M.K.O. Abiola, had since folded up. Some of the major *dramatis personae* in the work might also have died, as definitely the case in respect of the two personalities just mentioned; and names of places, including component state units in the federation, had also changed. But, then, many new retired military-businesses had since been incorporated too, and examples of their interlocking links with the subsidiaries of a number of multi-national companies also multiplied by fold. Other and much more fundamental changes that have taken place in the domain, including the circulation of ranks within the military hierarchy, growth in the size of top military retiree population, as well as increase in the number of "retired officer-gentlemen bankers", can be found treated in the Addendum that has just been written for that purpose. I insisted on the need for the study to be published exactly as originally submitted, while consigning whatever up-dating work one has to carry out to that new Addendum. It is hoped that readers going through the book will appreciate why.

Ibadan,
March 14, 1999.

Contents

Tables

Introduction

In September 1985, the first retired* senior-ranking army officer to hold a cabinet position in contemporary Nigeria, and a retired chief of defence staff, Lt.-General Julius Alani Akinrinade, was appointed the minister of agriculture by the new Federal military government of President Ibrahim Babangida. Under the preceding regime of Major-Generals Buhari and Idiagbon (both now retired), a number of diplomatic postings were made which included the appointment of retired Major-General Joseph Garba as Nigeria's permanent representative at the United Nations in New York; retired Col. Sanni Bello as high commissioner to Harare in Zimbabwe; and retired Rear-Admiral Benson Okujagu, as high commissioner to New Delhi, India.

Lest such appointments be considered a feature distinctive of military regimes only, it should be noted that high-ranking officers out-of-uniform had been similarly engaged politically under the short-lived civilian presidency of Shehu Shagari. For example, the period 1979–83 had seen a notable array of retired military officers going into politics or taking up political positions. Thus, the First Senate of that Second Republic had included in its membership two former senior military officers, retired Cols. Amadu Ali and Garba Musa Dada. Additional two were to be found in the First House of Representatives, namely Lt. J.C. Ojukwu and Lt.-Col. P.C. Amadu. The list of retired officers-turned-politicians included such house-hold names as Brigadier Benjamin Adekunle, the ex-Biafran secessionist leader Odumegwu-Ojukwu, ex-Brigadier U.J. Esuene, and ex-Brigadier George Kurubo; while a number, including two retired Major-Generals, Adeyinka Adebayo and Hassan Usman Katsina, were members of either national or state executives of political parties.

---

*   The adjective "retired", qualifying the term military officers throughout the book, is used interchangeably with "former", as with the prefix "ex-", following the universally accepted usage within this field of study. We do this, though mindful of the nuances maintained in the use of these terms in the vocabulary of contemporary Nigerian politics. We have also not bothered very much to differentiate between those officers" dismissed" from the force and others properly "retired".

By the time the controversial general elections of August 1983 were ended, Nigeria had produced its first elected ex-military, quasi-civilianised state governor in the person of ex-Brigadier Samuel Ogbemudia.

In the meantime, as a result of not just military developments going back to at least 1966 but also certain economic changes experienced in the 1970's, an increasing number of retired senior military officers found themselves appointed to the governing councils or boards of important government agencies, e.g. General I.B.M. Haruna as Chairman of the Council of the Nigerian Institute of International Affairs (NIIA) based at Victoria Island, Lagos. Retired senior military officers became members of boards of directors of the country's governmental commercial corporations, investment companies and industrial concerns. Also, a number of the multi-national companies, forced by the so-called economic "indigenisation" measures of the early 1970's to Nigerianise, began to open their various boards of directors to the highly prominent representation of Nigeria's former "top brass".

As if to complete this picture of growing military-economic linkage, many retired officers have emerged as dominant figures in certain sectors of private business, industry, and agriculture; e.g. the former military head of state retired General Olusegun Obasanjo with his Obasanjo Farms Nigeria Ltd., a multi-million naira poultry business, established at Ota in Ogun State; his immediate deputy in office, retired Maj.-General Shehu Musa Yar'Adua, now part owner of Habib Bank (Nigeria) Limited and of a shipping business concern African Oceans Lines Limited; and former chief of army staff, retired Lt.-General T.Y. Danjuma, whose group of companies called Medafrica Groups Limited based in Lagos runs a thriving shipping and importation business, among others.

Aims and Objectives

The foregoing are the kind of materials that constitute the subject matter of the present book. The major aim or objective of the book seeks to study systematically the growing power and influence of retired military officers in Nigerian society.[1] A number of postulations are advanced in the process. In the first place, the study holds that the traditional concept of civil-military relations in Nigeria as one involving the separation between civil society and military organisation is outmoded, and must be replaced by a new one which views the lines between the two spheres as increasingly blurred. The growing size and role of Nigeria's military retiree population are shown by the study to contribute significantly to the latter.

Besides, increasingly large number of retired military officers is fast assuming pivotal positions within the society, particularly in government and politics, the bureaucracy, the worlds of trade and commerce, business corporations, or companies, and even agriculture, where such retired senior officers develop interests or tentacles at once inter-locking and inter-changeable. Available to these top military retirees are resources like wealth, their ex-military connections, skill, prestige, and experience; and these they exploit to the maximum as bases of new influence.

Even though as yet unorganised politically, pluralistic in their membership, and not that self-conscious as a group, Nigeria's class of military retirees operating through a kind of "old-boy" networks are fast emerging as a new elite of power, whose members considerably influence decision-making regarding major issues of "high politics". Retired top military men may, or may not, be found occupying official, that is visible, decision-making organs within the format of government; nevertheless from the examples broached in the opening of the study, some have indeed come to be. Informally, however, retired top military men are beginning to wield enough actual power and influence to merit being studied as an emergent force in Nigerian society. This is what the present book is all about – the first detailed, scholarly, and systematic study of the role and influence of retired military officers in Nigeria.

Data and Sources

The data on which the book is based were obtained from so many sources, and these we indicate and evaluate as follows. Since the Nigerian military came into political prominence in January 1966, the present author as a specialist in the field has been compiling privately for his own library and research use a register of high-ranking retired military persons circulating in society. This provided us the first and foremost data source for the present study.

That compilation had, in turn, been aided by the use of the *Official Gazette* (of the Federal Republic of Nigeria), generally considered an indispensable source of data for any kind of research on circulation of officers among and within the Nigerian public bureaucracy and military establishment. The *Official Gazette* supplies, among other things, periodic lists of all Federal appointments (recruitments), promotions, retire- ments, and dismissals both civil and military. As regards the essentially military, the law requires that all resignations and retirements, as well as their effective dates, be first published in the army (navy, or airforce) orders and subsequently in the *Official Gazette*. From the various volumes of this Federal publication can be – and were by us – extracted the names of army generals, lieutenant-generals, major-generals, brigadiers, colonels, lieutenant-colonels, and majors, as well as their navy and airforce counterparts, who retired, were retired, or dismissed from active duty from 1966 to 1986. Our analysis of the growth and size of Nigeria's military retiree population benefited immensely from this particular source.

The chapter on the economics of military retirement considers military pension costs as an aspect of military expenditure, though dealing with military activities in the past. As such, it is related to an early piece by the author on "Nigeria Military and Social Expenditures" appearing as one of the chapters of his first book.[2] As with those dis- cussions on Nigeria's military expenditure patterns, our particular analysis of military pension costs presented in this book relied almost wholly on the facts and figures supplied by the *Recurrent and Capital Estimates* (of the Federal Republic of Nigeria). It is an invaluable public source of data for any research work on Nigeria's military expenditures past and present.[3] Of course, in this particular case, the facts and figures so obtained from the *Estimates* had to be supplemented by and cross-checked with other data from the Directorate of Military Pensions sources which also furnished useful information regarding the system of military allowances, benefits, gratuities, and pension or retirement plans.

The bulk of the data used for the study is of biographical nature; and for this we exploited all the available sources that we could lay our hands on, beginning with Dr. S.A. Orimoloye's *Bibliographica Nigeriana: A Biographical Dictionary of Eminent Nigerians* (Boston: G.K. Hall & Co., 1977). Of course, at the time Dr. Orimoloye wrote, there were few top retired military officers recognised as "eminent," which explains why none featured in his *biographical dictionary*. The Daily Times of Nigeria (DTN) annual series, *Nigeria Year Book,* especially beginning from 1977/78 issue and up to-date, proved more useful. For this annual contains regular "who's who" sketches on important Nigerian personalities in various walks of life. These are apart from that *Year Book's* regular section on "day-to-day events" (diary) for any given year, and occasional listing of board members of various government-owned corporations and companies, which we found also useful.

Related to the latter was the special publication edited by James O. Ojiaku and titled *Who's Who in Nigeria 1983* (also by Daily Times. Lagos, 1983). The distinctive feature of this special Daily Times edition of *Who's Who in Nigeria,* as we found, is that it includes the biographies of members of national and states' executives and assemblies after the military disengagement from government in 1979. Of similar value was the Federal Government publication, Nigeria *Who's Who in the Legislature (The House of Representatives) 1979–1983* (Ikoyi, Lagos: Executive Office of the President, Department of Information, Domestic Publicity Division, July 1983). Our chapter on the role of retired military officers in the politics of the Second Republic 1979–83 benefited from consulting these two particular sources, among others.

There is a newly-formed publishing company called the Biographical Centre for Nigeria (or BCN) Limited, Lagos, specialising in the business of biographical compilation, and with its series also titled *Who's Who in Nigeria* . Its first edition covering 1981–82 came out in 1981, the second in 1983, and the third in 1985. We found the detailed profiles provided by the new BCN series an important source of information for our discussions on the corporate links and other inter-locking directorships involving top retired military officers.

The office of the Registrar of Companies, Federal Ministry of Trade and Commerce, is, or rather should have been, a basic source of information for anyone studying ownership and control of registered companies in Nigeria, with which the present study is also partially concerned. However, the author found that office, when he visited it in the late 1986, to have been slightly disorganised, perhaps, understandably, since the Federal Ministry of Trade and Commerce was about to move offices from Lagos to the new Federal Capital, Abuja. So, we could not explore the Office of the Registrar of

Companies for its potential mine of information.

Fortunately, for the kind of data required for the core of the study, and for which the latter source would have been indispensable – i.e. the role of retired military officers in private business and their appointments to or memberships of boards of directors of private companies – alternative and equally reliable sources were available that could be tapped. These included the various *Annual Reports and Accounts* by the country's major companies, including the foreign-based ones, showing the who's who on their boards of directors. *The ICON Nigeria Company Hand-Book* (otherwise called the *INCH*) series, which was started in 1980 and especially the 3rd Edition *ICON Nigeria Company Handbook 1983* jointly produced by ICON (Merchant Bankers) and Jikonzult Management Services Limited, Lagos, proved exceedingly informative. The counterpart of the latter, in the banking business, is the Nigeria Banking Almanac series, a sort of "who's who in banking", particularly, the 1986 edition *Nigerian Banking Almanac 1985/86* published by the Research & Data Services Limited (or REDASEL), Lagos, which we also consulted.

From these last three sources, available in the Library of the Nigerian Institute of Social and Economic Research (NISER), Ibadan, information obtained was invaluable on the activities of some of the country's top retired military officers in various types of private business ventures. We also consulted, and found additional information from, Marie Lawn (ed.), *Major Companies of Nigeria 1980/81* (London: Graham & Trotman Limited, 1980). This book has the additional advantage that its company entries are listed alphabetically allowing any particular company to be located quickly, while its index also categorises various companies by major business activities.

National daily newspapers were another major source tapped for bits and pieces of information on the private lives of retired officers, as well as their occupational and institutional activities after retirement. It is amazing what volume of data one can obtain through perusal of the country's major newspapers, although their use requires considerable circumspection and critical approach, since they are also liable to misinformation and errors. Certainly, it was from newspaper reports based admittedly on government announcements that we got much of the information on intermittent appointments to, or changes in the composition of, boards of various government commissions and parastatals involving the retired military analysed in specific part(s) of the study.

Then, there are the occasional full-page newspaper advertisements by or involving top retired military officers among other Nigerians and their activities or interests, which can be very revealing indeed. To illustrate this point with three examples, when retired General Obasanjo's Temperance Farms Limited, Ota in Ogun State, was to undergo a change of name into what it is now known by, that is, Obasanjo Farms Nigeria Limited – and given the same acronym of OFN as "operation feed the nation" programme which he had helped to launch ten years earlier when he was head of state – it was by public notice placed on page nineteen (19) of the *Daily Times* (Lagos), October 8, 1986.

Similarly, a full-page advertisement placed in a number of Nigerian dailies, including the *Daily Times* and *National Concord* (Lagos) on April 19, 1986, heralded the launching of the African Oceans Lines Ltd., described as "Nigeria's largest independent shipping Company" and jointly owned by retired Maj.-Gen. Shehu Musa Yar'Adua and Chief M.K.O. Abiola, among others.

The third example to illustrate the significance of full-page newspaper advertisements as data source, was on the occasion of the installation of retired Maj.-Gen A.O. Aduloju as a traditional warrior chief "*Jagunmolu of* Ikare land" in Ondo State on Saturday, December 14, 1985, full-page congratulatory messages were placed same day on page seventeen (17) and thirteen (13) respectively of the *Daily Times* and *Daily Sketch* (Ibadan). The former message came from "the Board of Directors and Management of MEGPIN (NIGERIA) LIMITED, Makers of Air-king Air-conditioners." The latter was sent by "the Board of Directors and Management of Fred & Johnson Engineering Co. Limited, Alfreds Enterprises Limited, Long Acres Agro Complex Co. Limited, Flamo Petroleum Nigeria Limited, Alfa Manufacturing Co. Nigeria Limited." Heartily congratulated by both as "Chairman", retired Maj.-Gen. A.O. Aduloju could be presumed to have business links with the different group(s) of companies identified above. The same procedure of information-gathering was applied to many other top retired military officers studied here.

Finally, some personal interviews were conducted with a random sample of retired military officers based in Ibadan and Lagos. A number of the respondents included officers with whom the author had long enjoyed a good rapport. The interviews were designed not just to elicit survey data on various aspects of the subject of inquiry, but also to help correct possible errors of omission or commission to which the author was liable as a "non-insider." The answers, information volunteered on sensitive questions, and frank opinions expressed by those anonymous retired military officers interviewed proved very useful for our data analysis.

Plan of Work

Organisationally, the book is so structured as to cover the major relevant aspects of the subject central to our investigations. Chapter 1 not only details the growth, rate, and size of military retirement in Nigeria, especially at the senior officer level (i.e. army Lt.-Cols and above, as well as their navy and airforce equivalents), it also examines the major factors which explain the phenomenon, specifying in the process some of the important personalities involved.

The second chapter, as its title obviously suggests, looks at the economics of the phenomenon and its costs to society, as reflected in the growth and rate of military pensions and gratuities. In the chapter that immediately follows and titled "military-business complex" (a phrase borrowed from Lt.-General Danjuma, a former chief of army staff and himself now retired), we discus the role of retired military officers in various private ventures, either as contractors to the defence establishment, in retail trade and commerce, large-scale farming, or as newly registered professionals (lawyers, doctors, engineers, architects, etc.).

Chapter 4 analyses the overt political roles of retired military officers, particularly those of them who stood for election to various legislative and executive offices at Federal, State and even Local Government levels, during the civilian era of President Shehu Shagari (1979–83).

Related to the latter is the increase in the number of military men in mufti transferred to other government agencies and public bureaucracy, including external affairs and diplomacy, either as cabinet ministers, diplomats, advisers, re-employed public serv-ants, or executives of various government task-forces or think-tanks. Among them are the retired military officers who seek re-engagement in the teaching service, local government service, and even the judiciary. Details of these can be found in Chapter 5.

Military retirees appointed to the boards of directors of various public enterprises and corporations, including multi-national companies, are discussed in Chapter 6, where we also explore the hypothesis on the increasing linkage between military and industrial elites, including the foreign-based ones, as part of the political power dynamics in contemporary Nigerian society.

Chapter 7 points to the emergence of a new authority vacuum arising from the recent ban on the ex-politicians from participation in politics, and argues that the retired military are among the top contending social groups seeking to take over, if and when the present military administration leaves office.

The concluding Chapter 8 of the study takes off from the last point, while tying together the threads of the various arguments advanced in all the preceding chapters. Of central interest to our discussions here, and indeed to the study as a whole, is the influence that retired military men exert on the country's decision-making process, and how one begins to assess this. The discussions take us through a theoretical analysis of power, and an integrated social sciences method for its measurement.

It is assumed that formal decision-makers occupying organs of government may not always also be the actual wielders of power and influence; that the question of which elites make what decisions within a given political society, when, and how cannot be answered by merely examining the formal occupiers of governmental organs responsi-ble for the decision-making process. Very often we have to unearth the individuals or groups of individuals – in short, the *real* power wielders – who control or influence directly or indirectly the formally recognised decision-makers. Methodologists of comparative politics, especially those of them interested in elite studies,[4] have long considered this point crucial for the determination of which individuals or groups make what decisions in a given political society.

We focus in this study on the retired top military officers as one such emergent power factor in contemporary Nigerian society. Their growing numbers, share of the national budget (via gratuities and pensions), penetration into spheres of civilian activity, role as businessmen and large-scale farmers, membership of boards of directors of major industrial concerns, or involvement with companies or corporations vital to the country's economy, and of course their participation in government and politics: all these have combined to make Nigeria's retired military senior officers a new elite of power who exert influence both from and over the critical decision-making positions which they occupy in society. That is the central contention to whose elaboration and substantiation our present study is devoted.

NOTES

1. The popular press has recently, of course, been full of allusions to this phenomenon, as is clear from the following news-magazine headlines: "21 Years After: Will the Army Ever Go?" *This Week* (Lagos), Vol. 3, No. 3 January 19, 1987; "Obasanjo: Farmer, Leader, Writer," *Newswatch* (Lagos), Vol. 5, No. 2 January 12, 1987; "Retired Generals in Big Business," *New Horizon* (Yaba, Lagos) Vol. 7 No. 8, Aug–Sept 1987; "Military: Time for Reflection," *Hotline* (Kaduna), No. 31, January 25–February 7,1988, among others. But, while generally critical and well written, most of these journalistic pieces by their very nature tend to be rather casual, poorly researched, and unsystematic

2. J. 'Bayo Adekanye (Adekson), *Nigeria in Search of a Stable Civilian-Military System* (Aldershot, Eng.: Gower, & Boulder Co., U.S.A.: Westview, 1981 & 1982), ch. 3.

3. On the latter, see J. 'Bayo Adekanye, "Sources and Methods for the Nigerian Military Expenditure Data: A Research Note," *Nigerian Journal of International Affairs* (NIIA) Vol. 10, No. 1 1984, pp. 88–107.

4. See Roy C. Macridis, *The Study of Comparative Government* (New York: Random House, 1955), pp. 37–38.

1

Nigeria's Growing Military Retiree Population: The Whys and Wherefores

One of the paradoxes of the phenomenon of military retirement in Nigeria, especially in the decade that followed the end of the Civil War in 1970, is that it has come to involve two contradictory categories of servicemen: those who badly want retirement without having it, and those who have retirement without wanting it. At the risk of oversimplification, among the first category may be grouped senior-ranking military officers, who have made enough contacts in government, commerce and industry, banking and finance to be able to set up their own private post-retirement businesses, but who require to have put in the statutory 15 years' active service in order to qualify for full pension benefits, including the initial gratuity payments needed as a post-retirement working capital. Belonging to the second category, on the other hand, are the generality of the rank and file, re-enlisted ex-servicemen, and non-commissioned officers, who, being lower in the military remuneration structure, figure out their post-retirement benefits are not going to amount to much. Haunted by the poverty if not also the drabness that comes with a demobilised life, military personnel of the latter category would like to continue up to old age and possibly die in the service.

Yet the latter members are always the first to be affected in any general demobilisation by national policy, unlike personnel of the first category comprising mostly of high-ranking officers (i.e. Lt.-Colonels and above or their equivalents) whose exodus from the service at a relatively youthful age it is now the goal of national policy to prevent. One of the ways by which the latter is achieved is through constant improvement in officers' conditions of service, while maximising to advantage the bureaucratic bottlenecks, including long delays in processing the retirement applications of this class of personnel. This has not prevented, however, increasing numbers of Nigerian officers among other military personnel from joining the retirement rolls, as we shall soon see. In this first chapter of the book, we document the growth and rate of military retirement especially at the officer level, some of the major personalities involved, and the major factors explaining the trend.

The names of Nigerian servicemen joining the retired rolls are not very difficult to obtain. Even an otherwise casual public source of data like the *Nigeria Year-Book* (published by the Daily Times of Nigeria, Lagos) attempts a compilation of such names, although this particular publication is far from adequate, since it is rarely up-to-date. A much more reliable public source of information is the Federal government's *Official Gazette* periodically giving lists of all Federal appointments, promotions, retirements, and dismissals among others. The law required that all military resignations and retirements as well as their effective dates be first published in the Army (Navy or Air Force) Orders and subsequently in the *Official Gazette* of the Federal Republic of Nigeria. A study of various volumes of this *Gazette* going back to 1960 reveals that before 1966 there were very few Nigerian officers retired; certainly, not more than a dozen were retired during these first six years of the country's independence. But twenty-five years later, there were to be thousands of retirees drawing pensions.

Admittedly, no one knows precisely how many Nigerian military retirees there are, not even the old Military Pensions Assessment Board (M.P.A.B.), now called simply the Directorate of Military Pensions, currently located at No. 21 Ruxton Road, Ikoyi, Lagos. Neither does the pensions section of the Establishments Department under the office of the Head of Federal Civil Service. In a sense, the detachment of the Directorate from the Federal Establishments office in charge of pensions generally has contributed to this lack of good and up-to-date records on how many retirees are actually drawing pensions and/or gratuities.* So has the commonly alleged fraudulent practice whereby many "ghost" recipients are kept on military pensions.

Although we do not know the precise number of Nigerians on the retired rolls, because this information is difficult to obtain given the lack of reliable records on this, we do however have the facts and figures on how much the country had been expending on payments for military pensions since 1966. They can be obtained by combing such a public source as the *Recurrent and Capital Estimates of the Federal Republic of Nigeria,* published yearly by the Federal Information Ministry and based on requisite returns to and from the Federal Ministry of Finance. We also do have available from public source the formula for computing the pensions and/or gratuities payable to retired military personnel. The facts, figures and formula concerned will be found deployed for our analysis in Chapter 2 of the study.

In the meantime, information is not hard to come by on the growth of retirement at the high command level, its rate, and the major reasons for this. One is talking of the changes of the chiefs of staff of the three services (namely, army, navy and air force), their deputies, various service heads, general officer commanders, and other high-ranking officers. The ranks covered range from Lt.-Colonels, Colonel and Brigadier, to Major-General, Lt.-General, and General (for army); or their equivalents, namely

---

* Although, arguably, it has also helped to keep the military pensions affair purely military, excluding all civilians. Under the present arrangement, a civilian working in and retiring from ministry of defence is taken care of by the Establishments office, rather than by the Directorate of Military Pensions. Even the Defence Industries Corporation is regulated by civilian pensions rules.

from Commander, Captain, and Commodore to Rear-Admiral, Vice-Admiral, and Admiral (Navy); and, from Wing Commander, Group Captain, and Air Commodore to Air Vice-Marshal, Air Marshal, and Air Chief Marshal (Air Force). (Table 1.1 shows the comparative rank structure for the officer corps of the Nigerian armed forces.)

Table 1.1   Comparative Rank Structure of the Nigerian Armed Forces: The Officer Corps

ARMY	NAVY EQUIVALENT	AIR FORCE EQUIVALENT
Field Marshal	Admiral of The Fleet	Marshal of the Nigerian Air Force
General	Admiral	Air Chief Marshal
Lieut.-General	Vice-Admiral	Air Marshal
Major-General	Rear-Admiral	Air Vice-Marshal
Brigadier	Commodore	Air Commodore
Colonel	Captain	Group Captain
Lieut.-Colonel	Commander	Wing Commander
Major	Lieut.-Commander	Squadron Leader
Captain	Lieutenant	Flight Lieutenant
Lieutenant	Sub Lieutenant	Flying Officer
Second Lieutenant	Midshipman	Pilot Officer

Information on the growth, rate, and size of retiree population at this high command level has been readily available since the military came into limelight in 1966.

Factors Explaining High Rate of Military Retirement
As already remarked, although the precise figure on the size of Nigerian miliiary retirees as of 1985 is not available, we do know[1] that the raie of military retirement had been high and had shown an ever-increasing trend since 1966. This chapter of the study examines the major factors explaining the growth and rate of military retirement, especially at the senior officer level, detailing in the process some of the major personalities involved. The phenomenon can be explained by fourteen major factors at once chronological and analytical, and these we analyse as follows:

First, there were the many *coups, or counter-coups, including attempted ones* that Nigeria had experienced to-date, namely in January 1966, July 1966, July 1975, February 1976, December 1983, and August 1985.[2] The tendency of such events had been to heighten what this author has elsewhere called the "circulation of ranks" within the military, resulting almost invariably in the forced retirement of many personnel.[3]

Thus, to illustrate by examples beginning from one of the most recent and working our way back to previous ones, the military counter coup of August 27, 1985 ushering General Ibrahim B. Babangida to power not only brought about an immediate change of guards at Federal as well as State levels. But that event also led to the retirement of the then military head of state and his deputy, Generals Muhammadu Buhari and Tunde Idiagbon respectively. They were among the first batch of army officers totalling 42 in all retired within a month of the August 1985 coup. Those retired included Brigadier A. Ahmed; Colonels J.O. Adedipe and /O. Daramola; Lt- Colonels A. Gbadebo, C.F. Ugokwe, A.A.S. Aliyu, J.E. Idachaba, Y. Ibrahim, G.U Ugah, S.A. Olufemi, S.M. Okoh, R.O. Fashina, A. Daodu; as well as 25 majors, and a captain.[4] Other army generals and a brigadier were soon to join the post–1985 coup retired rolls, namely Generals Muhammadu Magoro, Mohammed D. Jega, Solomon Omojokun. Among the first on the navy's casualty list were Commodore Michael Bamidele Otiko, State military governor of Ondo, whose retirement was with effect from November 1, 1985, and Rear-Admiral Oduwaiye, with effect from January 1, 1986. Also retired from the navy following the Babangida coup were: Capt. T.U. Odibo (December 1, 1985), Commodore R.A. Oke (December 1, 1985), Commander J.R.T. Williams (December 1,1985), Commander T. Alabi (December 1,1985), Capt. M.O. Agbe (July 1), Capt. C.W. Ebere (July 1, 1985), Capt. E.E. Nsa (July 1, 1985), Commander O.R. Famuyiwa (December 1, 1985), Capt. F.O Bucknor. and Capt. M. Kentebe (widow of former chairman of the Nigerian Football Association, Edwin Kentebe).[5] Although not publicised until August 1986, all these retirements we associate directly with the aftermath of the August 1985 counter-coup.

One direct consequence of the earlier coup of December 31, 1983, which had toppled the sloppy civilian presidency of Shehu Shagari and returned the military to power, was the retirement of Lt.-Generals G.S. Jalo and M.I. Wushishi; Maj.-Generals R.M. Dumuje, A.R.A. Mamudu, A.O. Aduloju, G.O. Ejiga, J.U. Ekong; Brigadiers S.E. Tuoyo, M.S. Toki, and M.B. Jibril; Colonels J.A. Olubobokun and M.K. Olusanya; Lt.-Colonels A.U. Gombe and F.O. Ossai. In all, from the army alone 185 officers were affected by the December 31, 1983 coup,* although these retirements were not to be announced by the Buhari/Idiagbon regime until January 1985.[6]

While no retirements are known to have followed the counter-coup attempt which had assassinated General Murtala Mohammed on February 13, 1976, a number of the military personnel implicated in that abortive act were executed by firing squad. They included its leader Lt.-Col. Bukar Dimka and the defence chief Major-General I.D.

---

*   However, that this particular list of retirees announced in January 1985 comprised of not just the top army hierarchy, divisional commanders, and other senior-ranking officers, but even junior and petty ones – coupled with the size and timing of the retirement – suggests that the coup of December 31, 1983 could not have been the only cause. The general economic recession in the country, necessitating massive retrenchments in the various arms of the public service, was certain to have contributed, as we discuss towards the end of the chapter.

Bissalla; the remaining senior officers were Colonel D.S. Wya and Lt.-Colonels A.R. Aliyu, Tense, T.K. Adamu, and A.B. Omoru.[7] Obviously, because of their circumstances of leaving the army, akin to being dismissed from the force with ignominy, the legal personal representatives, relations, or dependants of the executed servicemen could not have been paid any pensions and gratuities.

In the wake of the successful counter-coup toppling the nine-year-long regime of Gowon, an *Official Gazette* No. 42 of August 1975 was published stating that General Gowon, all the military governors who served under him, and other top military officers above the rank of brigadier or its equivalent had been compulsorily retired with full benefits in accordance with the provisions of the terms and conditions of service. The senior-ranking officers, in addition to General Yakubu Gowon, who were specifically retired as a result of the July 1975 coup event, included: Vice-Admiral J.E.A. Wey, Maj.-Gen. Hassan Katsina, Major-Gen. David Ejoor (then chief of army staff), Rear-Admiral Nelson Soroh (then chief of naval staff), Brig. E.K. Ikwue (then chief of air staff), Maj.-Gens. R.A. Adebayo and E.O. Ekpo, and Brig. Godwin Ally.[8] The six, senior-ranking military men among the then 12–state governors also retired by the July 29, 1975 event were Brigs. Mobolaji Johnson, U.J. Esuene, Musa Usman, Oluwole Rotimi, Abba Kyari, and Samuel Ogbemudia, Commander Alfred Diete-Spiff, and Col. David Bamigboye.*

Of course, other coup or counter-coup events had brought their own increases and rates of military retirement, the first one of January 15, 1966 resulting in the *de facto* retirement, (detention) of the 32 junior officers and mostly of the rank of majors who were involved.[9] It is true that a number of the latter group were to die in the July 29, 1966 counter-coup, and others while fighting on the "Biafran" side of the Nigerian civil war; and that only two of the surviving officers Second-Lieutenants J.C. Ojukwu and Ozoemena Igbweze were properly retired and therefore qualified for some benefits, four and one years' benefits respectively. The remainder, including Majs. Ganiyu Adeleke and Adewale Ademoyega and Capt. Ben Gbulie were to be dismissed from the armed forces, all with effect from October 24, 1974.[10]

From the foregoing examples, there can be no doubt that coup and counter-coup events both successful and unsuccessful have been among the most important factors responsible generally for the changes in Nigeria's military command structure, and specifically for the growing size of Nigerian military retirees during the period covered by our study. Coups and counter-coups, including attempted ones, therefore, deserve the pride of place accorded to them in our scheme of explanations. (See Table 1.2 for the names of retired military heads of state as well as service chiefs, including dead ones, recorded over the period 1966–1986)

---

*   Apart from Brigadiers Rotimi and Johnson, all these state military governors of the Gowon Regime were dismissed, rather than retired, for an array of misdemeanours centering on probity in public office.

Table 1.2 Retired Military Heads of State and Service Chiefs, 1966 –1986.

(1)   MILITARY HEADS OF STATE & SUPREME COMMANDERS / COMMANDERS IN CHIEF

Aguiyi Ironsi (January – July 1966)
Yakubu Gowon (July, 1966 – July, 1975)
Murtala Mohammed (July, 1975 – February, 1976)
Olusegun Obasanjo (February, 1976 – October, 1979)
Muhammadu Buhari (December, 1983 – August, 1985)

(2)   CHIEF OF STAFF, SUPREME HEADQUARTERS

Babafemi Ogundipe (January – August, 1966)
E.O. Ekpo (August, 1966 – May, 1973)
J.E.A. Wey (May, 1973 – July, 1975)
Olusegun Obasanjo (July, 1975 – February, 1976)
Shehu Yar' Adua (February, 1976 – October, 1979)
Tunde Idiagbon (December, 1983 – August, 1985)
Ebitu Ukiwe (August, 1985 – October, 1986)

(3)   DEPUTY CHIEF OF STAFF, SUPREME HEADQUARTERS

Hassan Usman Katsina (May, 1973 – July, 1975)

(4)   CHIEF OF GENERAL/DEFENCE STAFF

Alani Akinrinade (1980 – 1981)
G.S. Jalo (1981 – 1983)

(5)   DEPUTY CHIEF OF GENERAL/DEFENCE STAFF

G.S. Jalo (Army) (1980 – 81)
Hussaini Abdulahi (Navy) (1980 – 83)

(6)   HEAD OF ARMY/CHIEF OF ARMY STAFF

Yakubu Gowon (January – July, 1966)
Joe Akahan (July, 1966 – July, 1967)
D. Bissala (Acting) (July, 1967 – May, 1968)
Hassan Usman Katsina (May, 1968 – 1971)
David Ejoor (1971 – July, 1975)
T.Y. Danjuma (July, 1975 – October, 1979)
Alani Akinrinade (October, 1979 – 1980)
M.I. Wushishi (1980 - 1983)

(7) HEAD OF NAVY/CHIEF OF NAVAL STAFF
J.E.A. Wey, (March, 1964 – May, 1973)
Nelson Soroh (May, 1973 – July, 1975)
Michael Adelanwa (July, 1975 – October, 1979)
Akin Aduwo (October, 1979 – December, 1983)

(8) HEAD OF AIR FORCE/CHIEF OF AIR STAFF
George Kurubo (1966 – July, 1967)
Shittu Alao (July, 1967 – October, 1969)
E.K. Ikwue (October, 1969 – July, 1975)
John Yissa-Doko (July, 1975 – October, 1979)
A.D. Bello (October, 1979 – December, 1983)

(9) INSPECTOR-GENERAL OF POLICE
Kam Salem (September, 1966 – July, 1975)
Maigari D. Yusuf (July, 1975 – October, 1979)
Sunday Adewusi (October, 1979 – December, 1983)
Etim Inyang (December, 1983 – November, 1986)

A second factor was *the thirty-months' civil war,* which had initially caused the Nigerian army among the other services to expand from its puny size of 10,500 to the astronomical level of 250,000, raising the necessity for some demobilisation in the immediate post-civil war period.[11] Among those affected here were thousands of newly trained recruits, although there is evidence suggesting that many of these would have liked to continue in service rather than be thrown onto the job market. There were also hundreds of ex-servicemen or reservists recalled during those civil war years, who till this day and albeit sporadically continue to be discharged in consequence of a reduction of the establishment of the army, but with enhanced pension and gratuities, thus adding to the population of military retirees. For the pension law, especially its revised version of 1979, permits any officer who had served in any of the armed forces of the Federation during the period May 27, 1967 and January 15, 1970 to count each completed year of "war service" as two years, a period of service exceeding four months but less than a completed year as a full year, and a period of service less than four months as half-a-year, for purposes of computation of pension or gratuity.

Thirdly, linked with aspects of the first two factors already examined, was the retirement in 1971 of most senior-ranking Ibo officers who had betrayed their oath of loyalty and fought for the defeated cause of secession. The retirement of this group of personnel was a sequel to a special inquiry by a Board of Officers, headed by Major-General Adeyinka Adebayo himself now retired. Set up soon after the war in 1970 to probe the *War activities of all ex-"Biafran" officers,* this Board had been charged to make recommendations as to whom among these "lost officers" to dismiss, retire, or reabsorb (wholesale court-martial being ruled out) under General Gowon's post-Civil War policy of reconciliation, rehabilitation, and reconstruction. In the process, some sixteen ex-"Biafran" officers, majority of whom were Ibos, were dismissed with ignominy, many others were allowed back into service. Among those affected by recommendations of the Board of Officers were Philip Effiong, Alexander Madiebo, Patrick Anwuna, David Ogunewe, Patrick Amadi, and Ogbugo Kalu, all Lieutenant-Colonels, in the Nigeria army before the war.

If the foregoing three factors explaining increases in the population of military retirees derive(d) from purely military sources, the fourth that we must look at has its root largely in the economic. It centres on the so-called *oil boom of 1973/74,* and the huge avenues of private commerce and industry that the latter was seen to have subsequently opened up all over the country. This induced many servicemen to want to get out of the armed forces in order to set up their own private businesses, including turning "contractors" to the ministry of defence. The expectation was that one could make it financially better and faster by "going private", as a popular slogan had it in the late 1970s, than remain in public employment and be dependent on salaries. Obviously, for a would-be retiree harbouring this kind of economic motivation, military service no longer had an intrinsic value about it, nor was commitment to asceticism, self-sacrifice, and *esprit de corps* believed any longer to have an intrinsic moral goodness than the pursuit of wealth, profit, and self.

Officers who came to be so oriented would, and did, get out of service the very moment they got the slightest opportunity. The latter included qualifying for sizeable gratuity or/and full pension which would allow them to set up on their own; or getting a business offer, especially in the wake of the Nigerian Enterprise Promotion, (or the so-called "Indigenisation") Decrees of 1972 and 1977, with their multiple promises of business purchases and partnerships.[12] A few such business-oriented officers on retirement were discovered to have in fact been running what turned out to be their post-retirement business even while they were still in service and under proxy, and merely took over those private practices formally and in person following their retirement.

Fifth, there was the military share in the *"Great Purge" of 1975* carried out by the reforming regime of General Murtala Mohammed following the overthrow of Gowon.* The fact that all the Nigerian public services, including the civil services, public corporations and parastatals, universities, the judiciary, the police force, and the armed forces, were affected by the exercise suggests that, for the military, the "purge" is, and ought to be treated as, an analytically separate factor from that of the July 29, 1975 coup itself considered earlier in the chapter. For the army, one of the first indications of the expected shape of things came on August 9, 1975 when the directoral-general of the

---

*   Of course, retirement or dismissal from service for acts of "insubordination," "inefficiency," or "fraud" – what we call here "purge" – has been a continuous feature of the military profession. This is one factor of retirement that recurs now and then, and for which countless examples abound.

armed forces medical service   Brig. O. Austen-Peters, army chief electrical and mechanical engineer Col. K.G. Lawson, and army paymaster-general Col. A.Z. Shielu were summarily retired.[13] But the first massive wave of military "purge" took place shortly thereafter when as many as 244 career officers from the three armed services were retired, breaking down into navy 13, air force 15, and army 216. Perhaps, this was the largest number of Nigerian military personnel ever to be retired in one fell swoop, with 47 out of the army number being actually dismissed.[14]

Of the 169 army officers retired in the November 1975 exercise, 3 were second-lieutenants, 34 first-lieutenants, 74 captains, 43 majors, 15 lieutenant-colonels, and 2 colonels. The names of the two colonels were Anthony Ochefu and S.P. Apolo (the latter retired for reason of inefficiency), while the 15 lieutenant-colonels were given as C.O. Agada, H.B. Greene, U Dikko, S. Gumut, J. Okandeji, M. Malunfashi, J.T. Bendega (for fraud), C.O. Adebiyi (for fraud), T. Oyedele, I. Imadonwiyi (for inefficiency), K. Ojomu, N.A. Anyaru, and G.O. Adenuga.[15]

Although the November 27, 1975 announcement, retiring such a large number of military officers in one fell swoop, was supposed to climax the mass "purge" of all the public services begun since the July counter-coup, in fact bits and pieces of the exercise continued, leading, for example, to the removal of three generals in February 1977, I.B. Haruna, John Obada, and O. Olutoye. The result was that an additional 265 officers are believed to have been affected, bringing the total army personnel retired in the process of the "purge" to a little over 500.[16]

The already mentioned effects of various coups or counter-coups, post Civil War discharges and retirements, and above all the traumatic "purge" of November 1975 and after – all combined to produce yet another factor that had contributed to the swelling of the number of Nigerians on the military retirement rolls. The factor at issue, and the sixth in our analysis, had been the potentially unstable nature of the civil-military environment and its *associated insecurity of tenure*. Even for a profession generally known to be full of risk and uncertainty, paradoxically enough, security of tenure (and of self) can be so highly priced by military men. Where both tenure and self are felt to be insecure, military members tend to contemplate actions which from the recent experience are known to include mutiny, coup, and counter-coup. Now, what we are saying is that this same factor has caused many anxious military members to contemplate leaving the profession both live and honourably, even if prematurely, rather than wait longer than necessary, which may mean being either forced by subsequent events to retire dishonourably, or even killed in service. Retired Major-General David Jemibewon was referring to this factor when, in a recent widely reported newspaper interview, he was quoted as saying "Nigerian generals retire early from the service to avoid being killed or removed with ignominy."[17] Perhaps Maj.-Gen. Jemibewon's statement here, in effect confessing to insecurity of life as a motive for top military retirement, correctly explains why and how he took his own and when he did in 1982.

The only problem with this particular motive is that, because considered somewhat unmilitary, it is rarely verbalised by the affected individuals as a ground for retirement; or, where verbalised by an individual or two, most officers both serving and retired are wont to deny its significance. Certainly, retired Maj-Gen. Jemibewon's August 1986 statement, earlier quoted, is known to have incurred the displeasure of the army chiefs, while provoking angry rejoinders from other fellow retired generals, including I.B.M. Haruna and Joe Garba. Nonetheless, it is possible, and in fact we would like to hazard the guess, that a number of the officers retiring from service on voluntary grounds may have been actuated by this motive of insecurity; that, in short, insecurity of tenure is a hidden factor behind some of the voluntary retirement that the Nigerian military had experienced to-date.

The converse of the factor just treated related to *promotion blockage/supercession in rank,* and the frustration that this brings to otherwise deserving officers, forcing a number of them to retire prematurely from service. It is understood from the recent inside account by retired Major-General Oluleye that one such senior officer affected by this had been Brigadier Godwin G. Ally. The latter was annoyed into retiring from the army following the promotion and appointment of a junior officer to the post of chief of army staff in January 1976.[18] But it is certain that there have been scores of others whose retirement could have been similarly brought about. In other words, retirement due to frustration over either lack of promotion or supercession in rank is widespread and important enough to be considered seventh in our category of factors.

Eighth, the hand-over of political power to civilians on October 1, 1979, meaning *the termination of military rule,* was another major factor that had contributed to the numerical increase in the population of retired military officers. As part of that previous process of return to civil rule or move towards complete de-politicisation, thirty-eight (38) military officers, including three brigadiers, were compulsorily retired on July 6, 1979. Among those retired officers were Brigadiers I.N. Obeya, B.M. Usman, and J.M. Gin.[19] It would be recalled that by the time of the hand-over, there was a generally felt need to have many of the top-ranking officers, who had been holding high political positions, to retire from service either simultaneously with or soon after the military withdrawal into the barracks.[20]

For those generals directly presiding over the liquidation of military rule, it was already clear as of July 14, 1978 that all were going to retire, and retired they did, by October 1, 1979. The list included General Olusegun Obasanjo (the head of the Federal military government and supreme commander of the Nigerian armed forces), Lt.-Gen Theophilus I. Danjuma (army chief of staff), Maj.-Gen. Shehu Musa Yar' Adua (chief of staff, supreme headquarters), Rear-Admiral M.A. Adelanwa (chief of navy), Air Commodore J. Yissa-Doko (chief of air force), and Maj.-Gens. Mohammed Shuwa, J.J. Oluleye, H.E.O. Adefope. Other senior-ranking officers, whose retirement had been influenced by the same consideration, and had taken place at various times between July 14, 1978 and October 1, 1979, were Maj.-Gens Martin Adamu and E.O. Abisoye, successively the general officer commanding the Ibadan-based Second Infantry (now

Mechanised) Army Division.

Ninth, with the return of civilian rule, *considerations of party political affiliation of a subtle kind* emerged as yet another factor affecting the retirement of many a senior officer after 1979. Admittedly, as we detail in Chapter 4 of the study, soldiers generally were constitutionally barred from expressing any open interest in or being associated with party politics. Specifically, soldiers were not supposed to show partiality toward any of the major competing parties that came to be active on the political scene between 1978 and 1983; namely, the National Party of Nigeria (NPN), Unity Party of Nigeria (UPN), Nigerian People's Party (NPP), Great Nigerian People's Party (GNPP), People's Redemption Party (PRP), and Nigerian Advanced Party (NAP).

It would seem, however, that the ruling NPN that succeeded to the military in power did not mind it having senior military officers manifest some interest in and even associate with their own party policies and programmes. After all, in ·a strictly instrumental definition of its role, an army was expected to support the party government that was in power. Thus, what the NPN government objected to was the idea of officers fraternising with others, meaning the opposition parties. Some officers suspected to harbour political views or loyalties, especially if different from those of ruling National Party of Nigeria (N.P.N) government of President Shehu Shagari, were known to have been quietly retired. A few might have been annoyed into taking their retirement on their own, after being removed ;rom key command posts or given redundant desk jobs, and in the process superseded by other officers whom they considered much junior.

Under the latter category must also be included the retirement of the three major-generals George Innih, Olu Bajowa, and Joseph Garba a few months after the return to civil rule, though apparently not so much for their party political views as for fear of their charismatic military personalities. No doubt, the three had been looking forward to further years of military service: the most senior of them, Innih, who had already been heading a full army division, must have been looking forward to the next highest army post open to any deserving professional soldier, that of army chief of staff, while Bajowa and Garba had gone abroad for further professional training. Significantly, all three were retired while on courses of instruction outside Nigeria.

Aspects of the ninth factor just treated had operated with the same effect as the new *federal character* principle of military selection, composition, and promotion that came to be entrenched in the Constitution of the Federal Republic of 1979.[21] Interpreted to mean state – and/or ethnic (or quota) – balancing among the constituent units of the federal political set-up, this principle has been invoked to effect a reduction in the number of representatives of states or/and ethnic groups thought to be predominant, especially at the officer command level. Considerations at once of ethnic – or state-balancing and politics (party loyalty) are generally believed to have contributed to the early retirement of Lt.-General Julius Alani Akinrinade from the army on October 1, 1981. For Lt.-Gen. Akinrinade hails from Ipetumodu, near Ile-Ife, in the former Oyo State of the federation, and belongs to the Yoruba group whose members were by the

Shagari presidency viewed as rather over-represented in the military high command as at 1979/80. Lt.-Gen. Akinrinade was actually promoted the chief of army staff on the eve of civilian restoration in October 1979, but removed within a year from the post, and given the less effective, freshly created, and rather ceremonial job of "chief of defence staff" from which he retired in 1981[22]. Retired Lt.-General Akinrinade's subsequent appointment to Federal cabinet ministerial position under the military presidency of General I.B. Babangida (1985), earlier alluded to, may have been intended as a compensation for that previous raw deal.

Nor has the *relative youthfulness* of much of the post-Civil War senior officer corps been a hindrance to the contemplation of early retirement. If anything, it has accentuated the trend, becoming the eleventh in our list of factors explaining retirement. Many officers are simply induced to leave the service in their prime of life when the officers concerned think they can better physically and more gainfully re-employ themselves than later. Hence the observable phenomenon of Nigerian senior officers, including quite a number on the rank of major-general and above or their equivalents, retiring in their early forties, some even in the late thirties. The following albeit official ages of a select number of army generals, navy rear-admirals, or air vice-marshals at the time of their retirement in 1979, are very instructive: Obasanjo 42, Danjuma 42, Yar' Adua 36, Adelanwa 39, Yissa-Diko 37, Shuwa 40, Oluleye 49, Adefope 53. The ages of others at the time of their retirement include I.B.M. Haruna (1977) 37, Joe Garba (1980) 37, Akinrinade (1981) 42, Martin Adamu (1978) 39, Olu Bajowa (1980) 40.

In a sense, the operation of the 1979 Armed Forces pensions Decree, sub-section 5, paragraph 1, currently regulating retirement policy in Nigeria, has further encouraged the phenomenon of senior officers joining the retired rolls in their early forties. The requirement of the paragraph of the said pension law states that it shall be lawful to require an officer holding a regular commission to retire from the service at any time after he has attained the age of 45 years, subject to three months' notice in writing. This particular stipulation has had the unintended consequence of encouraging many officers to consider 45 or thereabout as the magic retirement age, and to plan for this once they qualify for the nearest highest pensionable emoluments they can possibly collect by about that age. Of course, the phenomenon is not unique to the military, but can be found manifested also in other arms of the public service and, more recently, even the universities.

Admittedly, the ages at which military officers retire are considerably affected by the type of commission they hold. For one thing, the statutory length of service varies as between types of commission, whether "regular combatant", "short-service combatant", "direct regular", "direct short-service". "quartermaster", or "concessional". It also varies as between different ranks within a particular commission. Thus, within the regular combatant commission, as Table 1.3 shows, an army captain is required to retire after 35 years of service; major after 40, lt-colonel after 45, full colonel after 48, brigadier after 50, major-general and lt.-general after 55 and full general after 60. Except for their lack of the rank of full general, officers on direct regular commission have had stipulated for them the same age limits as those for the regular combatant. Officers on quartermaster commission otherwise considered regular officers rarely go beyond the rank of lieutenant-colonel, and are required to retire by 55, although their captains may remain in service until age 48.[23]

The latter considerations point to the twelfth factor that we must mention in our explanation of growth of military retirement in Nigeria namely: normal retirement based on *expiration of period of engagement.* A significant number of Nigeria's military retiree population left the force as a result of this. This includes those personnel considered as over-aged, with the "other ranks" (that is personnel on the rank of warrant officer or its equivalent and below) predominating among this category. Among the senior-ranking army officers retired in 1975 for reasons of this particular kind – officially classified as retirement "for old age" or/and "service no longer required" – may be mentioned Colonel P. Martins, and Lt.-Cols. B. Amusan, D. Bida, E.A. Williams, I.N.E. Onongha, and E.A. Utuk. But there are scores more to be counted from among military officers retired to-date on this ground.

Table 1.3   Statutory Age at Which Regular Officers are Retired on Particular Ranks

	Rank	Stipulated Age
1.	Captain	35
2.	Major	40
3.	Lt.-Col.	45
4.	Colonel	48
5.	Brigadier	50
6.	Maj.-Gen.	55
7.	Lt.-Gen.	55
8.	General	60

Source: Awodola – Peters, O.P. (1982), "On Post-Retirement Employment among Nigerian Army Officers" (B.Sc. Thesis: Department of Political Science, University of Ibadan) Table 1 (A), p. 21.

Next, there are the countless personnel retired as a result of injury during official duty and therefore qualified for *disability* pension. The immediate post-Civil War period saw many retiring for one disability or another. This ground of retirement is placed on the same footing as being retired for medical reason. That the latter is one of the important factors making for retirement can be gauged from the observation that medical fitness is a major qualification for the initial entry into military service. Consequently, military personnel who become unfit for duty are invariably given a medical discharge. There are no large-scale retirements announced in recent years which do not contain some examples of this.

Last but by no means the least, due to *recent economic recession* besetting the nation since about 1982 and more marked after the December 31, 1983 coup, the armed forces have come to share in the new wave of retrenchments (retirements) in the public service, including the civil services, public corporations, public-owned companies, and universities carried out in the name of rationalisation or structural adjustment programmes. Much of the military retirements carried out by the Buhari/Idiagbon regime, particularly of the 185 officers from the army, from the navy, and from the air force, covered earlier in our analysis of the effect of the 1983 coup, also fall under this last factor. But the effects of this factor, far from being already worked out, are still unfolding, and may in all probability last as long as the nation's economic recession persists.

Let us conclude the discussions of the chapter by recapitulating the fourteen major factors that have been responsible for the growing size of retired military personnel in Nigeria to-date. The factors involved are summarised as follows: (1) high circulation of ranks consequent upon the incidence of coups and counter-coups in recent past; (2) some discharge of re-enlisted reservists and new recruits, following the civil war (July 1967 – January 1970); (3) the retirement associated with the 1970 Special Board of Officers inquiring into the activities of ex-"Biafran" officers; (4) the oil boom of 1973/74, "indigenisation", and the economic prospects of leaving public employment and "going private"; (5) the "great purge" of November 27, 1975 and after; (6) exacerbating effects of insecurity of tenure; (7) frustration due to promotion blockage or supercession in rank; (8) retirement timed to coincide with the first return to civilian rule on October 1, 1979; (9) party political considerations and military loyalty; (10) the "federal character" principle enshrined in the 1979 Nigerian Constitution, its orientation to state and/or ethnic balancing, and contribution of this to military retirement; (11) relative youth as a consideration; (12) normal retirement based on expiration of period of engagement; (13) disability, injury, and such other medical grounds as a factor of retirement; and more recently (14) the factor of economic recession. By implication, those factors accounting for the high growth and rate of military retirement just analysed also explain, although not completely, the mounting economic costs of the phenonemon, the next topic in our study.

NOTES

1. Much of this first chapter, along with the second, was completed during the 1982/ 83 session when the author was Visiting Fellow at the Centre for the Study of Arms Control and International Security, Department of Politics, University of Lancaster, England. The manuscript had then appeared as "Growth of Military Retirement and Its Economic Costs: Nigeria (1966–81)," but has since been broken into two pieces, what constitute Chapters 1 & 2 of the present book.

2. The known cases of actual coup and counter-coup occurrences in Nigeria up-to 1987.

3. The concept of "circulation of ranks", borrowed from elite theory (see Chapter 8, was applied in one of my earliest writings in which I had traced the instabilities of comparative civil-military systems of Africa generally among other factors to the struggles within their officer corps, see "Toward Explaining Civil-Military Instability in Contemporary Sub-Saharan Africa: A Comparative Political Model", *Current Research on Peace and Violence* (Tampere), Vol. VIII, No. 3–4, 1978, pp. 195–5.

4. *The Punch* (Lagos), September 20, 1985, p. 1.

5. *Daily Times* (Lagos), August 30, 1986, pp.1, 13.

6. *Daily Times* (Lagos) January 9, 1985, p. 13.

7. Daily Times, *Nigeria Year Book 1977–78* (Lagos: Daily Times Publications, 1977), p. 242.

8. Of these, Brig. Godwin Ally is believed to have decided to leave the force on is own rather than continue under circumstances, which would have meant having to be carrying out instructions and orders from junior officers now catapulted by the 1975 coup event to positions of high command, Cf. James Óluleye, *Military Leadership in Nigeria 1966–1979* (Ibadan: University Press Ltd., 1985). p. 177.

9. See Ben Gbulie, *Nigeria's Five majors* (Enugu: Fourth Dimensions, 1981), p.158.

10. Adewale Ademoyega, *Why We Struck* (Ibadan: Evans 1981), pp. 189–190.

11. J. 'Bayo Adekanye (Adekson), *Nigeria in Search of a Stable Civil-Military System* (Aldershot, Engl.: Gower, & Boulder, Colorado, U.S.A.: Westview, 1981), pp. 10–12.

12. See Chapter 3 on "Military-Business Complex", below.

13. Daily Times, *Nigeria Year Book 1976* (Lagos: Daily Times Publications, 1976), p. 99

14. Daily Times, *Nigeria Year Book 1977-78* (Lagos: Daily Times Publications, 1977), pp. 167-8.

15. According to the Directorate of Military Pensions sources, further specifying the reasons for the inclusion of some of the officers in the November 1975 purge.

16. O.P. Awodola-Peters, "On Post-Retirement Employment Among Nigerian Army Officers", (Department of Political Science, University of Ibadan: B.Sc. Thesis, June 1982), p. 5.

17.   Quoted in *Newswatch* (Lagos), February 23, 1987, p. 27

18.   Same as fn. 8.

19.   Daily Times, *Nigeria Year Book 1980* (Lagos: Daily Times Publications, 1980) p. 437.

20.   To be sure, the effect of this particular factor goes back to the July 14, 1978 order by the then head of state General Obasanjo, reposting all the State military governors to the barracks; and asking the Federal military commissioners to choose between continuing as commissioners only to be retired by the planned hand-over date of October 1, 1979, and returning to the barracks immediately, in the hope of resuming their normal career after October 1, 1979, see J. 'Bayo Adekanye (Adekson), "Dilemma of Military Disengagement", in Oye Oyediran (ed), *Nigerian Government and Politics under Military Rule 1966–79* (London: Macmillan, 1979), pp. 221–2.

21.   See J 'Bayo Adekanye, "The Federal Character's Provisions of the 1979 Constitution and the Composition of the Nigerian Armed Forces", *Plural Societies* (The Hague), vol. 14 Nos. 1–2, 1983, pp. 66–78.

22.   Daily Times, *Nigeria Year Book 1982* (Lagos: Daily Times Publications, 1982) p. 299.

23.   See Awodola-Peters, "Post-Retirement Employment among Nigerian Army Officers" ... op cit., pp.21–25.

2

Economics of Military Retirement

In Chapter 1 of the study, we analysed the growth and rate of military retirement in Nigeria covering the period 1966 to 1986.[1] The present one examines the economic costs of the phenomenon over the same period. It is assumed here that many of the factors shown previously to explain the growth and high rate of Nigerian servicemen concerned going on retirement since the late 1960s – such as the incidence of coups and counter-coups, expansion of the armed forces during the civil war, demobilisation, opportunites for private business induced by both the "oil boom" and the "indigenisation" policies of the 1970s, the return to civil rule 1979–83, military share of retrenchments in the public service due to recent economic recession – also account for, though not fully, Nigeria's growing military pension burden. Other reasons for the latter can be traced to the periodic increases in pay approved for the military among other public servants in the post-1970 era, meaning the rises in personnel costs, and the upward revision of military pension conditions or benefits that invariably accompanied such pay increases.[2]

Thus, the exigency of the Civil War and the need to motivate the fighting men and women led to the promulgating of the Pensions and Gratuities (War Service) Decree No. 49 of 1969. In the aftermath of the Adebo Award of 1970/71 was enacted the Military Pensions (Amendment) Decree No. 18 of 1972. The Udoji Awards of 1974 and their military extensions became reflected in the Military Pensions (Amendment) Decree No. 13 for 1975. The enactment of Military Pensions (Disability Provisions) Decree No. 2 of 1976 came in the wake of the abortive Dimka counter-coup and its immediate aftermath. Consolidating these and all other previous enactments dealing with pensions, war pensions, and disability benefits for members of the armed forces came the Armed Forces Pensions Decree No. 103 of 1979, whose commencement was back-dated to April 1, 1974. The last of these enactments is of further interest to us here, being the regulation more or less currently operating in Nigeria. We proceed to highlight aspects of the said enactment as a step toward estimating the military pensions burden of Nigeria to-date.

Computation of Payable Pensions and Gratuities

For purposes of computing the pensions and gratuities payable to retired servicemen (see Table 2.1), and what cost Nigeria had been incurring on this particular expenditure heading, the circumstances of the retirement of the servicemen concerned must be taken into account. Generally, where a serviceman is dismissed (i.e. removed from service on the ground of inefficiency, fraud, and gross misconduct considered unbecoming of the military man), he forfeits any pension or gratuity under the 1979 military pension law. Retirement proper, on the other hand, may be voluntary or compulsory as we have previously shown, but for either to qualify for full pension benefits (meaning both pension and gratuity), the officer to whom it concerns must have completed not less than 15 years of continuous service. Where an officer is compulsorily retired, either for the purpose of facilitating improvements in the organisation of the armed forces or on medical grounds, if the officer has served for no less than 10 years but less than 15 years, he is entitled to only gratuity. If a compulsorily retired officer has served for a minimum of 3 years but less than 10 years, he is entitled to an *ex gratia* gratuity calculated on pro-rata basis at the rate of 100% per every completed year of service under the military pensions formula.

An other rank, meaning any military person on the rank of warrant officer or its equivalent and below, including the recruit, also qualifies for full pension on retirement, provided he has completed 15 years' continuous service; or if having been re-engaged after 10 years' continuous service, he is subsequently discharged in consequence of a reduction of size of the armed forces. A retiring other rank, who does not satisfy those service conditions, and is therefore not qualified for full pension, may be granted only a gratuity, provided the person has completed not less than 10 continuous years, as specified in the appropriate column of the pensions formular already cited.

There are provisions also for families on survivor benefits under section 7 of the Armed Forces Pensions Act (1979), stipulating the pension and gratuity payable to legal personal representatives, relations or dependants, *for life* in the case of wife/wives not re-married, where a serviceman dies in service; and under section 8, where a serviceman, during an active service, dies as a result of injuries received in the course of his or her duties, without his or her own default. Of course, the particular military pensions rule just cited is not a new one, but has been long-standing, proving beneficial to the legal

Table 2.1:   **Formula for Calculating Pensions and Gratuities Based on Percentage of Final Salary, Nigerian Armed Forces (1979)**

	GRATUITY PAYABLE		PENSION PAYABLE	
Years of Service	Officers %	Other Ranks %	Officers %	Other Ranks %
10(a)	100*	100	—	—
11	110	110	—	—
12(b)	120**	120	—	—
13	130	130	—	—
14	140	140	—	—
15	100	100	40	40
16	110	110	42	42
17	120	120	44	44
18	130	130	46	46
19	140	140	48	48
20	150	150	50	50
21	160	160	52	52
22	170	170	54	54
23	180	180	56	56
24	190	190	58	58
25	200	200	60	60
26	210	210	62	62
27	220	220	64	64
28	230	230	66	66
29	240	240	68	68
30	250	250	70	70
31	260	260	72	72
32	270	270	74	74
33	280	280	76	76
34	290	290	78	78
35	300	300	80	80

*   (a)   For ex-servicemen affected by Decree No. 13 of 1975 only.
** (b)   For colour servicemen.

Source: Armed Forces Pensions Decree (now Act) No. 103, 1979, *Official Gazette of the Federal Republic of Nigeria,* Vol. 66, No. 48, September 29, 1979, pp. 795–806.

personal representatives, relations or dependants of many Nigerian officers and men known to have been killed on duty in the recent past.[3] The current 1979 military pensions law ends with stipulations on various categories of disability retirements, and a complex of formulae for assessing the pensions and gratuities payable under each.

There is, however, both an upper and a lower limit to the pension payable to an officer or other rank under any circumstances. The total pension granted under the 1979 law cannot exceed 80% of the highest pensionable emoluments drawn by one at any time in the course of one's military career. The minimum may not also be less than ₦360 per annum. The latter minimum pension stipulated by the 1979 Act as payable to a retiree might have been slightly increased, during the Shehu Shagari civilian presidency, as a result of the salary increase from the so-called "Shagari award" approved for the other ranks. But it has not been possible to ascertain this.

On the whole, the retirement benefits that are payable to those personnel completing 15 years of active service are collected after leaving the service; the gratuities, or lump-sum benefits, almost immediately; and the pensions, collected monthly, and throughout the retired life. As regards the pensions proper, the benefits collected here can be calculated as equal to *twice the years spent in service plus ten and divided by hundred (and up to a maximum of 80%) times the annual basic military pay attained at the time of retirement.*[4]

Symbolically, the pension benefits payable under the 1979 Nigerian formula can be summarised as follows:

$$\left[\left(\frac{2x + 10}{100} \right) \ \dots 80\% \right] \ \text{₦SA}$$

where x = the length of service measured by number of years spent
                   on active service,
and ₦SA = military salary in Nigerian *naira* at the time of retirement.

Thus, a Nigerian military officer or other rank retiring after 15 years of service receives annually an amount of 40% of his annual basic pay at the time of retirement; a soldier serving 20 years receives annually an amount equal to 50% of his annual basic pay at the time of retirement; and so forth, up to a maximum percentage multiplier of 80%. From the equation given, it is obvious that no military person is allowed to claim pensions benefits for length of service in excess of 35 years, since two times the latter figure plus ten divided by a hundred equals exactly the maximum percentage multiplier of pensions benefits allowable.

With the formula just given, and using the 1981 officer salary scale (see Table 2.2), it should not be difficult at all to find out the actual pensions benefits being monthly drawn by generals like Obasanjo, Yar' Adua, Danjuma, and Shuwa who retired in October 1979, provided one knows the date of their initial commission, which we do.[5]

Also, using the formula for gratuity calculation that one finds attached to the 1979 pensions law, it is easy to determine how much gratuities, or lump-sum payments, these generals among other retirees were entitled to, and had processed for themselves immediately they left the service.

Of course, the above-mentioned are not the only benefits that senior-ranking military retirees receive. Although the 1979 Armed Forces Act does not mention them, retiring servicemen are known to retain many of those fringe benefits distinctive of the military compensation package enjoyed when they were in service, such as free medical attention, free education for servicemen's children, and some exemption from certain taxes, particularly duties.[6] At the same time, officers who retire at the rank of major-general or its equivalent and above, and especially those who once held either high political offices (viz retired military heads of state) under military rule, or command posts (including chiefs of army staff), but subject to certain conditions,[7] continue to enjoy the benefits of free drivers, personal servants, ADCs, batmen, cook stewards, and gardeners paid for at Federal public expense. These benefits were part of the improved service conditions specified for the top army officers under the "post-military" presidency of Alhaji Shehu Shagari.

In fact, according to the revised 1981 conditions of service, a four-star general retiring from the Nigerian army, is entitled to a general's salary for life (rather than pension), and car loan, in addition of course to all of the above-enumerated benefits. But since these other fringe benefits and related expenditures are normally accounted for in any analysis of other constituents of Nigeria's recurrent defence spending,[8] they may be omitted in the computation of pensions cost here so as to avoid double counting.

For the other ranks, however, such allowances are factored into the calculation of that portion of their pensionable emoluments referred to in the Armed Forces Pensions Act 1979 as the "free services element" (composed, by definition, of free facilities such as furnished lodging, fuel and light, personal services, rations, clothing and medical attention), the estimated value of which was fixed at ₦200 under the 1979 pension law.

Table 2.2:   Salary Scale for Nigerian Army Officers 1981 (Revised) in ₦ (Nigerian naira)

Ranks	*Annual Rates*						
Cadet	1,200	1,506	1,620				
2–Lt.	3,300						
Lt.	4,500	4,680	4,860	5,040	5,220	5,400	5,580
Captain	5,820	6,000	*6,180	6,360	6,540	6,720	6,900
Major	7,260	7,440	7,620	7,800	7,980	8,160	8,340
Lt.-Col.	8,676	8,916	9,156	9,396	9,636	9,876	10,116
Colonel	c10,344	10,584	10,824	11,064	11,304	11,544	11,784
Brigadier	s11,856	12,096	12,336	12,576	12,816	13,056	
Maj.-Gen.	14,159						
Lt.-Gen.	15,420						
General	16,260						

*   Entry point for Medical, Dental Officers, Accountants, Professional Architects.
c =   Entry point for Consultants (Medical)
s =   Entry point for Senior Consultants
cc =   Entry point for Chief Consultant

Source: Official Gazette of the Federal Republic of Nigeria

Cost of Military Retired Pay

The expenditure figures on payments for military pensions and gratuities are published annually in the Federal government publication titled the *Recurrent and Capital Estimates of the Government of the Federal Republic of Nigeria.*[9] Facts and figures on how much the country had been expending on payments for military pensions since 1966 can be obtained by combing this invaluable public source.

Expenditures on military pensions and gratuities can be found in various issues of that publication charged on and paid out under a special expenditure head labelled the "Consolidated Revenue Fund of the Federation", whereas the recording of other recurrent and capital military expenditure is done separately and under the expenditure heading of "ministry of defence". This procedure, while considered prudent as well as sound accounting, tends to mask two critical points of interest to us here. The first is that military retirement costs are in fact part of the recurrent defence expenditures a society incurs, although the payments in this case are not current, but deferred, payments meant for services rendered in the past. The second is that, considered as part of recurrent defence expenditure and in comparison with other items on the recurrent list, military pension and gratuity costs emerged after 1970/71 as one of the fastest growing components, and indeed the second greatest, of recurrent military expenditures, exceeded only by military emoluments and allowances for most of the fiscal years covered in the study.

Table 2.3 gives the figures of expenditures on the pensions and gratuities for the Nigerian armed forces as compared with those for other Federal establishments, including the civil service, covering the 21 years period 1966/67–1987. Of these, the figures for the first five fiscal years 1966/67 – 1970/71 are actual expenditures, while the rest are appropriations approved (or provisions) for respective fiscal years.[10] Analysis of the figures shows a generally increasing trend in Nigeria's expenditures on military pensions and gratuities. From the moderate level of ₦474,888 in 1966/67, and dipping slightly during the inter-Civil War years, pensions cost rose to the astronomical level of ₦9.0m in 1971/72 and then much higher still to ₦100.0m in 1981. The figures just quoted represented 16.2%, 41.7%, and 52.6% respectively of total Federal expenditures on pension and gratuities.

There was to be a further increase to an all-time high of ₦150.0m in 1983, and was to stay at the same level in 1984 and 1985; although in relation to the total Federal pensions and gratuities, the latter expenditure figure represented only 48.5%, 48.4% and 43.9% respectively, that is slightly lower than the military share of the total 1981 pension cost. The three rather general and most important factors explaining this rising trend of expenditure on military pensions and gratuities have already been suggested in the chapter, and relate to the numerical expansion of the Nigeria military establishment, growth of the military retiree population, and increase in military personnel costs.

But there are other, and more specific, causes that one can adduce by examining the high-lights of this rising trend of military pensions cost. We refer not only to the figure for 1966/67 and 1971/72 already quoted, but also the approved estimates of ₦20.0m for 1972/73, ₦30.0m for 1975/76, ₦50.0m for 1977/78, ₦60.0m for 1978/79, and ₦100.0m for 1980, the latter set of figures representing 54.3%, 54.2%, 65.0%, 63.9% and 60.2% of total Federal pensions cost. 1966/67 was the first fiscal year of the military in government; it naturally saw improvement in pensions benefits for the armed forces; it also saw the first wave of massive military retirement. All this is reflected in that year's military expenditure.

The 1971/72 figure reflects the increased cost of pensions benefits going both to military personnel retired on grounds of disability or injuries soon after the Civil War and to families of deceased military personnel. Associated with the 1972/73 figure were the Adebo and subsequent salary awards of the previous year, and the increased personnel expenditures, including pension costs, which accompanied those awards. The approved estimates of 1975/76 and 1976/77 reflected the increases not only in personnel cum retirement costs brought about by the Udoji and other related salary awards of 1975, but also the largest military retirements that followed the overthrow of General Gowon's regime.

The fiscal year 1978/79 saw the last budget exercise by the Obasanjo military regime before leaving office; the year also saw the pension vote being substantially increased in gross terms to take care of the top-ranking military officers retiring simultaneously from political power and active service, under the enhanced benefits of the Armed Forces Pensions Decree (now Act) No. 103 of 1979, promulgated as an extraordinary measure by General Obasanjo exactly two days before leaving office. The next were the already mentioned salary increases introduced under the new civilian presidency of Shehu Shagari from the 1975 salary grade levels:[11] resulting in an across-the-board increase of ₦300 per annum for all categories of officers, as well as considerable pay increases (the so-called "Shagari awards") for the other ranks. The latter was intended as an equalisation of, or rather to counter-balance, the national minimum wage demands of the Nigerian Labour Congress (N.L.C); the former was military officers' own share of new pay increases for all public employee, including the police, civil servants, and university lecturers wrenched from the Shagari government soon after taking office.

Table 2.3   Rising Economic Costs of Military Retirement, 1966–87

		Military Pensions & Gratuities N	Total Federal Pensions and Gratuities N	Military % of Total Federal
	Fiscal year			
	1966/67	474,888	2,940,347	16.2
Actual	1967/68	154,592	7,340,428	2.1
Expendi-	1968/69	205,006	7,020,474	2.9
tures	1969/70	142,324	6,585,782	2.2
	1970/71	155,036	7,021,434	2.2
	1971/72	9,000,000	21,600,000	41.7
	1972/73	20,000,000	36,850,000	54.3
	1973/74	20,000,000	36,850,000	54.3
	1974/75	20,000,000	36,850,000	54.3
	1975/76	30,000,000	55,275,000	54.2
Approved	1976/77	30,000,000	55,275,000	54.2
estimates	1977/78	50,000,000	76,900,000	65.0
	1978/79	60,000,000	93,900,000	63.9
	1979/80	55,000,000	93,900,000	58.6
	1980	100,000,000	166,720,290	60.2
	1981	100,000,000	190,000,000	52.6
	1982	100,000,000	245,290,500	40.8
	1983	150,000,000	309,435,750	48.5
	1984	150,000,000	309,755,750	48.4
	1985	150,000,000	342,457,340	43.9
	1986	150,000,000	367,700,180	40.8
	1987	170,000,000	616,620,520	25.9

Source: Relevant issues of the *Recurrent and Capital Estimates of the Government of the Federal Republic of Nigeria* (1966/67–1988), under the "Consolidated Revenue Fund of the Federation" heading of various recurrent expenditures.

These military salary increases, coupled with the continuing retirement of many senior-ranking officers between 1979 and 1981, have meant an even greater military personnel expenditure cum pensions cost, and the 1980 and 1981 figures in Table 2.3 partly reflect this. The further rise in retirement expenditure to the new high of 1983 was largely due to a combination of two factors: the depression in the nation's economy which persists up to the end of our period of study; and the new wave of military coups, including those of December 31, 1983 and August 27, 1985. Both events brought about more reductions in the size of not just the armed forces but the public service as a whole and resulted in further increases in budgetary outlays to take care of the personnel so retrenched. Hence, the allocations of ₦616.6m to total Federal pensions and gratuities in 1987, of which ₦170.00m were meant as military share, both being to-date the highest allocations ever made to these expenditure items in Nigeria's fiscal history. The pensions and gratuities costs as well as their military components are expected to jump even further after 1988, with the implementation of the so-called "elongated salary scheme for the public service" newly introduced by General Ibrahim Babangida's administration. Consideration of the effects of the latter, however, falls outside our period of study.

NOTES

1. Chapter 2 is an enlarged version of this author's article "Economics of Military Retirement in Nigeria, 1966–1983: A Research Note," (Department of Political Science, University of Ibadan: unpublished paper, 1983).

2. J. 'Bayo Adekanye (Adekson), *Nigeria in Search of Stable Civil Military System* (Aldershot, Engl.: Gower, & Boulder, Colorado, U.S.A.: West View, 1981), pp. 55, 58, 72–7, 192, 138–9.

3. Including officers and men killed in the January 15, 1966 coup (such as Brig. Maimalari, Col. Kur Mohammed, Lt.-Col. Pam, Lt.-Col Largema, Lt.-Col. Unegwe); in the July 29, 1966 counter-coup (Maj.-Gen. Aguyi Ironsi, and Lt.-Col. Francis Adekunle Fajuyi); the civil war of June 1967 – January 1970 (literally innumerable); in the February 13, 1976 counter-coup attempt (Gen. Murtala Mohammed, and Col. Taiwo among others); and in the December 31, 1983 coup (whose chief casualty was Brig. I.A. Bako).

4. Cf & Ct. this Nigerian formula for calculating military pensions with the American, as given by Richard V. Cooper *Military Manpower and the All-Volunteer Force* (Santa Monica, Calif.: Rand, September 1977), pp. 373–4.

5. See Robin Luckham, *The Nigerian Military 1960–1967* (Cambridge, Engl.: The University Press, 1971), pp. 343–46.

6. Of course, such fringe benefits are not peculiar to Nigeria, but general to the military the world over, and presumably derive from the uniqueness of the profession *qua* profession and the great harzards to life associated with it.

7. Top retired military officers including the commander in chief, chief of defence staff, chief of army staff, chief of naval staff, chief of air staff, and their various deputies, who hold the rank of a four-star general, are given certain special retirement benefits or privileges, provided such retired officers do not take up other appointments likely to be paid from public funds, or go into partisan politics. These were part of the revised terms and conditions of service approved for Nigerian army officers by the Shagari Presidency in 1981.

8. See J. 'Bayo Adekanye, "Sources and Methods for the Nigerian Military Expenditure Data: A Research Note," *Nigerian Journal of International Affairs* (N.J.I.A) Vol. 10, No. 1, 1984, pp. 88–101.

9. Apparently relying on returns from three Federal agencies: that is, the ministries of finance and establishments as well as the directorate of military pensions, or what used to be called the military pensions assessment board (MPAB).

10. Although the figures for the period 1970/71–87 shown on Table 2.3 are marked as 'approved estimates,' they are as good as 'actual expenditures.' In any case, the fact that pension appropriations go into the so-called Consolidated Revenue Fund of the Federation means that once appropriated, such resources are foregone by the

society, and cannot be used for other purposes than as specified, namely for military pensions only.

11. For the latter, see Adekanye, *Nigeria in Search of ...*, op. cit., pp. 73–76

3

The Military-Business Complex

The term 'military-business complex' was coined in 1978 by Lt.-Gen Theophilus Yakubu Danjuma,[1] then Chief of Army Staff under the military government of General Olusegun Obasanjo, both of whom have since retired. By the term, Lt.-Gen Danjuma was referring specifically to that section of the Nigerian business class — call it the transformed 'emergency contractors' from the Civil War years — upon which the military establishment had long depended for the procurement of its recurrent supplies, particularly fuel, food, uniforms and boots, furniture, the importation of arms, ammunition, and other equipment, and the construction of various capital projects, including barracks.[2]

The term 'military-business complex' is being broadened here to depict the complex of increasingly interlocking interests among representatives of the military establishment and private business in general, including businessmen specialising in defence contracts and procurement, and the recent contributions of the growing class of retired military officers in particular to the development of this phenomenon. We devote this third chapter of the book to analysing the phenomenon, its many dimensions, as well as operations.

1. Trend of (ex-) Military Involvement in Business

The tendency of military and business to become increasingly involved with each other has, since the Nigerian Civil War, reached a new point of articulation or explicitness. So much so that it is no longer realistic to regard the two as separate or distinct worlds. Time was, however, when military and business were viewed as existing in two separate or distinct worlds of their own. For example, up to 1966, senior army officers tended to consider 'business', coupled very often with 'politics', as a dirty kind of pursuit, characterised by excessive individualism, and unbecoming of the 'officer gentleman'.[3]

I suppose those pre-1966 views, regarding the activities of the businessmen as inconsistent with the character of an officer and a gentleman, were influenced both by British colonial legacy and the elaborate honour concepts derived from Western Europe's military feudal past.[4] Of course, the antipathy of the military toward businessmen had its own underlying self-interests. Being at the time economically poorer, professional soldiers were unable to equal the "conspicuous waste" of wealth of the *nouveaux riches,* and therefore needed something which would make them seem apart from and even superior over other rising elite groups or classes. That something, seized upon by professional soldiers to give them a striking trait as a distinct social group, was "honour". For their part, the Nigerian businessmen did not consider the defence sector an economically worthwhile area to invest in, but one unnecessarily restrictive of profit, and generally retardant of commercial and industrial growth. At the same time, the military profession tended to have been looked down upon by the intelligentsia, bureaucrats, and even the politicians as an inferior profession compared with the other professions.

But with the coup of January 15, 1966, and the consequent assumption of political power by the military, the old military versus business antipathy began to erode to the point that today the relations between the two are of mutual dependence, if not fusion, but certainly less of conflict or separation.

For one thing, the take-over of political power by the military also entailed the assumption by the latter of the major role of economic managers. With this began a process of "bridging that very dichotomy between the means of destruction and the means of production" through what Professor Ali A. Mazrui elsewhere aptly describes as "economization of the military" or better still "the *embourgeoisement* of the old *lumpen-militariat.* "[5]

That process saw the soldiers, by now turned rulers, take on additional functions in the industrial field as workers, managers, and owners; while completely replacing many of the top civil bureaucrats as government representatives on the boards of directors of various public corporations and State-owned companies (on the latter, see Chapter 6). In the private sector, the coming of the military to power brought soldiers into greater contacts with the world of business, including contractors, suppliers, traders, merchants, commissioned agents, and financiers. However, the emergent links between the military and private business did not become obvious until after the Civil War' 1967-70.

On the face of it, the operation of a "war economy"[6] during the latter period meant that all other interests, including those of private business, were supposedly subordinated to the war needs or exigencies. The quarter-master general's office, at the defence headquarters, was supposed to have monopolised the war business, being the military department statutorily charged with providing quarters, clothing, rations, ammunition, fuel, and transportation for troops. In actual fact, the war situation forged a new relationship of mutual dependence between the warlords, including field commanders, and the new 'emergency contractors' or suppliers, including arms dealers, thrown up by the war.[7] The acute needs for arms and ammunition, food and medical supplies, and transportation requisitions made the war-time military to be appreciative of and considerably dependent on the contributions of businessmen among others towards the war effort; especially since most of such supplies had to be financed by short-term borrowing from domestic sources through issuance of Treasury Bills and Treasury Certificates among other measures.[8] On the other hand, the new 'emergency contractors' awoke to the potentials of an increasingly large and profitable defence market and how their business as well as profit margin depended on it.[9] The result was the shattering of the old hostilities and the forging of a new economic *nexus* between the military and businessmen.

Admittedly, there were practically no retired military officers of significance involved in those military-business transactions of the civil war years, in part because only few military officers were on retirement at the time. But by the mid-1970s, a number of retired military officers could be counted among the class of transformed "emergency contractors" doing business with the defence ministry and other branches of government, including the various ministries of works and housing at Federal and State levels. For the mid-1970s which saw the first massive wave of military retirement also coincided with the era of huge public investment in building and construction programmes under the Third National Development Plan 1975–90, although begun from the Second National Development Plan 1970–74 period.

The first major area of private business venture for the retired military, however, was not in building and construction per se, but in real estate, although the two were inter-related. The sudden and astronomical increase in the size of the armed forces had created an acute problem of barrack and other accommodation shortages. At the same time, for countless civilians whose homes had been damaged during the war, there was the critical need to provide shelter as part of the immediate post-war rehabilitation programme. As a short-term solution to both problems, the government recoursed to the renting of private buildings mostly for the armed forces personnel spread across the federation, but also for some of the affected civilian population in the former Mid-West and Eastern parts of the country.

Thus, it was that many interested Nigerians whether in the private sector or public employment, both civilian and military, serving and retired, came to be involved in the business of procuring and renting houses and housing estates to the government at the Federal as well as State levels. In time, the real-estate business was to become a very big and lucrative business; with a few of the retired military officers in the business being actually involved in managing and directing this themselves, and many others engaging the services of professional estate managers, agents, or brokers to run the business for them.

Distributorships were the second major area of private business activity that attracted the interests of initial waves of retired military officers. The activity involved the wholesaling of essential goods, both imported and domestically produced, ranging from building materials such as cement, iron rods, and roofing sheets, through consignments of beer and soft drinks, and other food items like flour, milk, sugar, and rice, to motor vehicles, particularly cars. The structure of the Nigerian economy, characterised as it has been by chronic shortages of essential commodities even in the midst of plenty, has long made the sole agency system of trade in such commodities, and their bulk purchase and supply a money-spinning business indeed. Distributorships have also always been a cheap and convenient activity whose operation requires little or no skill, minimum or no direct supervision. Like the real-estate business noted previously, distributorships could be and were often run as a 'sideline', even while their owners whether in or out of service, carried on their other functions for which they were chiefly or officially employed.

Reference was made in Chapter 1 of the study to the "indigenisation" regime of 1972-77, and the attractive opportunity that the latter created for Nigerians either to purchase some of the nationalised businesses or go into (very often multiple) partnerships with the alien entrepreneurial class. The enterprises covered mostly business activities either exclusively reserved for Nigerians (e.g. road haulage, passenger and municipal bus services and taxis, bakeries and wholesale distribution of local manufactures, and other locally produced goods) or requiring not less than 60% equity participation by Nigerians (e.g. banking and insurance, construction industry, furniture making and interior decoration, mining and quarrying). The enterprises could be found listed under Schedule I & II of the Nigerian Enterprises Promotion Decree of 1972 and its Amendment of 1977.[10] The era of indigenisation coincided with the period of the so-called petroleum boom, with its huge avenues for profitable trade and commerce, and when 'soldiers and oil' combined in the transformation of Nigeria.[11]

The indigenisation policy was scarcely completed and its consequences fully worked out when the ambitious Third National Development Plan 1975-80 was launched, opening additional prospects for indigenous entrepreneurship, particularly in the building and construction field. For although it had completely banned private entre-preneurs both indigenous and foreign from enterprises connected with security printing cum minting as well as defence industries, the Third National Plan encouraged foreign private enterprises to come into partnerships with indigenous interests to set up industrial ventures, particularly for major exports, engineering and basic industrial chemicals. Even in such basic industries as crude mining, gas gathering and liquefac-tion, though not necessarily in down-stream petro-chemical industries, the Third National Plan insisted on the Federal government merely having majority shares.[12]

That was the economic environment in which the first massive wave of retirements took place in 1975. As previously remarked, such economic conditions were already inviting for serving military men, and saw many members voluntarily taking an early retirement in order 'to go private'. It was a period not only for acquiring, or setting up, and registering all sorts of businesses, but also entering into various partnerships with hitherto alien-controlled companies (including the Lebanese and Indian) operating in the country; while privileged Nigerians both in the private sector and public service came to acquire substantial shares in the Nigerian subsidiaries of a number of the multi-national corporations (MNCs).[13] But the said economic conditions also opened up areas of joint-industrial ventures with foreign technical partners. Along with the Nigerian business class, many military officers both serving and retired, as indeed their civilian bureaucratic counterparts, benefited from those government measures aimed at expanding the extent of indigenous participation in business establishments.

Meanwhile, there were those retired military officers with prior experiences, links, or interests in the area of defence procurements and supplies, who sought to exploit these by setting up and registering as contractors to the ministry of defence. Such retired officers now turned defence contractors were composed of two groups. First were those joining the ranks of transformed emergency contractors and suppliers earlier noted, and who must have been attracted into the defence contracts business by the sheer *naira* volume of defence orders for goods and services especially in the building and construction field, which was admittedly stupendous. Under the category belonged the over sixty or so agents and representatives of companies involved in the massive importation, what became known as the 'cement armada', into the country that took place between 1974 and 1975.[14] Then, there were those retired top military officers for whom doing business with the defence ministry was simply a way of making use of their acquired expertise in a post-retirement pursuit not markedly different from what they were used to.

A few branched off into the import/export business, a broad category that included such activities as shipping, operation of private jetties, clearing and forwarding, container service and warehousing. The petroleum industry, of course, particularly those aspects relating to exploration services, marketing, and distribution, including the running of petrol stations, also attracted the interest of a number of retired military officers. So did the consultancy services business, banking and insurance, especially the former, some manufacturing and industry.

Finally, since the launching of the national food production programme otherwise called 'Operation Feed the Nation' (acronymned OFN) in 1976, followed shortly after with promulgation of Land-Use Decree in 1978, a new profitable, though capital-intensive, line of private business activity had opened which was to prove so attractive to senior retired military officers. This was large-scale farming cum agro-allied industries. The rate of retired military investment in this particular business was to become the more marked after 1979 when the OFN was replaced with the "Green Revolution" programme. The latter not only further liberalised access to large farm holdings, but also made available to would-be investors, indigenous and foreign, large sums of loose money, increased fiscal incentives (e.g. income relief for pioneer enterprises, duty-free importation of farm equipment, etc.), as well as subsidised inputs (such as fertilisers, pesticides, improved seeds, and bank credits) for large-scale farming and food production.[15]

Not surprisingly, most of Nigeria's retired generals, especially those who left service after 1979, were induced to go into commercial farming. By 1985, the list of top retired military officers engaged in commercial farming as well as one agro-allied venture or the other included a former military head of state, and his deputy, seven other retired army generals and at least one air vice-marshal. Of late, middle and lower-ranking officers, 'noncoms', and even privates both serving and retired have also become increasingly interested in the farming business. Thanks to the new (1986) programme of 'Directorate of Food, Roads and Rural Infrastructures' (DFRRI) set-up under Babangida's military presidency, and the huge financial allocations made towards its execution.

The foregoing completes what roughly is a trend analysis of the kinds of private business pursuits or employments that retired military officers had been going into since the end of the Nigerian Civil War in 1970. One interesting generalisation that emerges from the historical materials just surveyed is that retired military business ventures tend to follow swings in national budget schedules.[16] To make the discussions of the chapter even more interesting, we must combine that synchronic analysis with a diachronic one, by examining the structure of retired military-business enterprises and their types, while at the same time providing more concrete details as to the names of which personalities have what business links (see Table 3.1 for a summary). These we proceed to treat in the next major part of the chapter

2.   The Structure of Retired Military Business Enterprises

Structurally, retired military businesses, as indeed those of indigenous Nigerian entrepreneurs generally, are characterised by three basic features.[17] First, such business activities have tended to be concentrated in softer areas of the economy, namely distributive trade and commerce, the service sectors (including consultancy), and small-scale and low technology industries. Until most recently, there had been very little interest shown in and attention given to agriculture, manufacturing and industry.

Second, the retired military business scene, as indeed indigenous entrepreneurship generally, is marked by the preponderance of one-man enterprises, sole proprietorships, and very limited partnerships. While some of the retired military businesses began as private limited companies, they were intended to be no more than proprietorship, to be closely held as family businesses. True, there exist a few which because of their large capital investment have gone into partnerships with others, mostly civilian-based. It is possible that the latter may well be indicative of what future developments to expect. But businesses of this kind are very few in number and remain rather an exception than the rule.

Third, a number of the business companies that have come to be established or owned by retired military officers, especially in the areas of large-scale farming, agro-allied production and processing, and manufacture, are linked to some foreign technical associates or others. The reasons responsible for such links are not difficult to find. Among these, paradoxically, is the very logic of the Nigerian Enterprises Promotion (or indigenisation) measure earlier discussed. This has driven many Nigerian businessmen into seeking all sorts of joint-venture arrangements with (and a few even fronting for) certain foreign interests invariably corporate. Of course, there are the familiar problems hampering indigenous businessmen generally such as lack of techno-industrial infrastructure, inadequate technical and managerial manpower though not necessarily also inadequate capital in the case of top retired military business ventures. But collaboration with foreign interests also serves the convenient purpose of helping to build up foreign exchange resources for a number of local business companies or their owners.[18] The latter, in turn, is to be understood partly in the light of the "dependent capitalist development" pattern followed by Nigeria since independence. Of most of these features characterising indigenous private sector generally, the retired military business scene partake.

There are thirteen major areas where retired military businessmen have become active:

(a)   defence procurement and contracts
(b)   large-scale farming and agro-allied ventures
(c)   import and export business, including shipping
(d)   distributive trade and commerce
(e)   building and construction
(f)   petroleum business, private mining and quarrying
(g)   motor industry, including transportation and haulage services
(h)   real estate or property development
(i)   manufacturing and industry (other than food processing)
(j)   banking and insurance
(k)   private security business
(l)   printing and publishing
(m)   law, medical and other professional practices and retainership.

We commence shortly an elaboration of these major business groups just categorised, giving names of the particular private companies, as well as their owners operating in those areas. But before then, one caveat or two must be introduced.

As with any scheme of classification, it is not possible in actual fact to have business interests of given retired military officers contained analytically within just one box. To be sure, a number of the top retired officers studied are known to have interests and pursuits cutting across the major business areas categorised here. For example, in December 1985, there were not less than six private companies with which retired Maj.-Gen. A.O. Aduloju was reported to be involved as Board Chairman: namely, Fred & Johnson Engineering Co. Ltd., Alfredo Enterprises Ltd., Long Acres Agro Complex Co. Ltd., Flamo Petroleum Nigeria Ltd., Alfa Manufacturing Co. Nigeria Ltd., and Megpin (Nigeria) Ltd.[19] The business activities of the companies concerned are multiple, and range from building and construction, commerce (distribution), large-scale farming, petroleum business, to manufacturing. An even better case illustrating the criss-crossing as well as multiple nature of retired military business interests is that of retired Maj.-Gen Shehu Yar' Adua, now director of Yar' Adua Group of Companies, and variously described as large-scale farmer, part-owner of a shipping line, manufacturer, part-owner of a bank, and more recently publisher.[20] It has not been possible for our classificatory scheme to (sufficiently) mirror such criss-crossing or multiple business interests of the latter retired officer and others.

Also, examples used in the analysis that follows should be taken as *merely illustrative*. But they are not meant to suggest that the retired military officers specified here are necessarily the ones who dominate the business groups under which they are listed. To be able to decide which retired military officers dominate what business groups, one needs to have information about the size of capital investment, scale of operations, and turn-over for all the business companies. But such information we did not have. The retired military officers named as examples of specific business activities are the only ones that our research efforts have been able to find from available public source. It may well be that the most influential retired military businessmen are not among the ones identified for some of the business groups categorised here. These are important caveats to bear in mind as we go through details of retired military business ventures, their types, owners or directors, company names, and principal business lines.

(a) Defence procurement and Contracts

When senior military officers retire to go into private business the world over, defence procurement and contracts are the most natural venture they generally branch into. Nigeria is not an exception to this generalisation. What seems to make defence business prospective for top retired military officers in Nigeria particularly is the size of annual budgetary allocations to the defence sector, capital and recurrent, which has remained consistently high compared to the outlays for such other sectors as education, health, transport, manufacturing, and agriculture since 1970.[21]

What kind(s) of activities are involved in the defence procurement cum contracts business? And who are the major firms and persons involved? To answer these questions, let us first define the nature of the defence business sector.

The defence procurement and contracts sector of Nigeria's military-business complex is based on the 'mixed economy' model, and comprises the following:

1. the government-owned Defence Industries Corporation and its subsidiaries, the Federal Ordinance Factory, and Armament Factory;
2. joint-public sector industry supplying defence and defence-related equipment to the ministry of defence (Steyr Nigeria Ltd., established partly as an armoured vehicle assembly plant);
3. private companies in the defence or defence-related business either owned by indigenous entrepreneurs (e.g. Nigeria Explosives and Plastic Company Ltd. owned by one of Nigeria's business magnates, Chief E.O. Asamu),[22] or some international corporate firms (of which there are quite a number)*, or by a combination of both;

---

*   Reference here is to the multi-national corporations (MNCs) in the arms-manufacturing or arms-sales business.

4.   a number of influential Nigerians conjoined with foreigners, acting as arms agents and dealers; and

5.   various contractors, consultants, and persons engaged in supplying defence recurrent needs, handling armed forces development projects, or both.

Obviously, it is with activities at the last three levels that our analysis is mostly concerned. Yet not all the components of the military-business complex just disentangled operate harmoniously with one another.

By the very nature of the defence business generally, however, most of the activities and operations are often a cloaked affair, and it is not easy for a researcher to come by the names of the companies and individuals involved. This is especially true of activities and operations connected with arms and equipment importation and supplies.

Nor, as regards the involvement of the retired military, is the problem of information made necessarily easier merely because such officers are no longer in public employment, and therefore absolved from official secrecy. Based on public sources, our research has been unable to find more than one person as being active in the area, namely retired Maj.-Gen. Emmanuel O. Abisoye whom a recent national publication described as "a private businessman specialising in a military soft-ware."[23] But there are certain to be many, many more retired military officers involved in the business than one has been able to discover. Some of these may have registered their companies and interests under business categories other than defence, such as import and export trade, including shipping, or simply advertised themselves as "general contractor and general merchants." My hunch is that some of the top retired officers in the import/export trade may have been doubling as licensed arms and equipment agents and suppliers. It is also possible that a few who serve as presidents of joint Nigerian and other countries' chambers of commerce and industry may be commissioned agents of foreign companies specialising in arms production or sales. But these are mere guesses that await to be confirmed by hard data.

The first public listing that one has of private companies, contractors, or individuals doing business with the ministry of defence (MOD) was provided on June 13, 1985 under the Buhari/Idiagbon military regime. It was issued to the press by a defence probe panel headed by Justice Mamman Nassir.[24] The contractors were those engaged in contracts for various armed forces development projects, particularly the construction of drainage, army sports centres, and military barracks between October 1 1979 and December 31, 1983. The list of the said defence contractors as well as the value of their contracts included the following: Messrs. B.C.C. Limited, ₦42.0m; Line Construction Ltd., ₦16.6m; M.I.A. & Sons, ₦14.3m; Inaolaji Builders, ₦7.9m; A.I. Gadama, ₦10.2m; Barau Yaro, ₦9.1m; Spie-Battingnollos, ₦103.6m; Gollard S.A, ₦13.2m; Strabag Bau A.G., ₦28.9; Rota Engineering Construction Ltd., ₦8.0m; Blohm and Voss, ₦234.8m; Itager Builders, ₦8.7m; Arbico Nigeria Ltd., ₦6.1m; Alhaj. M. Kabau, ₦1.0m; Alhaj. Ala Trading Co., ₦1.0m; J.U.J. Danjuma, ₦1.0m; Alli Kotoko & Sons, ₦1.1m; Musa Trading Co., ₦2.5m.[25]

It is probable that some of these private companies or persons contracting for the defence ministry might have had dealings with some top serving military officers of the Shagari civilian presidency, but we do not know. Neither do we know which of the defence contracting firms have had military officers whether serving or retired on their board of directors, as part-owners, or shareholders, although this is also probable. Of the companies listed, infact only one is known through other public source to have some retired senior military officers on its board. I refer to Arbico Nigeria Ltd., with a former Vice-Admiral Joseph E. Akinwale Wey and retired Maj.-Gen. Martin Adamu respectively as the Chairman and a member of Board of Directors.[26] Arbico Nigeria Ltd. is an active company in the building, civil engineering works and construction business as we show later.

But apart from arms and equipment imports and supplies, building and construction, there are many other lines for doing business with the MOD. There is the whole gamut of activities in meeting the recurrent needs of the military, such as providing or furnishing accommodation and quarters, clothing, footwear, rations, fuel, and transportation. A lot of business is involved in these other areas or line; and it is only reasonable to expect that quite a number of retired military officers would be interested and active here too.

(b)   Large-Scale Farming and Agro-Allied Ventures

Large-scale or commercial farming, including investment in agro and agro-allied industries, has become the favourite post-retirement pursuit of Nigeria's military generals. The number of retired senior military officers going into large-scale farming and agro-allied ventures is surpassed only by the list of multi-national companies turning to agribusiness. As earlier defined, this is a broad but capital-intensive business area that covers such particular business activities as poultry, feedmills; maize, rice, and soya beans production; citrus and other fruits cultivation; livestock rearing; fishery; land-clearing and preparation; food processing and other agro-allied industries; agricultural management and consultancy services.

Among the retired top military officers who have been active in this area since 1979 may be mentioned, the former head of state, retired Gen. Olusegun Obasanjo, with his multi-million *naira* farming company established at Sango Ota, near Abeokuta, in Ogun State of the federation. Incorporated originally in 1973 as *Temperance Enterprises Limited,* the company has since had its name changed to *Obasanjo Farms Nigeria Ltd.,*[27] with the same acronym of OFN as the "Operation Feed the Nation" programme which the general had himself launched while in office as head of state.

Admittedly, General Obasanjo would not be the first senior military officer to own or invest in large farms. For example, as early as 1975, Samuel Ogbemudia, even while still serving as brigadier in the Nigerian army and holding office as military governor of the former Mid-Western State under the Gowon regime, was known to own as many as ten farms located in various parts of that state, which were later confiscated following the July 29 counter-coup.[28] But the scale and rate of retired officers' involvement in farming and related ventures were to be much greater after 1979.

Apart from the Obasanjo case earlier mentioned, other retired army generals with big investments in this business included retired Maj.-Gen. Musa Yar' Adua, who throughout the early 1980s consistently introduced himself as, and was publicly considered, "a large-scale farmer", operating from his upper Kaduna State base. The venture was apparently launched from the 10,375,600 hectares of farmland along the Funtua-Birinin Gwari Road, which had been acquired by Maj.-Gen. Yar'Adua on the eye of his departure from office and retirement from the army in 1979.[29] In addition to being the owner of *Sambo Farms,* retired Maj.-Gen. Yar' Adua had acquired the *Mandara Farms;* a dairy firm located at Vom, Plateau state.[30] Other retired generals in the farming business are retired Maj.-Gen. George Innih, Chairman and Managing Director, *Niger Valley Agro Industries Ltd.* that owns the large farm at kilometre 2, Old Auchi/ Agenebode road, in Etsako Local Government area of the former Bendel State; retired Lt-Gen. Alani Akinrinade, though, subsequently employed in government as Federal Minister under the Babangida Presidency, but is also believed to own a complex of large-scale farms across the former Oyo State, including the Yakoyo-based *Niger Feeds & Agricultural Operations Ltd.,* near Ile-Ife; and retired Lt.-Gen. Gibson S. Jalo, owner of *Jalo Farms* located in the Numan Local Government area of Gongola State.

Another top army retiree Lt.-Gen. M.I. Wushishi has also been identified as the director of *Nigerfirst Integrated Farms.* Located at Kilometre 9 along Kaduna-Zaria Road in Kaduna State,[31] the latter has been described as an integrated farming scheme involving initially poultry production and a supportive feed-mills, but planned also for large-scale citrus and other fruits cultivation and processing.[32]

By 1986, at least one retired top air-force officer with the equivalent rank of general, and former air force boss under the Obasanjo regime, retired Air Vice-Marshal Yisa Doko was mentioned as being also interested in the farming business;[33] while his counterpart and former chief of army staff retired Lt.-Gen. T.Y. Danjuma, hitherto known to be operating in the shipping industry, was to be identified as Chairman, *Agricultural Managers and Consultants Ltd.,* with head office at Idah, Benue State. The latter was set up to provide a variety of agricultural management and consultancy services, including preparation of feasibility studies, land clearing and preparation, seasonal tractor-hiring services, and construction of farm roads and building.[34] Another high-ranking person newly emerging in the agribusiness is retired Maj.-Gen. A.O. Aduloju, identified as Chairman, *Long Acres Agro Complex Co. Ltd.*[35] A recent publication mentions retired Maj.-Gen David Jemibewon as being engaged in the rearing of cattle in Kwara State among others.[36]

These are but a few among the top retired military investors in large-scale farming. Nor are these big-time and ex-military farmers confined to the ranks of major-generals and above or their equivalent. There are scores of former brigadiers and colonels or the equivalent who are also known to be active in the business. The list includes former state military governors retired in 1975 with the Gowon regime. Of these, Samuel Ogbemudia, an ex-brigadier, is perhaps the most leading example. Although he was later to sell certain earlier acquired interests (that is the so-called *Ogbemudia Farms*) to *John Holt Nigeria Ltd*, as previously hinted, Chief Ogbemudia is still very much involved in farming and agro-allied business. He now has a business company by name *Sogalson Limted,* registered at 108 West Circular Road, Benin City, and which advertises itself as manufacturers of agro-based machinery including cassava grater, cassava dewatering press, garri frier, corn sheller, grinder, feed mill, etc.[37] Ex-Brigadier Ogbemudia has also been the owner of a huge farm in Iyenomo village, near Benin City.

A number of other brigadiers and colonels, or their equivalent, retired after 1979 have also gone into large-scale farming. For example, retired Brig. Abba Wali has an enterprise *Abba Wali Agriculture* or simply acronymed AWA operating in Kano State;[38] while retired Brig. Alabi Isamah is said to own a large farm in the upper-Ogun river basin area outside the boundaries of Ogun and Oyo State.[39] There are many more that space does not permit us to document.

No doubt, farming has become such a fashionable/profitable business activity as to attract all these retired military generals or their equivalent and the many others. But it has become a capital-intensive business requiring large landholdings, modern equipment, trained and varying management skills and techniques, and of course big money. That this is so can be gauged from the size of bank loans raised by many of the top officers involved to support their agro-allied ventures. For example, the *Obasanjo Farms Nigeria Ltd.,* formerly *Temperance Enterprises Nigeria Limited,* is said to have been started with a personal capital of about ₦1 million raised by General Obasanjo with his assets plus a heavy loan from his bank. This loan is believed to have been to the tune of ₦5 million taken from NAL Merchant Bank as well as the United Bank for Africa (UBA).[40] The *Nigerfirst Integrated Farms,* of which Lt.-Gen. Wushishi is the director, reportedly got a consortium of banks operating in the country, namely Savannah Bank, the International Bank for West Africa (IBWA), and the Merchant Bank, to grant to that company a ten-million naira (₦10.0m) loan for its integrated farm scheme.[41]

Retired Lt. Gen Alani Akinrinade, speaking then as the Federal Minister of Agriculture and Natural Resources in the Babangida administration, recently commented on this matter though not without his own interests here. On an official visit of inspection to the farm of a fellow retired top officer Major-Gen. Innih at Agenebode, former Bendel State, in early July, 1986, retired Lt.-Gen Akinrinade was quoted to have said that all the retired officers in large-scale farming, including himself, got their money from the bank as loans.[42] Of course, the statement by the retired general-turned-cabinet-minister would seem to have had an additional motive underlying it, which was to counter growing public query as to the source of the large funds invested by the retired generals in farming.

(c)   Import and Export Business, Including Shipping

The import and export business, including shipping, is the next major business area in which top retired military officers are to be found engaged. This business category covers a whole gamut of activities ranging from clearing and forwarding, or the import and export trade proper, container service, warehousing, and running of private jetties, to operation of shipping charter lines, and direct ownership of ocean-going vessels. Three top retired army general have come to be mentioned as the most dominant figures in this area of business activity: retired Major Gen. Emmanuel Abisoye, retired Maj.-Gen. Musa Yar' Adua, and retired Lt. Gen. T.Y. Danjuma. Of the three, retired Maj.-Gen Abisoye's immense interest in export trade became known through the activities of the Nigeria Exports Promotion Council, a Federal government-owned concern, as well as the Nigerian Exporters Association, both of which he came to head, though at various times, for several years. The private company of which retired Maj.-Gen Abisoye is the Managing Director, and through whose agency he pursues his interests in this particular business area, is called *Emmanoye Investments Limited,* located at 46, shopping Terrace, Tafawa Balewa Square, Lagos.

Retired Lt. Gen. Danjuma's interests in the export-import business, including shipping, first came to public attention through a press controversy in mid-1982.*[43] From the latter emerged a number of facts that interests us here. Retired Lt.-Gen. Danjuma had, since retiring as chief of army staff in October 1979, been in fact running a thriving shipping business. He had been Chairman of the *MEDAFRICA Group of Companies* that once owned and operated a number of private jetties, namely the Dantata Jetty (Apapa), Noli Jetty (Apapa), Wimpey Jetty (Port Harcourt), and yet another jetty at Warri.[44]

If *MEDAFRICA's* interest in the shipping business has been largely that of a terminal operator, the involvement of another company *Nigeria-America Line,* of which retired Lt.-Gen. Danjuma is also the Vice-President,[45] is as a carrier or ship operator. There are other companies operating in this and other related areas of activities, and in which the retired general has had business interests: i.e. *Eastern Bulkcem Company Ltd,* and *Sea Trucks (Nigeria) Ltd.*[46]

But it was not until December 1983 that was incorporated the largest independent shipping company involving one of Nigeria's retired army generals. The company was the *African Oceans Line* advertised as jointly owned by Maj. Gen. Yar' Adua and three

---

*   The background was the closure by President Shehu Shagari's government of all privately owned jetties suspected allegedly of being involved in smuggling activities. The latter measure provoked a public statement from retired Lt.-Gen. Danjuma, in his characteristic bluntness, accusing the Customs and Excise officials as in fact the "aiders and abbetors of smuggling;" followed, in turn, by a paid full-page advertisement placed by the then Department of Customs and Excise in the *National Concord* (Lagos) of Saturday, June 19, 1982 directed against retired Lt.-Gen. Danjuma's business Company operating in the area; and provoking yet another rejoinder in the form of a full-page newspaper article by the retired general; inter-spersed by various editorial press comments.

other eminent Nigerians. The three others are Chief M.K.O. Abiola, a business tycoon and for a long time Chairman, International Telephone & Telegraph (ITT) Nigeria; Alhaji Bamanga Tukur, a retired General Manager of the Nigeria Ports Authority (NPA); and Dr. Raymond A. Dokpesi. Established with its head office and management located at 30/32 Creek Road, Apapa, Lagos,[47] this company commenced full commercial operations in October 1984, and was reported by late 1986 to have a fleet of two large modern ships. It is a mark of the increasingly interlocking interests between the top retired military and the business class that the two ships initially making up the *African Ocean Line* were named after the relatives of two of its major partners, "Binta Yar' Adua" and "Atinuke Abiola", although the latter has since been sold off.

(d)   Distributive Trade and Commerce

But it is in the general area of distribution (commerce), wholesale and retail trade, and other related services that most retired military-business activities, as indeed those of the so-called household sector of the whole economy, are to be found concentrated. This had been facilitated by the indigenisation measure (in Schedule 1 of the Nigerian Enterprises Promotion Decree and its various amendments, 1972, 1977 and 1982) reserving the distributive trades for Nigerians and preventing domestic manufacturers both foreign and indigenous from appointing non-nationals (aliens) as "distributors" or "agents" within the country.

Of the many activities grouped under this particular business category, perhaps the most popular, and certainly the greatest money-spinner, at least until recently, has been the securing of multiple distributorships for the sale of certain scarce commodities. These include the following: (1) Cement, from any of the cement factories both old (Calabar, Ukpilla, Nkalagu, Sokoto) and new (Shagamu, Ashaka, Yandev), or from the Onigbolo Plant in the Benin Republic jointly owned by Nigeria; (2) a range of essential commodities, such as milk, sugar, non-alcoholic beverages, soaps and detergents, etc., manufactured/imported by multinational companies like U.A.C., U.T.C., Paterson Zochonis, Unilever, Leventis and Cadbury. (These are commodities whose supply suffers from chronic shortages); (3) Flour, from many of the country's flour-processing mills, including the Flour Mills of Nigeria, Northern Nigeria Flour Mills, Ideal Flour Mills among others; (4) Beer and Soft Drinks, from the various breweries or bottling companies, including the Nigerian Breweries, Guinness, Nigerian Bottling Company, etc.; (5) Peugeot and Volkswagen Cars, from the Kaduna and Lagos based assemblies, namely, the Peugeot Automobile of Nigeria (PAN) and Volkswagen of Nigeria (VON) among other passenger cars.

Our research shows that by the mid-1980's there were countless top military officers, senior civil bureaucrats, former politicians, and leading businessmen or their legal personal representatives, including wives, holding some distributorships or the other from the nation's large trading companies, cement factories, beer breweries, car assemblies, or flour mills.

Invariably, when retired military officers describe themselves or are described by others as "businessmen", the reference is to their activities in the distributive trade and commercial sector. The list here is interminable and includes: retired Maj. Michael Bibora Deinsah, a former airforce communications officer from Trofani town in Rivers State, as Managing Director, *Trofany Enterprises;*[48] Chief Alfred Diete-Spiff, the first military governor of the Rivers State, who has since 1975 been Managing Director/ President of the so-called *BZB Group of Companies.*[49]

Others are: retired Col. Mike N. Okwechime, with his *Tiki Group of Companies,* comprising engineering and sports promotion firms;[50] retired Maj.-Gen. David Ejoor, *Bensab (Nigeria) Ltd.,*[51] retired Brig. Benjamin Adekunle, often described by the newspapers as "a leading businessman".[52] We now know retired Brig. Adekunle to be the Managing Director of *Samak Industrial Holdings,* a Limited liability company registered under the Companies Act of 1968, and having its principal base of business at No. 2 Odutayo Street, Surulere, Lagos.[53] To be sure, a sizeable proportion of military officers retired to-date, including military state governors and senior-ranking officers either retired or dismissed with the overthrow of the Gowon regime, as well as those thrown out in the "great purge" of November 1975, could be conveniently assumed to have gone into various distributive trades, particularly at the wholesale or agency level.

Examples of retired military officers involved in distributorships are simply many. Sometimes the distributorships are held in the persons' own names, and at other times in the names of wives, relations, or friends. Nor is public information on such matters that difficult to obtain. For a random illustration of this, in July, 1987, the Benue Cement Company Ltd., Gboko, appointed some private companies, contractors and persons as Lion Brand Portland Cement distributors, customers or dealers.[54] On the list could easily be recognised the following retired military officers: Lt. Col. Gabriel Idoko, Maj. Peter Atsuku, Maj. Gabriel Entono, Maj. Riga Addingi, Capt. Aondoma S. Adom, Capt. C.A. Abayilo, Capt. Edward Kwaghkor Ula. This was not adding many of the business companies also featuring on that list as distributors known to belong to other military officers both retired and serving, or their wives, relations and friends.[55] Some of these had been regular distributors for the Benue Cement Company almost from its very inception; while others were first appointed in May, 1985, when they were listed alongside such others as retired Lt. Col. Adejoh Yakubu, retired Maj. Ita Okon, retired Maj. S.I. Myam, retired Capt. Maples Udo, retired Lt. Col. Christopher Ikwue.[56]

There have been retired military businessmen holding distributorships from not only other cement factories but also large trading and manufacturing companies dealing in other essential goods that we have previously discussed. But because of space we cannot detail these others here.

Closely related to distributorships, as a form of trade, was the import-licence business. Thus, along with some political influentials and businessmen, top retired military officers or their businesses had featured annually on the lists of import licenses allocated by government between 1979 and 1983.[57] Now, the import-licence business had long had seamy aspect to it. While many of the recipients might have used their import licence allocations honestly and genuinely for the purpose for which they were allocated, that is, for the import of essential food items, raw materials, industrial chemicals, pharmaceuticals, machinery and spare parts, quite a number of the businessmen were believed to have abused their allocations. For example, hawking of import licences, in order to make quick and excessive profits at public expense, was a notorious practice associated with the import-licence regime. The practice was general to the private sector. But we have no evidence linking any of the retired military enterprises or persons studied here with this and other related import-licence abuses. What we do know is that by fiscal years 1984 and 1985, the list of import-licence recipients contained many of the now familiar names of business companies that belong to some of the top generals,[58] although many of these later-year allocations could not be utilized because of shrunken foreign exchange earnings available to the nation.

A number of policy measures initiated in 1986 combined to make distributorships and the import-licence business no longer the lucrative lines of quick high profit they used to be.[59]

At the same time, however, the new observable trend toward "privatisation" of hitherto government-owned enterprises may well be opening up a new vista for profitable investment particularly in the area of exports. For, as part of the trend, moves have been embarked upon and measures initiated by the Babangida regime to liquidate among others the various Produce Marketing Boards and the Nigerian National Supply Company (NNSC). The former had long been vested with the responsibility for the shipment and sales abroad of the major Nigerian agricultural export crops, particularly cocoa, groundnuts, cotton, palm oil and palm kernels, while the latter Federal agency had been established since 1972 and charged specifically with the procurement and distribution of essential commodities. "Privatisation" of these two particular state-owned enterprises means new opportunities for the retired military among other businessmen active here.

Already, many of them are known to have followed up their interests by proceeding to purchase the assets owned by the two agencies, including useful food storage structures such as silos, cribe standard stores, warehouses, as well as motor trucks, dispersed throughout the Federation. These are facilities that can be put to good use especially in the area of exports promotion.

Meanwhile, there are other activities in the distributive and commercial sector where the retired military have also been investing. Banking and insurance is one such activity, but this we cover later in the chapter and under a separate category. Another is in the development of hotels. Nor are military interests in this venture a very recent phenomenon. For example, as far back as 1975, Brig. Samuel Ogbemudia, even while he was still in service and holding office as a state military governor, was known to own and run a lucrative hotel business, the Palm Royal Motel in Benin city.[60]

More retired military officers have gone into the hotel and catering business that can be documented in this study. Around the University of Ibadan area of the Oyo State, capital alone, I can think immediately of three: *Onile Aro Hotel*, off Oyo Road, Ojo, owned by retired Maj. J. Akinpelu; *Monad Motels,* located at Adetoro Crescent, off Adebajo Street, Kongi-Bodija, owned by a former military nurse retired Maj. Moni Esan; and *Joanis Guest House,* at 6 Ibrahim Taiwo Ave., off Oluyole Street, New Bodija, owned by retired Lt. Col. Y.M. Anifowoshe. There are certain to be a few more in Ibadan as a whole. Even greater concentrations of the business, in the form of guest houses, inns, motels, lodges and hotels owned by ex-military persons among others, can be found in the Lagos megapolis, Kaduna, Benin, Onitsha, Port-Harcourt, an additional number from the remainder of the various state capitals, not to mention a number of other major towns. We are talking of hotels and guest houses of medium to low international standards.

In response to an acute shortage of first-class hotel accommodation countrywide, a number of retired top military officers have sought the partnership of foreign private capital to build modern five-star grade hotels of international standard. Perhaps, the most recent, and the best known, example of this is *Golden Tulip-Agura Hotel* at the new Federal Capital of Abuja, of which retired Maj. Gen. George A. Innih, Chief Maxwell Onwuka Kalu (Chairman), Malam Saleh Jambo among others came to be identified as joint-owners, and in technical partnership with the Golden Tulip Group owned by KLM the Royal Dutch Airlines. Fag-Afrikana Services Limited was named the Nigerian holding company that owns the hotel.[61]

(e) Building and Construction

The Building and Construction Sector, as undoubtedly one of the most profitable areas of business over the last decade and half, has attracted large number of private entrepreneurs indigenous, foreign, or joint. The attraction has been the contracts from the huge public works launched under the three national development plans 1970–74, 1975–80, and 1980–85.

The contracts had not only been for the many and large roads and highways, fly-overs and bridges, sea and airport, dams, industries, new government offices, the new Federal Capital of Abuja, schools and hospitals, and of course barracks accommodation for armed forces and police personnel launched in the post-Civil War period, but also the massive orders for tonnes of cement and other building materials and equipment placed in pursuance of those construction programmes. Consequently, many private companies and contractors have emerged doing business in the area. There are a number of retired military officers to be counted among these.

Some of the firms, contractors or persons concerned have also been contracting for the ministry of defence. One such firm is *Arbico Nigeria Ltd.,* which we identified in a previous sub-section, while discussing the defence procurement business. *Arbico*

Nigeria Ltd. is a building construction company quoted on the Nigerian Stock Exchange and has a former Vice-Admiral Joseph E. Akinwale Wey as the Chairman and retired Maj. Gen. Martin Adamu also as one of its directors. This information is obtained from the Nigerian Stock Exchange sources.[62]

Among other companies quoted on the Nigeria Stock Exchange, and also said to be in the civil engineering (including road construction) business, are Julius Berger, Tailor Woodrow, Costain, Cappa and D'Alberto, and Dumez. But these are foreign-owned companies and among the most dominant in the construction industry; given their access to supply of capital goods, like machinery and equipment as well as technical personnel.[63] Presumably, as major and regular winners of prime contracts, these major foreign construction companies have been sub-contracting to smaller firms that may or may not include the indigenous competitors.

Then, there is *Roads Nigeria Ltd.*, a construction company incorporated in October 1974, which handles the building of roads, bridges, airfields, and dams mostly in the Northern part of the country, with technical management agreement with Volker Stevin Roads (a member of the Dutch based Royal Volker Stevin and International Construction Company). It had as Chairman of its Board of Directors Alhaji Musa Yar'Adua,[64] said to be the father of the retired army general known by that same name. But there is no evidence whatsoever that retired Maj. Gen. Musa Yar'Adua had had any financial interests in the business.[65] *Roads Nigeria Ltd.*, as a company, is also quoted on the Nigerian Stock Exchange.

But there are other examples of private civil engineering and construction firms in which retired military officers have come to acquire major shares. One of them is *Technical Constructions (Nigeria) Ltd.*, an electrical and associated contract engineering concern, which has retired Brig. E.E. Ikwue (Chairman) and two other retired public servants, Ambassadors Dr. Edwin Ogbu, and J.T.F. Iyalla among its major shareholders.[66] Among the earliest retired military-business establishments in the construction industry is that of retired Lt. Col. S.S. Adejoro said to be formerly of the army pay corps, who resigned soon after the civil war to set up *S.S. Adejoro & Co. Ltd., Engineers and Builders* based at 54–60 Opebi Road, Ikeja, Lagos.[67] And more recently, retired Maj. Gen. A.O. Aduloju has in a public advertisement been identified as Chairman, *Fred & Johnson Engineering Nigeria Ltd.* inter alia.[68]

(f)   Petroleum Business; and Other Mining Quarrying Activities

The petroleum industry has been the mainstay of Nigeria's economy since the end of the Civil War. Apart from being a major contributor to the gross domestic product, the petroleum industry has been the most important source of public revenue and foreign exchange for the economy. Consequently, the same industry has come to generate a lot of business opportunities for indigenous investors as well as foreign.

The activities here include petroleum exploration, prospecting, production; crude oil lifting and marketing, including exporting; oil refining; distribution of refined petroleum products (petrol, diesel, kerosine, engine oil and lubricants, and gas for home and industrial use); running of petrol and gas service stations for the latter purpose. While foreign-owned companies or "oil multi-nationals" dominate the first, most of all other activities which we have just listed have attracted indigenous private investors, though invariably with some foreign technical collaboration.

As is to be expected, an increasingly large number of top military officers both retired and serving, have moved into the petroleum business. The most obvious business area is the ownership and operation of petrol service stations. Such service stations carry either the trade marks of any of the seven major oil multinational corporations Shell, Gulf, Mobil, Agip, Elf, Total, Texaco, or are under the franchise of companies until now publicly-owned by the Nigerian National Petroleum Corporation (NNPC), namely the African Petroleum (AP), Unipetrol, or the National Oil Marketing Company (National for short). There are a few of the newly established privately owned indigenous oil service companies that use their own trade names. An example of the latter but by no means the most successful is retired Col. David Laoye. Appointed into the Oyo State military administration in 1984, retired Col. Laoye is said to be Deputy Chairman, Flora Group of Companies whose business activities apparently include the marketing of petroleum products under the registered trade name of FLORA Enterprises.[69]

But besides this rather obvious activity of running petrol service stations, there are military officers to be found in most of the other areas of the business as well.[70] Some top military officers together with other public functionaries had in the past been involved in the lifting and sale of crude oil. The latter includes the recent counter-trade, meaning petroleum-for-imports barter, deals struck in the period 1984-86, with all their seamy sides.[71] Admittedly, retired military officers are by and large new to the oil business, compared to their civilian counterparts. As such, they could not have been expected by now to achieve the level attained by some of the older established indigenous business companies such as Henry Stephens, the first indigenous oil producing company.[72] Nonetheless, at least one retired general is said to own an oil tanker run as part of a business outfit. There are companies owned by retired military officers in the building and construction industry already discussed, which also bid for and are awarded contracts in the petroleum sector; such contracts cover services like drilling, supply of equipment for drilling well logging, pipeline construction, and civil engineering works. A couple of others specialise in marine engineering related services.[73] A major service in the oil sector is marine and land transportation, where as a matter of course private indigenous interests are also pronounced.[74]

The problem with writing on business activities in this domain generally, though, is that information is a very guarded affair. In fact, the petroleum industry comes next after defence procurement and contracts in terms of sheer dearth of public information as to what interests, companies, and persons are involved. That is why our discussions thus far have had to be couched in such generalities.

The fact is that it has not been possible to get data from public sources as to which retired military officers have what business companies or interests in the petroleum industry; although it is generally believed there are retired officers possessing such companies or interests. The few examples that we know may, or may not necessarily, be among the companies or persons with the largest investment and turn-over in the business. The few example that we have in mind include retired Lt.-Gen. Danjuma, described as Director of and a major share-holder in *Sea Trucks (Nigeria) Ltd.,* a marine oilfield services company.[75] Another is retired Maj.-Gen. A.O. Aduloju, also recently advertised as Chairman, *Flamo Petroleum Nigeria Ltd.* among other companies.[76]

As for other private mining and quarrying operations and related services outside crude petroleum production, perhaps the best known example here is that of retired Brig. E.E. Ikwue identified at once as Chairman, Managing Director, and major share-holder, of the *Nigerian Swiss Construction and Quarrying Industries Ltd.,* a quarrying company established in 1976. But it surely cannot be the only example. Suffice it to add just one more, namely that of Brig. Atom Kpera who, although only most recently retired, is reported to already have a licence to mine coal in his native Benue State.[77]

(g)   Transport Industry, Including Haulage

The transport industry, including haulage – being the seventh in our categorisation of activities in the military-business scene – has long been a very large and profitable area for private business to invest in, and involves many lines. These include dealership in vehicles and spare parts,* repair and service stations or workshops; investment in passenger vehicles, vans, buses, lorries and trailers; operating transport companies engaged in long-distance road haulage; inter-city passenger transportation services; running of intra-city or intra-town taxi services; or, in the riverine areas, boat and ferry services for inland waterways. Among the more recent additions to business activities in the area are ownership of private airlines; operating passenger and cargo air/charter services; and courier message services of all sorts.

Retired military officers can be found branching into some of these – but not all – business lines categorised here under the transport industry.

Of course, it is impossible to detail all the names and companies of retired military officers with business interests in the area. Neither do we have the information required for such a task. The information available to us is limited mostly to activities of retired military officers in motor dealership which, the reader would have thought, is closer to the distributive trade previously covered than the transport industry, as a business line. Two big names come to mind. There is that of retired Maj.-Gen. E.S. Okai Armah, who was employed during the first year of his retirement 1980–81 as Executive Director, *Rutam Motor Ltd.,* Lagos.[78] *Rutam Motors* is a subsidiary company to the Ibru Organi-

---

*   Itself partly covered under "Distributive Trade and Commerce" above.

sation, and acts as a major distributor for among other Peugeot cars and Mercedes-Benz trucks assembled by Peugeot Automobile of Nigeria Company Ltd., (PAN, Kaduna) and Anambra Motor manufacturing Company Ltd., (ANAMCO, Enugu) respectively. Retired Maj.-Gen. Armah has since become the Managing Director, *Emene Motors Ltd.,* Airport Road, Enugu.[79] The other name is retired Maj.-Gen. Olu Bajowa, whom one bulletin published in May, 1987, described as the Managing Director, Trinity Motors, based at Oluyole area of Ibadan city.[80]

Indigenous entrepreneurs (transporters) had undoubtedly been long active in the transport industry, including road haulage. Their participation was to be further increased by the Nigerian enterprises promotion (i.e. indigenisation) decree barring aliens, meaning Levantine interest principally, from the sector. Thus, between 1972 and 1982 many Nigerian businessmen, including some retired military, came to acquire some of the businesses and shares until now held by those aliens. The enterprises here concern haulage of goods by road, municipal bus services of every kind (including inter-state), and commercial transportation (wet and dry cargo and fuel). The enterprises were among those progressively reserved exclusively for Nigerians.

Even while this was going on, a number of retired generals were moving into the directorships of Nigerian subsidiaries of such large foreign-owned companies as SCOA, UTC, and even UAC (via two of its associated companies, Niger Motors and the Federated Motor Industries) known to have vested interests in the transport industry. At the same time, between 1984 and 1987, retired military officers were appointed by government as Chairmen or Board Members of almost all of the country's vehicle assembly plants; i.e., the Peugeot Automobile Nigeria Ltd. (PAN, Kaduna), Volkswagen of Nigeria (VON, Ikeja), Anambra Motor manufacturing Company Ltd. (ANAMCO, Enugu), National Trucks Manufacturers Company (NTMC, Kano), Leyland Nigeria Ltd. (Ibadan), and Steyr Nigeria Ltd. (Bauchi), though at varying times. Such measures could only have helped to strengthen those retired military members with business interests in the area.[81]

There are examples of retired military engaged in water transport business, including the running of boat and ferry services. Among them is that of a former naval officer and governor of the Rivers State, Chief Alfred Diete-Spiff said to own a Port-Harcourt-based riverine transport service,[82] run perhaps as part of his *BZB Group of Companies,*[83] But we have not been able to cross-check this information. Other and much more definitive examples reveal retired Lt.-Gen. Danjuma to be Director, *Sea Trucks (Nigeria) Ltd.,* being a transport and other related company in the marine oil field service.[84] But the latter retired general has also been identified as Director, *Motor Tyre Services Company of Nigeria Ltd.,*[85] again a business concern falling under the motor and road transport sub-category discussed earlier.

Within the last five years or so, private investment in air transport has been on the increase. This is clear from not only the emergence of private airlines such as Okada, Kabo, and the Inter-Continental now competing with the national carrier, Nigerian

Airways, but also increase in the number of applications by newly incorporated private companies for permit to operate non-scheduled passenger and cargo charter services within and outside Nigeria. Public information on who owns which ones of these emerging private air lines or air charter services is as yet unavailable. But it would be surprising if retired military members, including former airforce officers, were not among the new investors in the private air transport business, as the experience in shipping previously discussed has shown.

(h)   Real Estate

As remarked in the first major section of the chapter, property development or real estate were among the first major areas of private business venture for the military whether serving or retired. The sudden and astronomical increase in the size of the armed forces consequent upon the Civil War had created an actual problem of barracks accommodation shortage country-wide. There was also the need to resettle many of the citizens whose dwellings had been damaged by the war. Coupled with these was the high and rising demand for industrial buildings and residential accommodation in many of the urban areas. The result was to make provision of rental accommodation a very profitable area for investment. Many interested Nigerians whether in the private sector or public employment, both civilian and military, came to be involved in the business of procuring and renting houses and housing estates to government, state-owned agencies or corporations, industries, private establishments, and individuals. The retired military were not left out. Obviously, activities here are very closely tied to the goings-on in the building and construction sector (including the building materials industry).

But unlike the latter, examples of retired military investors in real estate are not easy to document, given the nature of this particular activity and the general lack of researchable data on it. The number of retired military investors in the business are believed however to be countless. In fact, the generalisation can be advanced that every retired military officer of the rank of Colonel and above or the equivalent has one interest or the other in property development or the real estate business whether actual or potential. This should suggest the extent of involvement by the retired military in this business.

Some of the properties concerned are run by the individual investors themselves, others by professional estate managers, agents, or brokers specifically employed by the owners to help run their business for them. There is also the procedure involving contractor financing. According to the latter, a contractor both finances and carries out the building project; as part of agreed terms of repayment, goes on to lease the building out to prospective tenant, and does actually take the rent for the initial years, handing over the property to the owner only after realising the principal and interest on the building. The latter practice is general to the properties developed on Victorial Island, a suburb of Lagos. Yet another practice is that involving (retired) military officer going into partnership with other, and most invariably civilian, investors in the property or real estate business.

An example of this would seem to be *Seaview Investments Ltd.,* a real estate development company that owns among others the vast property known as Beachland Estate in Apapa, near Lagos, and in which retired General Olusegun Obasanjo was once said to have some interest.[86] But there are certain to be many more of the latter and other examples

(i)   Manufacturing (Other Than Agro-Allied)

Within the last decade, many agro-allied industries have been established in Nigeria under the aegis of the retired military among other investors. Ventures of the kind referred to here involve miscellaneous food preparations (Soya milk production, dairy, fruit and vegetable canning and preservation, meat and fish processing, and preservation, grain milling, bread making) as well as fabrication of agro-based machinery (cassava grater, cassava dewatering press, garri frier, corn sheller, grinder feed mill, etc.).[87] But since manufacturing activities of the kind just described has already been covered in a previous sub-section of the chapter sub-headed "Large-Scale Farming & Agro-Allied Ventures", they need not be repeated here. Some manufacturing ventures dealing with building as well as cement and other concrete products can also be assumed to have been touched upon in some of our previous discussion.

Outside agro-allied ventures and investment in cement and other concrete products industries, not many retired military officers, or for that matter Nigerian businessmen as a whole, can be found in manufacturing *per se* as a business line. The few examples of retired military officers in other areas of manufacturing that I know include retired Maj.-Gen. R.A. Adebayo, Chairman and major share-holder, *Mag Furniture and Interior Designs Ltd.,* an Ikeja-based company in the furniture and fixtures making business which he owns,[88] in addition to being a Director in *Nigerian Sewing Machine Manufacturing Co. Ltd.,* which manufactures and assembles sewing machines and allied equipment. The latter company, which has the Estate of late Chief Henry Fajemirokun as one of the major Nigerian shareholders, is a subsidiary of Singer International.[89]

There is also the example of *Anchor Products Limited,* a plastic and rubber products manufacturing company established in April, 1979, and based at 11, Eleruwa Street, Ikeja near Lagos. It has retired Lt.-Col. A.A. Keshi as its Managing Director.[90] Also manufacturing foam mattresses, cushions and pillows was *Kojusola Foam Industries (Nig) Ltd.,* in Osogbo, now Osun State, set up by retired Lt.-Col. S.S. Adejoro and as a subsidiary of his engineering and building firm.[91] Still another example, and a more recent one for that matter, which we have come across, is that of retired Maj.-Gen. A.O. Aduloju, mentioned among other things as Chairman, *MEGPIN Nigeria Ltd.,* a company in manufacturing of air-conditioning units based in Ikare, Akoko, Ondo State.[92]

The fact is that manufacturing generally is not as quick and high yielding a line as other businesses. Thus, we have not seen any retired military businessman invest in the very heavy-industrial sector such as engineering and transport industries for the manufacturing of component parts of vehicle assembly plants; the metallurgical, i.e., iron and steel related works; and petro-chemical projects. What "manufacturers" there are among Nigerian businessmen remain oriented mostly towards distribution and services, rather than production. It is one major reason for characterising all the major ventures described in the present chapter of study as military-business complex with emphasis on business. Thus defined, the notion of military-business complex is not the same as, but sharply contrasted with, that of military-industrial complex.

The implication of this is that the structure of Nigeria's defence and defence-related enterprises can scarcely be expected to undergo any transformation from a military-business complex into a "military-industrial complex",[93] until and unless there is a re-orientation towards the more productive or industrial ventures.

This is the more so, since the state-owned Defence Industries Corporation (or DIC), which could have been spear-heading the expected transformation, is itself very much steeped in the imports cum commercial culture, rather than oriented to production and technology development.[94]

(j)   Banking and Insurance

With the overthrow of the import-licence regime, consequent on the initiation of the "second-tier foreign exchange market" (SFEM) along with subsequent variants, and the move towards trade and payments liberalisation introduced as part of the 'structural adjustment programme' (SAP), interested businessmen, including the top retired military, soon shifted their attention to banking as the latest and very lucrative business line. Investment by the retired military in the private banking business, however, slightly antedates SAP, SFEM, FEM, or for that matter the new variant called the Inter-Bank Foreign Exchange Market (IFEM).

The banking annual *Nigeria Banking Almanac* for the year 1985/86 named retired Lt-Gen. T.Y. Danjuma as Chairman of *Universal Trust Bank of Nigeria*, a private bank, first incorporated on 21 June 1981, under the old name of Credit Commercial de France Bank (Nigeria). It began operations in April 1985, with 40% foreign share-holding and the remaining 60% owned by individual Nigerians.[95] This was among the earliest attempts by retired top military officers to establish a private banking business. Admittedly, there is a stipulation in the banking regulation that forbids a single Nigerian individual from owning more than 5% of a given bank's equity.[96]

From that same source, we obtain the information that retired Maj.-Gen. Musa Yar' Adua is Chairman, and presumably part-owner with Chief M.K.O. Abiola among others, of the *Habib Bank (Nigeria) Ltd.*[97] Also a private commercial bank with head office at 28 Ahmadu Bello Way, Kaduna, the latter is affiliated to the *Habib Bank Limited*, Pakistan, as the main foreign shareholder (40%) and with individual Nigerians owning the remaining 60%. By December 31, 1985, *Habib Nigeria Bank Ltd.* had built up a share capital of ₦234.9m.[98]

More banks have been established within the last two years alone than in any other period of Nigeria's economic history; and many more still are believed to be in the pipeline. Although the details of these new private banks mushrooming all over the country are not yet available, a sizeable number of them are believed to have top military persons both serving and retired either as their sponsors, patrons, or (part) owners. It remains to be seen, however, whether these private banks mushrooming all over the place can survive very long without the injection of loose money derived from state-based transactions on which they obviously depend.

Meanwhile, for retired Maj.-Gen. Yar'Adua and Chief M.K.O. Abiola earlier mentioned, their joint-private interests in the banking business are but one out of many and increasingly interlocking interests in other areas, including shipping, as we saw. As for the two retired generals involved here, their branching into banking and finance represents yet another example of their ever-widening interests in important sectors of the national economy.

Activities grouped under the present business category are not confined to banking and finance, but do also include the establishment and running of finance houses investment trust, trade in stocks and shares, and part-ownership of insurance companies, or insurance-broking firms. Of these, the insurance business is known to have attracted the interests of at least two of the retired army generals: retired Maj.-Gen. David Ejoor, long identified as the Chairman, *West African Provincial Insurance Co. Ltd.,* a Nigerian subsidiary of a multi-national company;[99] and Maj.-Gen. Olu Bajowa, Director, *Roverton Insurance Co. Ltd.,* established in 1979 to handle general insurance business except life.[100] The above-mentioned are examples of top retired military persons in the banking and insurance business that we know. But there are certain to be many more.

(k) Private Security Business

Thus far, most of the private business activities of Nigeria's retired military men analysed above bear little or no relation to their previous profession of soldiering.* However, as the Nigerian economy and society grew at once more complex and unequal, with its attendant rising wave of crime (including armed robberies), there had emerged a number of private companies recruiting and relying on retired military cum police personnel for their private security business. These were companies specialising in providing the services of watching, guarding, and patrolling persons, property, and other business premises, or the carrying of money, for the purpose of ensuring protection

---

* Nor should this be surprising. For soldiering *per se* is not an easily transferable and marketable skill. Besides, the near-monopoly of the coercive machinery of the Nigerian State limits the opportunities for making private use of the unique skill or special expertise that goes with the profession. The converse of this is that it is only in government-owned agencies, especially at the federal level, that one can find job vacancies which have need for the use and hire of the military man's special expertise. See chapter 5 for details.

against crime.[101]   Demand for such services came to be heightened after the Structural Adjustment Programme (SAP) was introduced in 1986 and in response to the burden of external debt. The rising state of general insecurities, tensions and conflicts generated by both pressures, coupled with the declining capacity of regular armed and police forces in coping with the latter, created need for privatising much of security functions.

Among the first indigenous firms to be recognised in the field are *Vanni Holdings Ltd.,* and *Nigerian Explosives & Plastics Co. Ltd.,* although both have corporate links with certain multi-national business interest; the former with Vanni International,[102] and the latter with *Remington Arms Inc.,* U.S.A. among others.[103] Other companies in the private security business include *Don International Ltd., Metropolitan Guards Ltd., United Security Group.* But retired military personnel working as employees in such private security companies are invariably of low rank and rarely higher than major or the equivalent.

Some retired top officers have of recent moved into the business, not as employees or workers but as employers or owners. Two names readily come to mind: (1) a former Vice-Admiral, Joseph Edet Akinwale Wey, named as the foundation President of the recently (August 1987) inaugurated Nigerian Professional Security Association;[104] and (2) retired Maj.-Gen. Joseph Garba, named as Director, *Montgomery Vaults Ltd.,* Yaba, also a very new company in the private security business.[105] But there could be more.

(l)   Printing and Publishing

Printing and Publishing are the last but one major business area which has come to attract the interests of the top retired military. We know at least two retired generals with investment in this business, although there are certain to be many others involved.

But before naming them as well as their companies, a brief description of the nature of the business is necessary. There is a myriad of ventures grouped under this business category, and it includes not only printing and publishing proper, but also ownership of printing press, newspaper proprietorship, and such other allied activities as bindery, book trade, etc.

One of the first known top retired military officers to have invested in this area is retired Maj.-Gen. A. Mohammed, described as Managing Director of the *Atoto Press Ltd.,* situated along Oko Erin Road in Ilorin, the capital of Kwara State. However, the size of investment and operation involving the latter venture is relatively small compared to that of retired Maj.-Gen. Shehu Musa Yar'Adua.

Retired Maj.-Gen. Yar'Adua is the owner of The *Nationhouse Press Limited,* which publishes the recently (1987) launched national daily *The Reporter,* of which the retired general is also the proprietor. With this, retired Maj.-Gen. Yar'Adua thus ranks among the few most leading Nigerian businessmen or/and ex-politicians known to own and run national daily newspapers.*

(m) Law, Medical, and Other Professional Practice

Lastly, there are the businesses that relate to law, medical and other professional practice, retainership, and consulting services, including those of engineers, accountants, architects, and surveyors. But retired military officers practising these skills as a post-retirement activity must have trained, received the necessary qualifications, and been so registered by the appropriate professional bodies.**

Retired Officers practising such skills could either have retired as military lawyers, military doctors, and from other professinal corps of the armed forces, or gone back to school after retirement in order to receive these qualifications.

But we are not interested in pursuing this distinction here. Suffice it here to simply point out the examples of retired military officers in various professional practices. The examples we have in mind include (1) from LAW: those of retired Maj.-Gen. I.B.M. Haruna,[106] *Ibrahim Haruna & Co., Solicitors & Advocates,* with chambers in Lagos; retired Maj.-Gen. David Jemibewon,[107] *David M. Jemibewon & Co., Legal Practitioners,* also based in Lagos; and more recently retired Col. Yohanna Madaki,[108] *Kabeyan Chambers Legal Practitioners,* Kaduna; (2) From MEDICAL practice, retired Brig. Adeniyi Austen-Peters,[109] proprietor of both *The Clinic and Austen·Restaurant* being run at the Tafawa Balewa Shopping Complex, Lagos; Retired Grp.-Capt. James Adebayo Ogunro,[110] retired Col. E.W.O. Thomas,[111] and retired E.E. Bassey-Inyang,[112] all running medical practices of various kinds in Lagos, including the *Akan Clinic* of which the third is Medical Director; (3) from ENGINEERING, retired Brigadier M.S. Toki,[113] recently appointed the Executive Secretary, Nigerian Society of Engineers, but also believed to have a private engineering consulting or contracting firm of his own; and discharged Captain A.A. Adegun, Technical Director, *Lee Fakino Nigeria Ltd., Construction Engineers,* located near Bishop Phillip Academy, Monatan-Iwo Road, Ibadan. These are but a few examples of retired military officers practising their various professional skills or specialisations other than military. There are many more that we have not mentioned here, including perhaps those with larger and more successful practice, particularly in medicine and engineering.

Conclusion

The foregoing discussions of the chapter have sought to demonstrate what we hypothesised as the complex of increasingly interlocking interests among representatives of the

---

* These are the Estate of Late Chief Obafemi Awolowo, Proprietor of the African Newspapers of Nigeria Ltd., and Publisher of *Nigerian Tribune;* Michael Ibru, owner of the Guardian Press Ltd., and Guardian Newspapers, and Printer and Publisher of the Guardian Group of Newspapers; The Estate of late Chief Aboderin, owner Punch (Nig) Ltd., and publisher of *The Punch;* and Chief M.K.O. Abiola, owner of Concord press of Nigeria Ltd., and Publisher of the *Concord* Group of Newspapers.

** Although nothing prevents anyone without these qualifications from setting up a private medical (including X-ray diagnostic) Centre, or a firm of consulting engineers, and running this as a purely business proposition, while employing others to work for him or her. But examples of this are rare.

military establishment and private business generally, including businessmen special-ising in defence contracts and procurement, and the recent contributions of the growing class of retired military officers particularly to the development of this phenomenon. This hypothesis on inter-penetration of the military and business spheres, the reader would recall, was central to our definition of the "military-business complex."

The strategy of analysis has been to detail the activities of retired military officers in major areas of the private sector; namely, defence procurement and contracts, large-scale farming and agro-allied ventures, import and export business (particularly shipping), distributive trade and commerce, building and construction, petroleum business, transport industry (including haulage), property or real estate, manufacturing (other than food processing), banking and insurance, private security business, printing and publishing, and professional practice and retainership (including legal and medi-cal). Of course, that analysis cannot be considered complete. For it leaves out the matter of retired military appointments to corporate positions, i.e., directorships, on govern-ment boards and multi-national companies, which dovetail with the activities just described. Fortunately, there is a whole chapter of the study devoted to this other matter (see chapter 6) and intended necessarily as a companion piece to the present one.

Let us conclude our discussions here by indicating one other important way of gauging the extent of retired military officers' involvement in business. This is the large and growing number of trade associations, business societies, and special-interest groups, in whose affairs retired military officers have come to play leading roles. Admittedly, membership of some of these associations is of professional nature; and, as such, may not have been new, but infact carried over from the service or even pre-service days.

We have in mind professional bodies such as the Nigerian Medical Association (NMA), and Nigerian Society of Engineers (NSE). Military officers who retire as trained doctors and engineers, and have not been previously debarred, are certain to be members of these two bodies respectively. We have already pointed out some examples of both. There are also retired military officers to be found enrolled as members of the Nigerian Bar Association (NBA). The Nigerian Institute of Town Planners (NITP) has as its current President one retired Lt.-Col. Tomi Asenuga, formerly of the civil engineering and town planning unit of the army corps of engineers.[114]

Some retired military elements can be counted among other professional associations, representing dentists, pharmacists, nurses, and possibly architects, surveyors, and accountants possessing recognised-registrable qualifications by various professional councils. For, as if borrowing from the American experience, Nigeria is fast becoming a nation of "joiners." The tendency or propensity to form or belong to one special-interest organisation or another is in the ascendant.

But it is in their membership of businessmen's unions – various trade, business, and commercial organisations as well as chambers of commerce and industry – that the interests of the retired military in business have become most publicised. For example, retired Lt.-Col. Keshi, has for some time now been active in the Lagos State Chapter of the Manufacturers Association of Nigeria (MAN), and was its Chairman up to December 1986. At the same time, retired Maj.-Gen. Olufemi Olutoye was mentioned as Chairman of the Akure Chamber of Commerce. The names of some of the officers already mentioned, as well as those of former Brigadier Samuel O. Ogbemudia and retired Maj.-Gen. George A. Innih regularly feature in the activities and quarterly news of the Nigerian Association of Chambers of Commerce, Industry, Mines, and Agriculture (or NACCIMA).[115] Retired Maj.-Gen. David Ejoor has for some time now been President of the Nigeria-Belgium Chamber of Commerce;[116] while retired Maj.-Gen. Emmanuel Abisoye was for many years the President, and remains an important member, of the Nigerian Exporters Association (NEA), as we saw. Retired Maj.-Gen. Olu Bajowa is said to be a member of National Association of Peugeot Distributors of Nigeria (NAPDN).[117]

Even more interesting is the observation that almost every major line of industrial cum agro-allied and commercial activity involving the retired military now has its association. Thus, retired General Obasanjo became a foundation member as well as the first President of the Nigerian Association of Poultry Breeders and Hatchery (or NAPBH) established in 1985, which also has retired Maj.-Gen. Innih as a member. The latter was also the first National Vice-President, Poultry Association of Nigeria for 1984–86,[118] and at the same time Executive Member, Bendel State Poultry Association of Nigeria.[119] Both retired Lt.-Gen Danjuma and retired Maj.-Gen. Yar'Adua are assumed to have been involved in founding the newly (September 1987) established Nigerian Shipping Companies Association (N.S.C.A),[120] if only because of their interests in the shipping business. A former Vice-Admiral Joseph Akinwale Wey was named in August 1987 as the foundation President of the newly inaugurated Nigerian Professional Security Association.[121] There could be more.

In the meantime, this joining tendency of the retired military at once reflects and reinforces the power of their business and propertied interests, while helping to strengthen the social solidarity among members. At the same time, the joining tendency just described is one further proof of the increasingly inter-locking relationships involving the business and retired military elites. It is an outgrowth of what one foreign weekly magazine in a recent issue aptly calls "the Military Incorporated phenomenon" rearing its head in much of today's Third World.[122]

Table 3.1   Retired Military Officers in Private Business Ventures, 1970–1986

TYPES OF PRIVATE VENTURES	EXAMPLES OF RETIRED MILITARY INVOLVEMENTS AND THEIR BUSINESS NAMES
1. **DEFENCE PROCUREMENT & CONTRACTS:** Defence procurement and supplies (fuels, food and medicaments, apparel, boots and furniture); arms and equipment imports; building and construction contracts for the MOD.	The most natural venture for top retired military officers the world over; specific Nigerian examples not easy to come by, but certain to involve countless private companies or individuals both civilian and military, foreign and indigenous.
2. **LARGE-SCALE FARMING & AGRO-ALLIED VENTURES:** particularly poultry, feed-mills, maize, rice and soya beans production; citrus and other fruits cultivation; livestock, and fishery; food processing and other agro-allied industries	The favourite post-retirement pursuits of Nigeria's military generals, including such well-known examples as Gen. Obasanjo, *Temperance Farms* (now christened *Obasanjo Farms Nigeria Ltd.*); Maj.-Gen. Yar'Adua, *Sambo Farms;* Maj.-Gen. Innih, *Niger Valley Agro Industries;* Lt.-Gen. Akinrinade, *Niger Feeds & Agricultural Operations;* Lt.-Gen Jalo, *Jalo Farms;* Lt.-Gen. Wushishi, *Nigerfirst Integrated Farms.*
3. **IMPORT & EXPORT BUSINESS, INCLUDING SHIPPING:** Import and export business, clearing and forwarding, container services, warehousing, running of private jetties, operation of shipping charter lines, ownership of ocean-going vessels.	Maj.Gen. Abisoye, *Emmanoye Investments Company Ltd.;* Lt.-Gen. Danjuma, Chairman *Nigeria-America Line,* & Vice-President, *Medafrica Groups;* Maj.-Gen. Yar'Adua, *African Oceans Lines* (jointly owned with Chief M.K.O. Abiola and others).
4. **DISTRIBUTIVE TRADE AND COMMERCE AS WELL AS OTHER ALLIED PURSUITS (INCLUDING HOTEL DEVELOPMENT):** Distributive trade in essential goods, whether produced at home or imported, wholesale or retail, otherwise called the distributorships business, hotel development and catering services.	Top among the many examples are Maj.-Gen. Ejoor, *Bensab (Nigeria) Ltd.;* Col. Okechime, *Tiki Group of Companies;* Brig. Adekunle, *Samak Industrial Holdings;* Maj.-Gen. Innih, part-owner of *Golden Tulip-Agura Hotel.*

TYPES OF PRIVATE VENTURES	EXAMPLES OF RETIRED MILITARY INVOLVEMENTS AND THEIR BUSINESS NAMES
5. **BUILDING & CONSTRUCTION (OTHER THAN DEFENCE):** Contracting for building, civil engineering and construction projects of all kinds, together with their allied services.	Former Vice-Admiral Wey, & Maj.-Gen. Martins Adamu, both Directors, *Arbico Nigeria Ltd.,;* Brig. E.E. Ikwue, Chairman & major shareholder, *Technical Constructions Nigeria Ltd.*; former Lt.-Col. Adejoro, *S.S. Adejoro & Co. Ltd. Engineers and Builders;* Maj.-Gen. Aduloju, Chairman, *Fred & Johnson Engineering Nigeria Ltd.*
6. **PETROLEUM BUSINESS; OTHER QUARRYING & MINING ACTIVITIES:** Petroleum & gas exploration, production services; bunkering, marketing & distribution; running of petrol stations; other private mining & quarrying operations.	Some top retired military officers are believed to be involved in the lifting and sale of crude oil; and a number have their own oil tankers. Besides, there are the examples of Lt.-Gen. Danjuma, director and major shareholder of the marine oilfield company *Sea Trucks (Nigeria) Ltd.;* and Maj.-Gen. Aduloju, named chairman of *Flamo Petroleum Nigeria Ltd.* Regarding other mining and quarrying activities, Brig. E.E. Ikwue, Chairman & Managing Director, *Nigerian Swiss Construction and Quarrying Industries.*
7. **MOTOR INDUSTRY, TRANSPORTATION & HAULAGE SERVICES (OTHER THAN SHIPPING):** Private transportation & haulage business; motor transport companies, boat and ferry services for inland waterways; air services; courier services.	Maj.Gen. Bajowa, Managing Director, *Trinity Motors;* Maj.-Gen. Armah, Managing Director, *Emene Motors Ltd.;* former Lt-Cdr. Diete-Spiff, Managing Director/President of *BZB Group of Companies.*
8. **PROPERTY OR REAL-ESTATE BUSINESS:** (Partly related to 5 above): property and real-estate investment, building and management; provision and renting of house and office accommodation (other than defence already covered by 1 above).	Most military officers of the rank of lieutenant-colonel and above or their equivalents, whether serving or retired, have one interest or the other in real-estate business. Thus, examples of retired military involvement here are so numerous that it makes no sense to list any.

TYPES OF PRIVATE VENTURES	EXAMPLES OF RETIRED MILITARY INVOLVEMENTS AND THEIR BUSINESS NAMES
9. **MANUFACTURING (OTHER THAN FOOD PROCESSING):** Setting up industries in the productive sectors of the economy (other than food processing), but including metal and wooden furniture & fixtures; structural metal products; agricultural and industrial tools and equipment; household electrical apparatus; plastic goods; textiles, tyres and tubes, etc.	Maj.-Gen. Adebayo, *MAG Furniture and Interior Designs Ltd.;* Lt.-Col. Keshi, Managing Director of a plastic processing company *Anchor Products;* ex-Brig. Ogbemudia, owner of *Sogalson Limited,* an agricultural implements and spare parts fabrication company; Maj.-Gen. Aduloju, Chairman of *Megpin (Nigeria) Ltd* and *Alfa Manufacturing Co. Nigeria Ltd.* manufacturing air-conditioner electrical sets.
10. **FINANCE, BANKING & INSURANCE:** Business in the banking and finance sector, particularly financial investment and lending, including ownership of banking institutions; stock-broking firms; investments in the insurance sub-sector.	Maj.-Gen. Yar'Adua, part-owner of *Habib Bank (Nigeria) Ltd.;* Lt.-Gen. Danjuma, Chairman, *Universal Trust Bank of Nigeria Ltd.;* Maj.-Gen. Olu Bajowa, Director, *Roverton Insurance Co. Ltd.*
11. **PRIVATE SECURITY BUSINESS:** Companies specialising in providing security services for persons, property, or other businesses	Maj.Gen. Joseph Garba, Director, *Montgomery Vaults Ltd.*
12. **PRINTING AND PUBLISHING:** Printing and publishing proper; ownership of printing press; newspaper proprietorship; investment in book trade.	Maj.-Gen. Abdulahi Mohammed, Managing Director, *Atoto Press Ltd.*; Maj.-Gen. Yar'Adua, owner *Nationhouse Press Limited,* and publisher of the new national daily *The Reporter.*
13. **LAW, MEDICAL, & OTHER PROFESSIONAL PRACTICE, RETAINERSHIP, & CONSULTANCY** Retired military doctors, lawyers, engineers and other professionals setting up their various private practices and retainerships	Maj.-Gen. Haruna, *Ibrahim Haruna & Co., Solicitors & Advocates;* Maj.-Gen. Jemibewon, *David M. Jemibewon & Co. Legal Practitioners;* Col. E.E. Inyang, Medical Director, *Akan Clinic,* Lagos; Brig. Austen-Peters, Director, *The Clinic,* Tafawa Balewa Complex, Lagos; Capt. Adegun, Technical Director, *Lee Fakino Nig. Ltd. Construction Engineers.*

Sources: Marie Lawn (ed.), *Major Companies of Nigeria 1980/81* (London: Graham & Trotman Ltd., 1980); ICON Limited (Merchant Bankers), *ICON Nigeria Company Handbook 1983* (Lagos); Research & Data Services Ltd. (or REDASEL), *Nigeria Banking Almanac 1985/86* (Lagos); Alfa Communications, *Nigeria Banking Annual Incorporating WHO'S WHO in Banking 1987* (Lagos); Nigerian Stock Exchange, *The Nigerian Stock Exchange Handbook,* Vol. 2 (Lagos, 1985) among others

NOTES

1. See *New Nigerian*, January 3, 1978, pp. 1-5; First quoted in J. 'Bayo Adekanye, "The Role of Private Sector and the Universities in the Development of Military Technology", *Nigerian Journal of Policy and Strategy,* June 1986, p.55

2. *Ibid.*

3. On the importance attached to this concept by the pre-1966 Nigerian military, see Robin Luckham, *The Nigerian Military 1960–67* (Cambridge, Eng.: The University Press, 1971), pp. 109–14.

4. The Western European sources of these elaborate honour concepts are analysed in Alfred Vagts, *A History of Militarism: Civilian and Military* (New York: Free Press, 1959), pp. 66–74, 175–9. Also, see Samuel P. Huntington, *The Soldier and the State* (Cambridge: Harvard University Press, 1958) pp. 222–26, 289–94

5. Ali A. Mazrui, "The Lumpen Proletariat and the Lumpen Militariat: African Soldiers as New Political Class", *Political Studies,* Vol. 21, No. 1, 1973, pp 1-12

6. See O. Aboyade & A. Ayida, "The War Economy in Perspective", *Nigerian Jounrnal of Economic and Social Studies,* Vol. 13, No. 1, March 1971, pp.13–38.

7. In addition to inducing a new sense of urgency that resulted in some military technological innovations see Adekanye, "Role of Private Sector and Universities in Development ...", *op. cit.,* pp. 52–3.

8. See Obafemi Awolowo, *AWO on the Nigerian Civil War* (Lagos: John West Publications 1981), especially the last chapter dealing with "Financing The War", pp. 124–40.

9. There were many Nigerians known to have profited from those business transactions of the civil war period, rising to become prominent businessmen and politicians in later years, among them were Chief Arthur Nzeribe and Alhaji Ibrahim Waziri.

10. See B. Onimode, J. Ohiorhenuan, and T. Adeniran, *Multinational Corporations in Nigeria,* (Ibadan: Les Shyraden Nigeria Ltd., 1983), pp. 110–12.

11. To adapt the very apt title of S.K. Panter-Brick's (ed.), *Work, Soldiers and Oil: The Political Transformation of Nigeria,* (London: Frank Cass, 1978).

12. Federal Republic of Nigeria, *Third National Development Plan 1979–80* (Lagos: Central Planning Office, 1975), Vol. 1, p. 153.

13. Onimode *et.al, Multinational Corporations in Nigeria,* op.cit., passim.

14. Those involved were reported on October 31, 1975 to have been ordered to appear before the Belgore Tribunal set up to probe the massive cement importation affair, Daily Times, *Nigeria Year Book* 1976 (Lagos: Daily Times Publication, 1976), p. 168.

15. Federal Republic of Nigeria, *The Green Revolution: A Food Produciton Plan for*

Nigeria (Federal Ministry of Agriculture, 1980), and *Fourth National Development Plan 1981–85* (Lagos: National Planning Office, 1981), pp. 85ff. However, for a critique of the use to which came to be put the huge sums of money allocated to agriculture during the period, see Yusuf Bala Usman *et al., The Nigerian Economic Crisis: Causes and Solutions,* (Zaria: Gaskiya Corporation Ltd., for ASUU, 1985), p. 30ff.

16. This is, of course, true of civilian business ventures as well.

17. For some of the descriptions of Nigerian indigenoius entrepreneurship applied here, see E.O. Akeredolu-Ale, *The Underdevelopment of Indigenous Entrepreneurship in Nigeria* (Ibadan: The University Press, 1975), & S.P. Schatz, *Nigerian Capitalism* (Berkeley & Los Angeles: University of California Press, 1978).

18. Onimode *et al., Multinational Corporations in Nigeria...,* op. cit., pp. 123 -25.See also John Ohiorhenuan, *Capital and the State in Nigeria* (New York: Westport, Conn. & London: Greenwood Press, chs. 3, 4 & 6.

19. As reported separately, though on the same day, in *Daily Times* (Lagos), December 14, 1985, p. 17, and *Daily Sketch* (Ibadan), December 14, 1985, p. 13.

20. Retired Maj.-Gen. Shehu Yar'Adua's business involvements are known to include the following: *Habib Bank* (in partnership with M.K.O. Abiola and others); *African Ocean Lines Ltd.* (with M.K.O. Abiola and Bamanga Tukur and others); *Sambo Farms* (outside Funtua); *Madara Ltd.,* a dairy firm recently acquired (at Vom, Plateau State); *Spring Waters Nigeria Ltd* (SWAN); proprietor of *Nation House Press Ltd.* (publishers of the national daily *Reporter*) among others.

21. The central argument of my first book *Nigeria in Search of a Stable Civil-Military System,* (Aldershot, Engl.: Gower, & Boulder, Colorado, U.S.A.: Westview, 1981), ch. 3.

22. Four other Nigerian companies classified in 1980 as operating in this business area were Industrial & Safety Equipment (Nigeria) Limited; Nabena, LR. & Sons Ltd.; Sonnar Nigeria Limited; and, of course, the Defence Industries Corporation of Nigeria; See Marie Lawn (ed.), *Major Companies of Nigeria 1980/81* (London: Graham & Trotman Limited, 1980), p. 257.

23. *The Guardian* (Lagos), June 29, 1986, p.9.

24. See "49 Contractors Summoned: Panel to Probe ₦600m awards", *Daily Sketch* (Ibadan), June 14, 1985, p.1

25. *ibid.*

26. ICON Limited (Merchant Bankers), *ICON Nigeria Company Handbook 1983,* (Lagos: ICON & Jikonzult Management Services Ltd., 1982), p.34.

27. By public notice, appearing in *Daily Times* (Lagos), October 8, 1986, p.19.

28. In addition to running a lucrative multi-million naira Palm Royal Motel, see Daily Times, *Nigeria Year Book* (Lagos: Daily Times Publication, 1977–78), p.234. It

is not clear whether those farms seized by the state's new military government were later recovered by Ogbemudia during the short-lived political come-back as state governor between October and December 1983, nor are we certain of their relationship with what became known as the Ogbemudia Farms subsequently sold to John Holt Nigeria Ltd.

29. As subsequently reported in the *Daily Times,* Lagos), December 17, 1979, p. 1.

30. Information about the latter deal was first brought to public notice by an article "MANDARA LIMITED: Sold Out or Given Out?", published in *The Analyst* (Jos), Vol. 2 No. 1, 1987, pp. 19–21.

31. *National Concord* (Lagos), September 12, 1986, p. 20.

32. *New Nigerian* (Lagos) May 29, 1986, p.2

33. See *New Nigerian* (Lagos), May 29, 1986, p.2

34. *Daily Times* (Lagos), March 12, 1986, p.8.

35. *Daily Sketch* (Ibadan), December 14, 1985, p 13.

36. See the recent special issue on "Military Inc.: The Military Forces in Business", appearing in the monthly publication *SOUTH* (London), March 1988, p.17.

37. Also advertised as a manufacturing company, see fn. 87 below.

38. *The Guardian*, (Lagos), June 1, 1987, p. 13.

39. This is one of the very few items of information volunteered by an anonymous respondent, which we have been unable to confirm.

40. Information from "Obasanjo: Farmer, Leader, Writer", being special issue of *Newswatch* (Lagos), Vol. 5, No. 2, January 12, 1982, p. 13.

41. *New Nigerian* (Lagos), May 29, 1986, p.2.

42. Retired Lt.-Gen. Akinrinade, reported in *Nigerian Observer* (Benin City), July 3, 1986, pp. I & II.

43. *Daily Times* (Lagos), June 2, 1982, p. 1; *National Concord* (Lagos), June 19, 1982; *Sunday Tribune,* (Ibadan), June 27, 1982. p. 5; *National Concord,* June 29, 1982, p. 2; *Nigerian Tribune* (Ibadan), July 16, 1982, p.7.

44. *Ibid.*

45. Bibliographic Centre of Nigeria Ltd., *Who's Who in Nigeria,* 3rd Edition (Lagos, 1985), pp. 42–3.

46. *ibid.*

47. *Daily Times* (Lagos), April 19, 1986, p.11.

48. Biographical Centre of Nigeria Ltd., *Who's Who in Nigeria, ...* op. cit., p. 40.

49. *ibid.,* p. 41

50. *The Guardian* (Lagos), December 22, 1985, p. 3.

51. *The Guardian* (Lagos), August 29, 1986, p.3

52. Since being ordered, together with an associate Brig. Folusho Sotomi to go on compulsory retirement in late August 1974, see Daily Times, *Nigeria Year Book 1975* (Lagos: Daily Times Publications, 1975), p. 40

53. *The Guardian* (Lagos), November 23, 1985, p. 12.

54. As published in *The Guardian* (Lagos), July 28, 1987, p.12; July 30, 1987, pp. 12–13; July 31, 1987, p.6.

55. *Ibid*

56. Ibid.

57. Especially under the Shagari presidency (1979–83) when the import-licence business became or rather got converted into a really big business, see "the seamy side of politics" of the period as we describe it in Chapter 4.

58. See, for examle, *Daily Times* (Lagos), March 29, 1986, p. 12; March 31, 1986, p. 12; April 1, 1986, p. 12; April 2, 1986, p.12; April 3, 1986, p. 12; April 4, April 5, 1986, p.7.

59. We refer here to the establishment of the "second-tier foreign exchange market" (or SFEM), later replaced by one "foreign exchange market" or (FEM); reliance on "market forces" for determining pricing of goods and services; and the government's move towards trade and payments liberation – all as part of the so-called "structural adjustment programme" (SAP) aimed at restructuring the nation's economy and rescuing it from the massive debts and recession with which it is faced. Though inspired by the International Monetary Fund (IMF) philosophy, and not without their own great attendant costs particularly social, these measures have succeeded in dealing a death blow to the old import licence system as well as distributorships as a business activity. But it is believed that some of the old interests thus displaced as well as newly generated ones soon moved into the banking business as shown below.

60. One of the properties belonging to the ex-army brigadier and confiscated by the Murtala regime following he counter-coup of July 29, 1975, see fn. 28 above.

61. The Golden Tulip-Agura Hotel at Abuja was inaugurated with a big advertisement placed in *Daily Times* (Lagos), May 3, 1986, pp. 6–8. However, it has since run into financial troubles and gone under receivership.

62. Nigerian Stock exchange, *The Nigerian Stock Exchange Handbook.,* Vol. 2, (Lagos, 1984), p. 148. Also see ICON, *ICON Nigeria Company Handbook,.* op. cit., p 34.

63. Nigerian Stock Exchange, loc. cit., passim.

64. *ibid.*, p.. 140

65. Alhaji Musa Yar'Adua is said to have taken over the chairmanship of Roads (Nig.) Ltd. from Alhaji Shehu Shagari, before the latter became President of the Federal Republic of Nigera in 1979, see Y.B. Usman *et al.*, *The Nigerian Economic Crisis* ..., op.cit., pp. 111–112.

66. ICON Ltd., *ICON Nigeria Company Handbook 1983* ... op cit., 315.

67. While the information as regards this business concern is substantially correct, I have not been abe to cross-check that on the owner's ex-military background or links.

68. *Daily Sketch* (Ibadan), December 14, 1985, p. 13.

69. Flora Enterprises apparently owned the petrol station that used to be located at the Ede Junction on the Gbongon-Osogbo Road.

70. According to the Nigerian National Petroleum Corporation (or N.N.P.C.) sources.

71. Which the Aboyade Committee of Investigation into Counter-Trade, headed by Professor O. Aboyade, was set up to probe, and later reported on in 1987.

72. This information was obtained from B. Onimode *et. al.*, *Multinational Corporations in Nigeria* ..., op. cit., p. 32.

73. And are therefore likely to have been cross-listed under "building and construction" as a business line, see the sub-section of our discussions so titled.

74. See sub-section on "transport industry, including haulage" immediately below.

75. ICON Ltd., *ICON Nigeria Company handbook 1983* ..., op. cit., p. 300.

76. *Daily Sketch* (Ibadan), December 14, 1985, p. 13.

77. *This Week* (Lagos), Vol. 8, No. 9, May 9, 1988, p. 23.

78. Biographical Centre of Nigeria Ltd., *Who's Who in Nigeria* ..., op. cit., pp. 26–27.

79. *Ibid.*

80. This information, which was initially obtained from *University of Ibadan Official Bulletin,* No. 791, May 29, 1987, p.2, has since been cross-checked with other sources and found to be true.

81. See Chapter 6.

82. It has not been possible to establish the authenticity of this particular information volunteered to the author by an army officer student at one time on course here at Ibadan.

83. See fn. 43 above.

84. See fn. 66 above.

85. Biographical Centre of Nigeria , *Who's Who in Nigeria* ..., op. cit., pp. 42–43.

86. And reported recently to have become a subject of litigation in a law court, *The*

Guardian (Lagos), December 11, 1986, p.3.

87. An example of this particular kind of business is Chief Ogbemudia's Sogalson Limited, registered at 108 West Circular Rd., Benin City, here classified under manufacturing as a business activity, but known to be also involved in agriculture, see fn. 31n above.

88. *Sunday Vanguard* (Lagos), October 27, 1985, pp. 5, 19; Lawn (ed.), *Major Companies of Nigeria 1980/81 ...*, op. cit., p. 113.

89. ICON, *ICON Nigeria Company Handbook 1983. ...*, op. cit., p. 242.

90. *ibid.*, p. 33.

91. Lawn (ed.), *Major Companies of Nigeria 1980/81... op. cit.*, p.104, but which has since folded up.

92. *Daily Times* (Lagos), December 14, 1985, p. 17; *New Nigerian* (Lagos), October 3, 1985, p.26.

93. Something wished for by the President of the Federal Republic, General Ibarahim Babangida, as clear from his widely reported national policy address, "Defence Policy Within the Framework of our National Planning", delivered at Eko Hotel, Lagos, and reproduced in two parts in the *Daily Times* (Lagos), March 5 & 6, 1985, p. 5 each. Babangida had delievered this some six months before becoming head of state and in his capacity then as the Chief of Army Staff.

94. See J. 'Bayo Adekanye, "Domestic Production of Arms and the Defence Industries Corporation of Nigeria", *Current Research on Peace and Violence*, 4, 1983, pp. 258–69.

95. Research & Data Services Ltd., *Nigeria Banking Almanac 1985/86* (Lagos: REDASEL, 1986), p. 159; Alfa Communications Limited, *Nigeria Banking Annual Incorporating WHO's WHO in Banking 1987*, (Lagos: Alfa Communications), p. 131.

96. Research & Data Services Ltd., *ibid.*, p. 265.

97. *Ibid.*, pp. 83–84; Alfa Communications, loc. cit., pp. 81–82; *New Nigerian* (Lagos), January 9, 1986, p.3.

98   See *National Concord* (Lagos), April 25, 1986, p. 8.

99. ICON, *ICON Nigeria Company Handbook 1983...*, op. cit., p. 351.

100. *ibid.*, p. 292.

101. And, as if to acknowledge that business in this area has come to stay, a decree was recently promulgated – the Private Guard Companies Decree No. 33 of 1986 – aimed at regulating the practices of private security companies.

102. Lawn (ed.), *Major Companies of Nigeria 1980/81 ...*, op. cit., pp. 223–4.

103. *ibid.*, p.148.

104. Suggesting that the former vice-admiral may have business interests or involvement in the area.

105. *Daily Times* (Lagos), September 8, 1987, p.7.

106 L.L.E., (ABU, Zaria).

107. L.L.B. (UNILAG)

108. L.L.B. (UNIBADAN)

109. B.A. (Cantab, 1945), M.A. (Cambr. 1956) M.R.C.S. (Engl), L.C., C.P. (London), M.B., B.Ch. (Cantab 1952).

110. M.B., Ch.B (Edinburgh 1958).

111. L.R., C.P. & L.M. (Ireland 1953).

112. M.R.C.S. (Engl. 1957), L.R.G.P. (London 1957), F.M.C.G.P. (Nig. 1975).

113. Retired Brig. M.S. Toki has training qualifications and is duly registered as an engineer.

114. Retired Lt.-Col. Tomi Asenuga, who is a trained architect specialising in urban design and planning, holds Dip. Arch (Cantab), M. Arch. in U.D, MC.P. (Harvard) qualifications. He is the Managing Director/Chairman of *UDA Urban Design Associates,* a Firm of Architects, planners and development consultants

115. As a reading of the Association's magazine *NACCIMA NEWS* issued from 15A Ikorodu Road, Maryland, Lagos, shows.

116. *The Guardian* (Lagos), August 29, 1986, p.3

117. I am grateful to the chairman/managing director of Confidence Automobile Engineering Co. Ltd., Chief M.O. Adewakun, for this information.

118. Biographical Centre of Nigeria, *Who's Who in Nigeria,* 3rd Edition (Lagos, Biographical Centre of Nigeria, 1985), pp. 70–71.

119. *Ibid.*

120. See *The Guardian* (Lagos), September 24, 1987, p.10. It is significant that on the Executive Council of the new shipping association were among others: (1) Dr. Raymond Dokpesi (Executive Secretary), himself part-owner with retired Maj.-Gen. Yar'Adua and Chief M.K.O. Abiola, of the *African Oceans Line*; and (2) Mallam Musa Danjuma (Member), representing in a corporate capacity the *Nigeria-America Line Ltd.*, of which retired Lt.-Gen Danjuma is the Director.

121. See fn. 104 above.

122. *South* (London), March 1988, pp. 9ff.

4

Phenomenon of ex-Military Officers in Politics

In this chapter of the study we analyse the role of retired military officers in the politics and government of the Second Republic, that is under the Shehu Shagari civilian presidency (1979–83), leaving their more recent role to be treated later in a separate chapter (see Chapter 6). We look at four things: (1) participation of ex-officers in the 1976–79 electoral struggles preparatory to the first return to civilian rule on October 1, 1979; (2) the political pardon granted to the one-time head of state ex-General Gowon as well as the ex-"Biafran" leader Ojukwu, and its effects upon the Nigerian army, politics, and society; (3) retired military officers' role in governance, both as public office or party political office holders, and, if any, in the seamy side of politics of the times; and (4) retired military involvement in the controversial elections of 1983 and the immediate aftermath. These issues are discussed below in the order in which they have just been broached.

1. Participation in the Struggle For Power, 1976–79

The pattern of active involvement by the retired military in the politics and government of the Second Republic, 1979–83, had been set towards the terminal phase of the preceding military rule. Admittedly, at the very initial stage of that transition to civil rule involving the drafting of new constitutional proposals for post-military Nigeria, not a single retired military officer could be seen to be active on the political scene.[1] However, between the time the Constitution Drafting Committee (CDC) submitted its Draft Constitution for public debate in late 1976 and the summoning of a Constituent Assembly in 1978 to deliberate on the Draft Constitution, a number of retired military officers emerged active politically. Let us follow the major stages of political involvement by the retired military more closely and in greater details.

Public Debates on Draft Constitution

We have suggested that retired military officers did not play any visible role in the making of the Draft Constitution (1976). Nor in the list of three hundred and forty-six (346) or so memoranda submitted to the CDC by members of the public could a single one be pointed out as having come from a retired military person;[2] although there was a memorandum submitted by one top retired police officer and former Deputy Inspector-General of Police, Chief T.A. Fagbola.[3]

Also, initially, when the Draft Constitution was thrown open for public debates, only a very few retired military officers could be found taking part in the exercise, and mostly at the state level. A notable example among the few was Hillary M. Njoku, an ex-army colonel, who participated in the Imo State Seminar on the Draft Constitution held at Owerri on September 8, 1977, at which he was said to have distributed leaflets titled "Freedom of the Press and the Nigerian Draft Constitution".[4] The low participation by the retired military was in marked contrast to other social groups such as organised labour, the intelligentsia, various professional associations, and women's societies, whose members participated very actively in the public debates on the 1976 Draft Constitution.

Two major reasons could be advanced for this initially low participation of retired military officers at this stage of the politics of return to civil rule. First, by the time of commencement of the draft constitutional debates in December 1976, the first massive wave of retirees from the armed forces (see chapter 2) had barely re-adjusted to their civilian life. This factor of timing alone, coupled with the paucity of officers as yet on retirement rolls, meant that not many could have been available psychologically and physically for recruitment to this initial political role.

Second, since political debates involve discussions and soldiers are generally ill-equipped for these,[5] a number of retired military officers, otherwise interested in going into active politics, might have found the general debate of 1976/77 particularly uncongenial. Nor had a generality of the military profession as yet acquired sufficient political training or intellectual confidence to be able to discourse on the major constitutional issues of the day, such as the merits or demerits of executive presidential government; what party cum electoral system to prescribe and based on what criteria; the role of the judiciary; fundamental objectives and directive principles of state policy, etc.

One of the first high-ranking officers to venture into the field of contest of political ideas was Maj.-General I.B.M. Haruna. Although retired from the army barely a month earlier, Maj.-Gen. Haruna found time to participate actively in the National Conference on Issues in the Draft Constitution organised under the auspices of the Institute of Administration, Ahmadu Bello University, Zaria, March 21–24, 1977.[6] But the said retired general was not to play any active role in the politics and government of the Second Republic or the events immediately preceding its inauguration.

Local Government Elections, December 1976

About the same time the CDC was submitting its Draft Constitution report for public debates, a programme of Local government re-organisation and reforms was being commenced by the Federal military government. This offered ex-military officers among other interested groups, including retired civil servants, lawyers, businessmen, and of course some former politicians, the prospect of being elected into some of the new local government bodies, municipal councils or management boards opening up.

In December 1976, elections were held countrywide to constitute the newly created three hundred and four (304) odd local councils organised under the auspices of the Federal Electoral Commission (or FEDECO). Countless number of retired military and police officers among others contested in the local government elections across the country. The contestants included retired Capt. E.K. George, standing for councillorship in the fourth ward of Port Harcourt city, capital of Rivers State,[7] and retired Commissioner of Police Joseph Adeola, seeking a seat in the Owan Local Council of the old Bendel State,[8] to mention just two examples.

By early 1977, a sizeable number of retired military officers had emerged holding political office at this third tier of government. The number included those whose selection for local political office was done through outright nominations by State governments. An example was Kaduna State where, of the sixty-nine (69) councillors nominated by the state government for all the local government areas, there were as many as thirty (30) or 43.48% names of retired officers, including retired Lt.-Col. U.O. Dikko, prominent on the list.[9] An additional number or retired officers were to be found elected/nominated into the local government councils of the remaining northern states.

For some southern examples, from Oyo State, retired Lt.-Col. Tunde Oyeleke stood for and was elected to the post of Chairman of Ifelodun local government council, with headquarters at Ikirun;[10] while retired (now the late) Lt.-Col. Ayo Ariyo emerged as the Chairman of Ijero local government council in Ondo State.[11] From the Rivers State came the example of retired Brig. George Kurubo, and the story of how he became the Chairman of the Management Board of the Bonny local government council that needs a brief elaboration. Retired Brig. Kurubo had been elected from the Bonny district into the Bonny local government council which also had representatives from three other districts – Okrika, Adoni, and Opobo, all of them sworn into office on March 9, 1977. But the councillors soon began to quarrel among themselves and along lines that made it possible for them to appeal for factional support from the component communities. This forced the state military government to dissolve the council and appoint a management board to run its affairs; and retired Brig. Kurubo became its Chairman.[12]

Meanwhile, for many of the retired officers specified above, these local councillorship positions and/or chairmanships, which they had just won, were to provide a useful training ground, if not the spring board, for being launched into state and national politics. The subsequent political careers of a number of the ex-officers show this.

Constituent Assembly Elections and Deliberations, August 1977 – September 1978

The next stage in the planned programme of transition to civil rule under the Murtala/

Obasanjo regime was the summoning of a Constituent Assembly to deliberate upon, ratify, or produce a new Constitution out of, the Draft Constitutional proposals. The elections into the Constituent Assembly were conducted on August 31, 1977, with the newly reorganised local governments acting as electoral colleges. Many retired military personnel again filed their papers to contest. The list included many who had participated in the previous local government elections, but a number were entering political competition for the first time.

By the time the results of the Constituent Assembly election were announced, two former top military officers had been elected – George T. Kurubo, a retired army brigadier and one-time head of air force, representing the Bonny local government council area of the Rivers State; and Hillary M. Njoku, a former army colonel and ex-"Biafran" officer, elected from the Owerri/Ikeduru local government area of Imo State. In addition, the Constituent Assembly had elected into its membership the late Alhaji Kam Salem, an ex-Inspector General of Police, representing the Munguno/Ngala area of Borno State; and one Mr. A. Yerima Balla, from Gombi in Gongola State, who claimed to have "spent five years in military college in India,"[13] and had actually seen action in the Burma campaigns of World War II.[14] Also elected were two distinguished members who, though civilians, had been intimately involved in the administration of military affairs going back to the late Balewa era: Alhaji Musa Daggash (a nominated member), a one-time permanent secretary in the Ministry of Defence; and Alhaji Ali Monguno (Maiduguri, Borno State), a one-time Minister in charge of the Nigerian Air Force.

Of the first three ex-military cum police officers elected Constituent Assemblymen, retired Brig. Kurubo was of course not completely new to politics. He had in fact been "in" politics since his first posting as Nigerian's Ambassador to Moscow shortly after the July 1966 counter-coup. Admittedly, his involvement then was as a soldier-turned-diplomat and therefore at the international level, where he had operated until he was compulsorily retired in August 1975. As we saw, his debut in national politics began on March 2, 1977, when the retired army brigadier, and himself an indigene of the Bonny district, won one of the councillorship seats in that local government, becoming chairman of its management board shortly thereafter. It was from the last position that retired Brig. Kurubo got elected into the Constituent Assembly.

The other ex-army senior officer who got elected into that Assembly, ex-Col. Hillary M. Njoku, cannot be described as a completely fresh comer to politics either, judging from R.C. Ohale's biographic study appositely titled "An Ex-Army Officer Turned Politician: The Election of Col. Njoku (Owerri Local Government) to the Constituent Assembly".[15] Sent out of the Nigerian army for his participation in the "Biafran" war after 1970, ex-Col. Njoku had been engaged in the transport business before going into active politics. But even before 1976, the former Colonel had been playing a leading role in organising the activities of the Catholic Church in the diocese of Owerri, and this in a part of the country where religion has long been inextricably bound with political power. During the nation-wide local government elections of December 1976, although he had stayed out of the contest, Njoku is said to have campaigned openly for some of the major candidates, in the hope that if and when elected those councillors would support his own subsequent political ambition for a Constituent Assembly seat.

Ex-Col. Njoku also showed himself very much conversant with the "issues in the politics of Owerri," such as the Catholic versus Protestant church divisions, the "*Osu*" versus "free-born" caste conflict, and various intercommunal rivalries; and had a good calculation as to how the use of such issues could make, or mar, a would-be politician's community power base.[16] At the state level, as we previously pointed out, Njoku had participated in the Imo State seminar on the Draft Constitution held in September 1977. Those, in a nutsehll, were the kinds of preparations that had gone into the making of both Kurubo and Njoku as elected Constituent Assembly members.

Meanwhile, the two former senior officers, along with the other ex-military connected persons named, played an active part in the Constituent Assembly deliberations on the Draft Constitution. Their contributions touched on almost all the major national issues of constitutional interest. But it was on military issues (i.e. deliberations on the essentially military clauses of the Draft Constitution) that these members played their most prominent role, even if occasionally talking at cross purposes with one another. The central problem here concerned political control of the military, discussions of which came to involve other issues, like the war-making powers of the president; control and composition of the National Defence Council, the National Security Council, and the National Security Organisation; relationship between the Nigerian police and the armed forces; quota system of recruitment into the armed forces; operational control of the force; and constitutional contrivance against future coups.[17]

I have in my first book covered much of the ground touched upon here, including which Constituent Assembly members said what, when, and in what context.[18] There is, therefore, no need to repeat the same here. Suffice it to point out that the ex-military persons identified above contributed significantly to these debates relating to the role of the armed forces in society. What was more, because of their past experience, training, and knowledge on such matters, the views expressed by these ex-military members bore the air of being both definitive and authoritative. An example was ex-Col. Njoku's remark pointing out the contradiction between the demands for "quota" system and the proposed "compulsory military training or military service for Nigerian citizens".[19] Another was the reminder by the same person to fellow Constituent Assembly members, in the course of the debate on the so-called "anti-coup" constitutional proposal, that "by the provision or manner of military law, a soldier is forbidden from participating in partisan politics".[20]

Of course, the retired military representatives were not always speaking in agreement with one another. Thus, Njoku and Kurubo disagreed as to whether or not to insert a clause on the composition of National Defence Council in the emergent Constitution;[21] while Mr. Yerima Balla argued for further increase in the size of the Nigerian armed forces, against overwhelming shouts of opposition or interruptions from other members of the Constituent Assembly, including the two retired military.[22] From the contributions of the retired Inspector General of Police, Alhaji Kam Salem, one discerned attempts to get the Constituent Assembly in particular and the Nigerian public at large to appreciate the disparity in the working conditions between the police and the armed forces, and to use the occasion of the debates to argue the necessity for improved pay and other working conditions for the Nigerian police force.[23]

Formation and Membership of Political Parties

In the meantime, helping to further deepen the interest and involvement of retired military officers in the emergent politics was the military order of July 14, 1978.[24] Promulgated by the departing Obasanjo regime a little before the lifting of the ban on political party activities, the order had been intended to achieve complete political disengagement by October 1, 1979. But its unintended effect had been to encourage increased political participation by ex-officers. For the said promulgation did not just re-post all the state military governors as well as Federal military commissioners (ministers) to the barracks, leaving only the military top brass to preside over the remaining process of authority transfer. The July 14, 1978 order also advised those serving military officers who might have been nursing any political ambitions to first resign their commissions. Admittedly, not many senior serving officers in response were known to have resigned in order to compete for political office; perhaps, the only known major exception was Col. Ahmadu Ali, a senior army medical doctor then holding the portfolio of Federal Commissioner (Minister) of Education.[25] For many of the long-retired military officers, including generals, though, the proclamation appeared to have been construed as an invitation to participate, judging from the large numbers that emerged active politically almost soon after.

Of this new class of ex-officers in the process of turning professional politicians, the present author had, in a previous (1979) book contribution, defined as "including Major-Generals Adeyinka Adebayo, Hassan Usman Katsina and Olufemi Olutoye; Brigadiers George Kurubo and Benjamin Adekunle; Colonels Hillary Njoku and Anthony Ochefu; Lieutenant-Colonel T. Oyedele; as well as Inspector-General of Police T.A. Fagbola. These are the most visible ones. Besides, there are hundreds of other senior officers either dismissed or retired for their participation in the 'Biafran' war after 1970, for involvement with the former Gowon regime immediately following the July 29, 1975 coup, or as a part of the 'general purge' of November 1975. For now, most of these are politically dormant. In addition, one should mention the thousands of NCOs, infantry men, temporarily recalled ex-servicemen discharged, though, in piecemeal, as part of the post-war demobilisation exercise. The political role of these ex-military individuals will make a very interesting study, but can probably not be done thoroughly until more details of their involvement become available."[26]

Those words were written in early 1979 when information on retired military interests and involvement in politics was still sketchy. But we now do have sufficient details to be able to write more authoritatively on the subject matter. In a sense, this is what the remaining analysis of the present chapter is all about.

On September 21, 1978 the ban on active politics, which had been in force since January 15, 1966, was lifted by the Obasanjo military regime, and the Constituent Assembly dissolved. In no time, the formation of six major political parties was announced which were to dominate the politics of the Second Republic. The political parties concerned were the Unity Party of Nigeria (UPN), National Party of Nigeria (NPN), Nigerian People's Party (NPP), Great Nigerian People's Party (GNPP), People's Redemption Party (PRP), and Nigerian Advance Party (NAP), most of which had palpable links with the banned parties of the pre-1966 period.[27] These parties came to be led by Chief Obafemi Awolowo (now deceased), Alhaji Shehu Shagari, the late Dr. Nnamdi Azikiwe, Alhaji Ibrahim Waziri, the late Malam Aminu Kano, and Mr. O.A. Braithwaite respectively. Soon, Nigeria's retired military officer scene began to throw up UPN officers, NPN officers, NPP officers, GNPP officers, PRP officers, and even NAP officers following the major lines of emergent political party divisions.

To begin with, a number of the retired military officers played a central role in the formation as well as subsequent operations of these parties. For example, two notable generals of the Gowon era, retired Maj.-Gens. R.A. Adebayo and Usman Katsina, as well as a former police chief retired Inspector-General of Police, Kam Salem, were prominent among the foundation members of the NPN.[28] Of these, the first and third persons came to occupy top posts within the party's emergent political pyramid as National Vice-Chairman for Ondo and Borno states respectively. Ex-Col. Njoku was also named as one of the early supporters of the NPN – itself born out of a national movement of certain Constituent Assembly members – and certainly came to compete for the NPN gubernatorial position in Imo State in December 1978.[29]

Retired Brig. Benjamin Adekunle, otherwise known as the "Black Scorpion" and hero of the Nigerian civil war, was, initially, identified with the NPP, and said to have been present when that new party held its convention in December 1978.[30] The GNPP, a break-away party formed out of the original NPP, also attracted top ex-officers at its inception. These included: the former naval commander and governor of the Rivers State, Alfred Diete-Spiff, who became the Chairman of the Rivers State GNPP in February 1979;[31] retired Brig. George Kurubo, also a Rivers State foundation member;[32] retired Lt-Col. I. Orpin, one of the early GNPP members from Benue State;[33] and retired Lt.-Col. Tunde Oyedele, who came to compete for the GNPP gubernatorial position in Oyo State in January 1979.[34]

Nor were the three remaining major parties the UPN, PRP and NAP without any retired military inputs into their initial formation as well as subsequent operations. For example, retired Maj. U.S Unemegba was long identified as a close aide to Mr. Tunji Braithwaite, the NAP presidential aspirant,[35] although the latter party was not to be officially permitted to run in 1979 but in 1983. The UPN (or rather its leader, Chief Obafemi Awolowo) has from the very beginning attracted retired Lt.-Col. S.D. Gumut of Plateau State into the party's caucus, and gone on to field the said retired officer as the UPN gubernatorial candidate for the Plateau State in the 1979 elections.[36] Also, by mid-June 1979, the PRP could lay claim to ex-Col. Phillip Effiong as the latter party's top notcher in the Cross River State.[37]

The spirited tussle between the PRP and UPN for Phillip Effiong's support in the Cross River State, climaxed by the ex-colonel formally declaring for the PRP on July 16, 1979, pointed to the political importance that all of Nigeria's party leaders had come to attach to top retired military officers in certain States of the federation. We elaborate. Ex-Col. Effiong had been an officer of the Nigerian army before 1966, but became Chief Emeka Ojukwu's second-in-command during the civil war, attaining the rank of "major-general" in the "Biafran" army. Effiong in fact it was who signed the instrument of surrender of the "Biafran" regime in January 1970. He was formally discharged from the Nigerian army in 1971.

A minority-ethnic soldier now turned politician, ex-Col. Effiong was first nominated in May 1979 by the UPN as its Senatorial Candidate for the Itu-Etinan district of what then was Cross River State. This nomination he initially accepted, but subsequently declined after being apparently attracted by a better and higher political position by another party, the PRP, which offered the discharged colonel the prospect of being fielded as its gubernatorial candidate in the state. Another retired officer by name Col. Akpan Utuk was to be his running mate. Ex-Col. Effiong would have so stood in the Governorship Elections of August 1979, but for FEDECO which disqualified him from participation and thereby dashed his political ambition.[38]

Elections to Federal and State Legislative Offices, 1979

As already implied, there were many retired military officers involved at the various parties nomination levels as well as primaries. But their numbers got considerably reduced by the time of the actual general elections. Even so, retired military participation remained sizeable. While no retired military officer won the nomination of any of the five registered parties to stand as the chief flag bearer in the Presidential elections of August 11, 1979, many were available to contest in all of the other elections, namely into the Senate, State Governorships, House of Representatives, and various State Assemblies.

There were retired military officers to be found contesting in four of the ninety-five seats at stake in the Senatorial elections of July 7, 1979. Of these, two were in the Benue State alone, one in Niger, and the fourth in the Rivers, but all under the banner of either the NPN or GNPP. Specifically, retired Col. Ahmadu Ali, a qualified army medical doctor and former Federal Commissioner of Education in the Obasanjo regime, contested the senatorial seat in Benue-West under the NPN; retired Lt-Col. I. Orpin, the Benue-East Senatorial constituency, under the GNPP banner; retired Col. Garba Dada, the senatorial district of Chanchaga/ Rafi in Niger State, as an NPN; and retired Brig.

George T. Kurubo, an ex-Constituent Assemblyman, but this time contesting to represent the Phalga senatorial district of the Rivers State under the GNPP. By the time the Senate elections were over and the results of the voting counted, Nigeria had elected its first crop of retired military officers turned senior law-makers: namely, Cols. Ali and Dada, both of the NPN.[39] They were after October 1, 1979 to take their seats in the new Senate whose membership comprised a total of thirty-six (36) NPN, twenty-eight (28) UPN, sixteen (16) NPP, eight (8) GNPP, and seven (7) PRP.[40]

For the *State Governorships,* three of the political parties the UPN, NPP, and NPN fielded retired senior military/police officers as candidates in the July 28, 1979 elections in three of the then nineteen states of the federation. To be specific, retired Lt.-Col. Sati Gumut was the UPN candidate for the governorship elections in Plateau State; retired Col. A.P. Sawa, the NPP gubernatorial candidate in Gongola State; and the former Inspector-General of Police Kam Salem, the NPN gubernatorial candidate for Borno State. Two of the gubernatorial aspirants concerned, Gumut and Salem, had been foundation members of their respective parties, as we saw. However, all three lost their gubernatorial contests – one of them, retired Col. A.P. Sawa of the NPP, by a very narrow margin in Gongola State.[41]

But it was in the elections into not only the 445-member (Federal) *House of Representatives,* but also the various *State Assemblies,* held on July 14 and 21, 1979, respectively, that the retired military featured the most. The lists included (a) ex-officers who filed papers with FEDECO, but were disqualified from contesting; (b) those who contested, but lost; and lastly (c) the successful others, who got elected into either the House of Representatives or any of the then nineteen State Assemblies.

To take the first two categories of contesting ex-officers first: For example, Emeka Odumegu-Ojukwu, the ex-"Biafran" military leader, although still a refugee in Ivory Coast at the time, had his election papers presented on his behalf by his legal adviser Mr. Edele Nnokoye, but was rejected. Ojukwu had wanted to contest into the House of Representatives from the Nnewi constituency of Anambra State and under the platform of GNPP. The reason given by FEDECO for rejecting the papers, and which was later unsuccessfully challenged by Ojukwu's counsel at an Enugu High Court, was that Ojukwu had been dismissed from the Nigerian army.[42] This was one of the few cases – the Effiong one mentioned earlier was another, and both of them controversial cases no doubt – where a former senior military officer was disqualified by FEDECO from standing for political office in the 1979 elections.

Among those who stood but lost in the elections into the House of Representatives may be mentioned retired Lt.-Col I.U Ratakka, of Kaduna State, who contested but failed to win the Katsina-Tsagero constituency under the NPN ticket. Also, retired Col. M.N. Okwechime under NPN contested but failed in his bid to represent the Oshimili North constituency of old Bendel State in the House of Representatives.[43]

In the end, not more than two ex-military men are known to have been elected into the House of Representatives.[44] The names of the two officers are retired Lt.-Col. P.C.

Amadi and J.C. Ojukwu, both on NPP platform, elected into the House of Representatives from the Owerri-North and Idemili constituencies of Imo and Anambra states respectively.[45] Of these, J.C. Ojukwu is known to have retired as a second-lieutenant.

Retired military participation in the elections into the various State Assemblies was the highest. Not surprisingly, it was also here that were elected the highest number of retired military personnel turned legislators. They were to be found in six different states scattered throughout the federation, and came from three of the major parties – the NPN, UPN, and NPP. The elected state legislators concerned were: retired Maj. J.E.A. Ighodaro, UPN, representing the Orhionomwon East constituency in the Bendel State Assembly; retired Capt. N. Ocheja, NPN, representing the Dekina constituency in the Benue State Assembly; retired Maj. F.A.C. Osuji, NPP, representing the Mgboko constituency of the Obioma-Ngwa local government area in the Imo State Assembly; retired Maj. A. Abdu, NPN, representing the Ikara constituency in the Kaduna State Assembly; retired Lt.-Col. Kojoe Anthony A. Ojumu, UPN, representing part of the Owo constituency in the Ondo State Assembly; and retired Lt.-Col. L.P. Nyam, NPN, representing the Jos-South constituency in Platcau State Assembly.[46]

All these retired military representatives along with the others were to be sworn to office after the August 11, 1979 Presidential elections that made Alhaji Shehu Shagari and his NPN the winner of the nation's presidency, though not without some "help" by the departing Obasanjo regime.[47] The Second Republic was formally inaugurated on October 1, 1979.

2.   Gowon, Ojukwu, and other ex-Military Crisis Phenomena

By 1982, politics had ceased to be a mere pastime for the few rather bored top ex-military officers, which was what it was at the beginning of the first transition to civil rule in 1976. It had become a full-time second-career, if not in fact big business, for many more ex-officers. This was clear from the daily reports that we read at the time in the national newspapers carrying bold head-lines of some ex-brigadiers or ex-generals joining (declaring for) one political party or the other. So much so that one retired army officer Lt.-Col. Ayo Ariyo (now deceased) had to comment, rather sarcastically, that he would not be surprised at all if one of those days he read of an application to FEDECO for the registration of what he coined as a "Retired Generals' Party" (or "RGP" for short).[48]

The names of top retired officers in politics included, paradoxically, that of retired Lt.-Col. Ariyo. For he had himself been on the fringes of politics and the political more or less since 1976. As we saw, the retired lieutenant-colonel had contested election into and won the chairmanship of the Ijero local government council of Ondo State. Nor after 1979 was it possible for him to disguise where, and to which of the parties, he leaned politically (for he was said to have been a member of UPN). And although by December 1980 retired Lt.Col. Ariyo had taken up a supposedly non-partisan FEDECO job as the Resident Electoral Commissioner for Ondo State, the very "sensitive and controversial" character of some of the "political statement" that he continued to make (including the one of July 9, 1982 just referred to) could not but have provoked angry rejoinders from others with opposing political views or interests; for example, that by retired Maj.-Gen. Olu Bajowa.[49] Retired Maj-Gen. Bajowa was to vie for the NPN candidacy for the Ondo State governorship election of 1983.[50]

Retired Lt.-Col. Ariyo's July 1982 statement had appeared as a national newspaper article under the caption "Ojukwu, Gowon and Other Ex-Soldiers in Politics".[51] In that article, retired Lt.Col. Ariyo had lamented: "It is a sad situation to have so many young brigadiers and generals who retired or were retired into the community with so much money and time for so much mischief, using their ranks and former military assignment as a weapon to compete with civilians for election".[52] But Ariyo would not be the first to voice such concern over the increasing number of ex-soldiers involved in trading their former ranks for political power or fame. Similar misgivings had been expressed before by some legislators of the Second Republic, public officials, and of course serving military officers concerned over the deleterious effects of the phenomenon on the military profession *qua* profession.

For example, the Army in June 1982 had taken a decision to publish the names of all dismissed, convicted and retired soldiers. The move as explained, was aimed at checking dismissed and convicted military personnel from parading the streets as if they were retired with full benefits.[53] A year earlier on March 9, 1981 to be precise, the Minister of Defence, Professor Iya Abubakar had been ordered to compile the list of dismissed military officers. He had received the order from the Senate Committee on Defence, which wanted to know the offences of every dismissed officer. The Committee Chairman, Senator Jacob Madaki, had said that the list of names and offences of officers dismissed was required for record purposes.[54]

Nonetheless, there could be no denying that the latter exercise was also part of the issue raised by the rush of retired military officers into politics. It was to acquire even greater meaning and significance after Gowon and Ojukwu had both been given state pardon within six months of each other – the former on October 1, 1981, and the latter in May 1982. Let me elaborate.

Emeka Odumegwu-Ojukwu had been a senior officer of the Nigerian Army, a lieutenant-colonel by rank, and military governor of what used to be the Eastern Region of Nigeria until May 1967, when he was dismissed with ignominy for various acts of insubordination. These included rebellion, declaration of the territory under his command as a new and independent "Republic of Biafra" to be excised from the Federation of Nigeria, and levying war on the Federation then headed by Lt. Col. (later Gen) Yakubu Gowon.

The conflict between the two leaders had taken place against the background of personal differences over claims to military seniority, as well as acute inter-regional cum ethnic hostility and violence that eventually led to war. After thirty agonising months the war of Nigerian unity was won on January 12, 1970, and the rump of the

"Biafran" leadership agreed to renounce secession. Shortly before then, the head of the secessionist regime and *generalissimo* of the "Biafran armed forces," Ojukwu had fled the country to the neighbouring West African State of Cote d'Ivoire. There he lived as a fugitive for twelve and a half years until his return to Nigeria on June 18, 1982 after being pardoned.

By some irony of fate, General Gowon was to go through a parallel course. He had presided over the affairs of the Federation for nine years beginning from July 29, 1966. His period of rule included the Civil War years 1967–70 which he had fought "to keep Nigeria One," and from which he had emerged with the aura of a Lincoln. After his rather long stay in office, General Gowon was toppled in a counter-coup which brought Brig. (later Gen.) Murtala Mohammed to power. Initially, following the July 29, 1975 event, a government notice simply listed General Gowon as "compulsorily retired with full benefits". A slight modification to that notice on November 12, 1975 placed Gowon on the reserve list as a full General.

But retired Gen. Gowon's status soon changed from that of an elder military statesman-turned-student comfortably pensioned off in far-away England to that of a "a wanted person". This was sequel to the February 13, 1976 counter-coup which, although nipped in the bud, had succeeded in assassinating Gowon's successor in office General Murtala among others. On February 18, 1976, the Federal government by now headed by General Olusegun Obasanjo issued a statement in which it said that retired Gen. Gowon knew of the abortive coup. Request was made to Britain for retired Gen. Gowon to be extradited to Nigeria to stand trial (court-martial), but this was turned down by the new British prime minister Mr. James Callaghan on April 22, 1976. Consequently, Gowon was stripped of his rank as full General together with his retirement benefits.

On February 1, 1979, the Nigerian police renewed their search for those they called the four most wanted "fugitive offenders": Yakubu Gowon, Emeka Ojukwu, Capt. Dauda Usman, and Sgt. Clement Yilda (Usman and Yilda were wanted along with Gowon for their alleged roles in the abortive counter-coup of February 13, 1976).[55] Ex-General Gowon continued to be so officially classified until October 1, 1981 when he was granted state pardon.

As was to be expected, the granting of state pardon to Gowon and Ojukwu by the civilian administration of President Shehu Shagari – followed shortly after by their home-coming, and the loud publicity surrounding it all-provoked a serious crisis phenomenon or controversy in the retired military sphere. Newspaper accounts of the events showed this; and, in fact, the earlier cited piece by retired Lt. Col. Ariyo was among the first to fire criticisms. To follow his arguments a little further, retired Lt. Col. Ariyo was unhappy that "ex-Generals Gowon and Ojukwu," " who up to 1979 were regarded as villains", "suddenly .... became heroes". Ariyo was particularly irked by the observation that "individuals, groups, political parties have been falling over one another to gain some political credit for the humane action of the executive President."[56]

As the retired Colonel reminded: "The truth of the matter is that these two great 'heroes' of today were responsible through acts of commission or omission for the death of many, for those who became disabled. Many homes lost their bread-winners. Some are now roaming the streets helplessly while these ex-this and ex-that are collecting accolades, chieftancy titles, contracts, million naira edifices, elected post nominations all over the place".[57] That was the central message which retired Lt. Col Ariyo sought to convey by his obviously angry piece.

Retired Lt. Col. Ayo Ariyo then warned: "Both ex-Generals Gowon and Ojukwu deserve a very long rest from publicity. They have as many friends upstairs as they have enemies downstairs among the silent majority and many unknown soldiers. I want to warn the nation that using these men for any political effect and purpose may precipitate unpleasant consequences."[58]

Other top retired military officers interviewed by newspaper correspondents on the Gowon/Ojukwu pardon and its subsequent politicalisation expressed similar misgivings. One such person was retired Lt. Gen. T.Y. Danjuma, a former chief of army staff in the Obasanjo regime. Asked by two separate newspaper reporters to comment on the pardon granted to Ojukwu in particular, retired Lt. Gen. Danjuma replied separately thus: "My views are irrelevant, since the pardon has already been granted. I have no comments. But if you expect me to sing halleluyah, you are talking to the wrong person.... why? Well, I have thousands of my colleagues who died during the Nigerian Civil War and I am not happy about that."[59] "I took part in the war," Danjuma retorted, in another context, "and I have responsibility for my colleagues maimed and those killed during the civil war while the government has responsibility for the people and citizens of the country."[60] Pressed further, retired Lt. Gen. Danjuma said the pardon was President Shehu Shagari's fulfilment of an election promise made in 1979.[61] The latter was another way of saying that the state pardon was a purely political matter and bore little or no relation to concerns of the military.

There were numerous other reactions against Ojukwu from top retired military men among whom were retired Maj.-Gens. Joe Garba and I.B.M. Haruna, retired Brig. Benjamin Adekunle, and retired Col. Sani Bello.[62]

To be sure, there were others from among the retired military ranks who supported the move. They fall into many categories. One category of supporters comprised retired military officers identified in a politically partisan way with the policies and programmes of the ruling NPN. Retired Maj.-Gens. Olu Bajowa[63] and R.A. Adebayo[64] are probably two examples of this. Then, there were those who came to be involved, due to their long-standing association with either or both of the returning ex-military "heroes". One such supporter was ex-Col. Phillip Effiong, who in his own words was to have accompanied the initial Federal government delegation to negotiate with Ojukwu in Abidjan.[65] Ex-Col. Effiong, as previously pointed out, had been Ojukwu's second-in-command during the "Biafran" war.

The third group of supporters consisted of Ojukwu's or/and Gowon's loyal friends from among the retired military officers, some of who came to serve as members of one "committee of friends" or others involved in arranging either the state pardon itself or subsequent events associated with the home-coming of the two ex-leaders. I have in mind here the example of retired Maj. Afolabi Olagunju involved in Gowon's subsequent home-coming in 1983.[66] Finally, of course, there were retired officers whose support for the pardon was based simply on ethnic cum sub-regional identities. Most Ibo-speaking elements, majority of who also happened to have been ex-"Biafran" officers, obviously empathised with their former military leader. On the other hand, those areas now constituted as the Benue and Plateau States, as well as the Kaduna State (or to be more specific the southern Zaria areas of the latter state) tended to see ex-Gen. Gowon still as their man and more sinned against politically and militarily than sinning.

In short, the Gowon/Ojukwu pardon did not only evoke mixed reactions from the retired military personnel, but tended on the whole to fragment rather than unite the members. Serving officers and men interviewed at the time on the issue revealed attitudes and feelings parallelling those of their retired military counterparts just sketched, ranging from downright opposition, if not hostility, through cool or lukewarm attitude, to sympathetic understanding, and outright support. Another way of putting this is that, for the serving as well as non-serving military, the state pardon had a politically divisive impact; although it is unimaginable that President Shehu Shagari could have taken such a crucial decision without first taking into confidence or briefing his service chiefs whether formally or informally.

Among the civilian population at large, of course, there were many who did not like the whole idea of Gowon and Ojukwu being placed on the same footing for treatment, as though their circumstances of being forced out of the country as self-exiles were the same. The Ojukwu pardon, for one, provoked a sullen, passively resentful, reaction from some of the people of the Rivers State and what then was the Cross-River State (or formerly still the South-Eastern State). For these, the Ojukwu pardon not only brought back bitter memories of both their travail and heroic struggles as minority-ethnic opponents of secession.[67] But it also struck the "sad irony", so wrote Dr. Nabo S. Graham Douglas (S.A.N) on July 11, 1982, as if voicing the feelings of these groups, "that whilst a reprieved Ojukwu marches triumphantly on the road of national recognition and honour, and whilst the political parties woo him for what material political advantage they may derive from his partisanship, and whilst our legislative houses engage in deliberations about restoring him to his former rank in the Nigerian Army (which may be senseless, for Ojukwu would not now wish to be mere Lt. Col.), and so on, the memories of those true patriots of Nigeria are allowed to slide irretrievably into the foggy distance of a nation's unacknowledged history."[68]

President Shehu Shagari had denied that partisan politics had anything to do with the decision to grant the two ex-military leaders pardon. But even if that was initially true, two considerations soon belied it. One was the political use of pardon by the ruling NPN, whose chieftains saw the factor of Ojukwu's presence as well as that of Gowon as a means of penetrating the strongholds of NPP influence particularly in Anambra, Imo

Benue and Plateau, and for adding to the NPN's political strength nationally. For general elections were due to be held before the end of 1983.

Then, there was the political behaviour of the pardoned officers themselves, particularly that of Ojukwu, soon after receiving the pardon. Whereas ex-General Gowon was not to return home until late 1983, and, on returning, limited himself to conducting countrywide tours intended perhaps at building up a potentially new political base for future use,[69] the ex-"Biafran" leader arrived back to Nigeria within a month of being pardoned in 1982, and almost immediately plunged straight into national politics, after being conferred with a chiefly title as the *Ikemba* of Nnewi. He formally declared for the NPN, and expressed the intention to contest one of Anambra's senatorial seats into the National Assembly in the forth-coming 1983 elections. He had a private retinue of young and dedicated followers the so-called *Ikemba* Front established in order to aid his political goal. In doing all this, Ojukwu apparently thought the ruling NPN needed him as much as he needed the NPN. He was to be proved wrong by the 1983 election results.[70]

To conclude this important part of the chapter, there was in the meantime a "Boulanger"-like potential[71] in the tumultous welcome which greeted Ojukwu and Gowon on their return to Nigeria. For their ardent supporters at least, including millions of their ethnic partisans, the return of the two former military leaders brought out the mass tendencies towards welcoming dictatorship, the kind often offered to generals on horseback, especially when returning home from some foreign war exploits.[72] Civilian rulers everywhere tend to fear the growing dangers inherent in the phenomenon; and the NPN government, including President Shehu Shagari himself, was no exception. That government could not have pardoned and brought back Gowon and Ojukwu from their self-exile, in order to have either or both of them take over the presidency. Neither could the Shagari government, although itself fathered by a previous military regime, have been at all eager to see an organisation led by top ex-military officers grow up that might well contain "the gems of military menace to civilian supremacy"[73] Considerations such as the foregoing meant that the NPN government's interests in Gowon and Ojukwu were bound to be short-lived.

3.   Role in the Governance of the Second Republic

From focus on the pardon of Gowon and Ojukwu and its reverberations in the political and military spheres, we move on to consider the role of retired military officers generally in the governance of the Second Republic. Here we are interested in looking at two things: who held what public or/and party political officers and when; and the contributions of retired military officers if any to the seamy side of the politics of the era. We discuss them in that order.

Holders of Public or/and Party Political Offices

In a sense, this section returns us to the discussions in the first part of the chapter. There, retired military (and police) officers were shown not only to have contested almost all the contestable, that is to say elective, posts opened up by the transition from military to civil rule in 1976–79. But indications were also given showing a number of the ex-officers to have been involved in the actual governance of the Second Republic at all levels. – Federal, State, and Local. In order to further substantiate this point, we proceed shortly to document some of the important public or/and political party offices held by retired military officers between 1979 and 1983.

In the meantime, perhaps the first and highest public office to be formally held by any retired military officer under the Shagari presidency was that of retired General Obasanjo's membership of the Council of State[74] although this was supposedly a non-partisan role and derived from the stipulation of the 1979 Constitution. The nature of composition of the Council of State demands that elder statesmen – precisely the President, former heads of state, former chief justices, governors, and high traditional rulers – must converge to bring collective wisdom to bear on the governance of the country. As one of the former heads of state, retired Gen. Obasanjo automatically qualified as a member of the Council of State. Being an important member of that Council, and as the immediate predecessor of President Shagari in office, retired Gen. Obasanjo had an important role of advising the latter's government on vast, complex but sensitive issues affecting the welfare of the country.[75] But whether retired Gen. Obasanjo did actually do this is quite another matter. We simply do not know. Neither do we have information to suggest President Shagari being influenced one way or the other in the conduct of government business.[76]

Much more partisan were posts held by certain top retired military and police officers within the hierarchies of a number of the political parties of the Second Republic. References were previously made to some of these in another context, but there is need now for them to be formally listed here. By 1982, the most notable examples of top retired military and police officers holding high positions within the various party organisations were known to include the following: retired Maj.-Gen. R.A. Adebayo, NPN national Vice-Chairman for Ondo State; retired Inspector-General of Police the late Alhaji Kam Salem, NPN National Vice-Chairman for Borno State; ex-Brig. U.J. Esuene, Member of UPN National Executive Council; retired Lt.-Col. Sati Gumut, Chairman of UPN Plateau State Executive; retired Maj. A. Usman, Member of UPN Sokoto State Executive; retired Capt Adenekan, Publicity Secretary of UPN Ogun State Executive; retired Col. A. Ochefu, Member of NPN Benue State Executive; retired Maj. Ndachaba, Member of NPN Niger State Executive; retired Maj. Danthoso, Member of NPP Kaduna State Executive; retired Capt. U. Ekpo, Deputy Publicity Secretary of NPP Rivers State Executive.[77] There could be more.

Next to come to public glare were those retired military officers holding top party political posts within the Senate, House of Representatives, or the various State Houses of Assembly. We are talking of leadership in policy adoption within the major law-making organs of government at both Federal and State levels; with the posts involved here including such ones as Leader of Party, Chairmanship/Membership of Senate

Committees, Chairmanship/Membership of House Committees, Chairmanship/Membership of State Assembly Committees among others. These posts carrying considerable influence were an inevitable part of the Presidential structure of government adopted in 1979. Obviously, no retired military officer or for that matter any other person could aspire to holding any or most of the posts just categorised, unless he had first been elected into the major legislative organs of government concerned.

As a corollary, retired military officers found occupying such positions were drawn from among those shown to have been elected in 1979. For some of the examples we have in mind, retired Lt.-Col. P.C. Amadi, an NPP member representing the Owerri-North constituency of Imo State in the House of Representatives, emerged after 1979 as the Leader of NPP in the House of Representatives.[78] He also served on the House Special Committee of Selection,[79] and was a Member of two other House Standing Committees, namely the Committee on Defence[80] as well as that on Petroleum and Energy Conservation.[81] Also serving with retired Lt.-Col. Amadi on the House Committee on Defence was another NPP representative from Idemili constituency of Anambra State, and a former army officer of the rank of 2/Lt., J.C. Ojukwu.[82]

At the Senate, the two retired army colonels from Benue West (Benue State) and Minna/Kagara (Niger State), Dr. Ahmadu Adah Ali and Garba Musa respectively and both of the NPN, came to hold important positions within the system of committees. Retired Col. Dada was the Chairman of the Senate Committee on Internal Affairs, which also had retired Col. A.A. Ali as one of its members; while the latter for his part headed the important Senate Committee on Petroleum and Energy.[84] In addition, retired Col. Dada was a Member of three other Senate Committees, namely those on Defence,[85] Agriculture and Natural Resources,[86] and Labour.[87] Besides those already mentioned, retired Col. Ali held the membership of yet another Senate Committee, that on Banking and Currency.[88]

A number of retired military officers elected into the various State Assemblies might be found serving similarly on legislative committees set up at the State level.

Within the Presidency and under the various State Executives also served a number of retired military officers, some of them as heads of executive staff, others as special advisers, special assistants, or liaison officers, and others still on specialised government agencies. We leave out those of them appointed to chairmanship/membership of Federal and State boards, statutory corporations, or government-owned companies during the period, as they will be considered along with others in a separate chapter of the study (see Chapter 6). Thus, among the examples that interest us here was that of retired Maj. M.B. Ndayako, who had been a post-graduate student at the University of Ibadan's Department of Political Science in 1979 and was known to have abandoned his studies to join the President's staff.[89] Also, by 1983 retired Maj. Paul Dickson had been appointed one of the nineteen Presidential Liaison Officers (P.L.O) and placed in charge of Plateau State.[90] These are a few of the examples at the Federal level that come to mind.

At the State level could also be found a number of military officers – both serving and retired – appointed to special or advisory posts with the various state executives. For example, on taking over the Cross River State government in 1979, Dr. Clement Isong the NPN Governor appointed among others three senior military and police officers based in the state, that is Brig. A.R.A Mammudu (Army Commander), Capt. Promise Fingesi (Navy Commander), and Alhaji R.A. Laleye (Ag. Commissioner of Police), each to the portfolio of Special Duties in the State executive.[91] By 1982, Capt Fingesi and Alhaji Laleye were to be replaced with Capt. E. Buba (Navy Commander) and E.J. Umoren (Commissioner of Police) respectively in Governor Isong's executive.[92] Of course, for the Cross River State in particular, such military appointments to civil posts, apparently continuing a long-established practice going back to the previous military rule era, would seem to have been dictated by the volatile security situation of that state, combined with perceived military threats coming from the neighbouring Republic of Cameroun.

To continue with examples of military officers involved with the governance of the Second Republic, retired Rear-Admiral Nelson Soroh served as Special Adviser on Security to the NPN-controlled Rivers State cabinet of Governor Melford Okilo.[93] In the same Rivers State cabinet was also to be found by 1983 retired Lt.-Col. L.D. Ayah appointed as Commissioner for "Functional Committees" (sic) under Governor Okilo.[94] Retired Col. Joseph Selong Madagu served as one of the special Advisers (Legislative Liaison) to the NPP Governor of Plateau State, Solomon Lar, beginning from 1979,[95] and apparently continued into 1983.[96] The UPN governor of Oyo State, Chief Bola Ige, retained retired Maj. R. Salawu as head of the Oyo State Road Safety Corps, which had been carried over from the administration of then Brigadier David Jemibewon. Institutions similar to the Oyo State one just mentioned were to be established by two other UPN-controlled States, Ogun and Lagos, as well as by the NPP Governors Jim Nwobodo and Sam Mbakwe of Anambra and Imo States respectively, which relied on retired military and police personnel for their operations.[97]

Finally, we must point out the Federal Electoral Commission (or FEDECO), that Federal agency statutorily charged with the conduct and administration of election during the Second Republic, and the key role that at least two top retired military officers came to play in the Commission's set-up as well as operation. These were retired Lt. Col. Ayo Ariyo (deceased since June 1987) and retired Brig. Ignatius Obeya, both nominated by President Shehu Shagari and confirmed by the First Senate in 1980 as the Resident Electoral Commissioners for the States of Ondo and Cross River respectively.[98] They were to remain in their States of posting until the Elections year 1983 when the two retired military officers got re-assigned to Bendel and Anambra States respectively.[99] We shall have cause to return to an aspect of this in the concluding part of the chapter.

The Seamy Side of Politics

On June 1, 1982 a former chief of army staff was asked by a journalist if he would follow the footsteps of his ex-military colleagues then flocking in their scores into politics. Retired Lt. Gen. Danjuma's response was as perceptive as most of his responses and comments whether prepared or off-the-cuff are wont to be. "I have neither the inclination nor the money to take part in politics," the retired general retorted. "I don't have the stomach for politics"[100] On the face of it, retired Lt. Gen. Danjuma's view here regarding the role of money in politics might read like an earlier one expressed by retired Maj.-Gen. Joseph Garba while answering a similar question. The colourful former commissioner of external affairs in the Obasanjo regime had on December 5, 1981 said that money was "one big constraint" to his political ambition, saying "I have no money, and in Nigeria, you can't do anything including politics without money."[101] Note, however, that retired Maj. Gen. Garba did not here say outright "no" to politics, only that for the meantime lack of money was a political handicap. And herein lies the difference in the two responses just quoted.

This is not the place to investigate the claims of retired Lt. Gen. Danjuma about not having money; nor did he want to suggest from the above comment that he was poor.[102] What he meant was not that he was not rich, but that he had not the kind of *slush money* that the profession of politics requires. Besides, there was the very nature of politics in Nigeria marked by intense conflicts, passions, and personal ambitions in competition, for which Lt. Gen. Danjuma implied he had no "stomach" as a professional soldier though now retired. For him, the code of honour and conduct of politics were inherently incompatible, with "politics" being seen as a dirty, uncertain, and ungentlemanly kind of game. Of course, by the time retired Lt. Gen. Danjuma was talking, the two points implied in his observation – the factor of slush money and the increasingly distasteful nature of politics – had become a familiar manifestation of the seamy side of political rule under the Second Republic.

The Shagari era 1979-83 has been characterised by the present author in a paper done elsewhere as "one of the most brazen-faced systems of kelptocracy known to the contemporary world, given the extent and depth of graft that it came to manifest".[103] While there is no evidence that President Shehu Shagari was himself personally involved, it was shown that "practically all facets of Nigerian public life, including administration, legislature, judiciary, government, the wider society itself, and of course the economy, were permeated by this massive plague of graft distinctive of the Shagari era."[104]

Nor was the military sector spared these depradations of the politicians of the Second Republic.[105] We had no evidence that retired military officers engaged at the time in politics also contributed to these depredations, although a number probably did. After all a number of the retired military officers in politics were also engaged as big businessmen. And big business in the Second Republic was mostly about import licence, contracts and cuts (or commissions). It was, therefore, inevitable that some of the top retired military officer politicians in business, like their civilian counterparts, would have been involved in those seamy transactions. But we do not know.

However, what we know was that most of the retired military officers who went into politics between 1976 and 1983 became increasingly steeped, like their civilian counterparts, in "excessive individualism," "fractionalism", "dissensions", "mercenarism", indiscipline", "opportunism", and even "crookedness". These are vices which the ideal professional soldier would regard as distinctive of the ways of the "bloody civilians" and "their dirty politicians," and corrupting of a typical military organisation.[106]

One manifestation of this could be found in the countless examples of retired military officers in politics decamping from one party to another, or changing their political leaders as often as they changed their party loyalties and affiliations, and then invoking some ideological rationalisations or another in order to justify such changes, just as the civilian politicians were wont to do. Among the early examples here were ex-Col. Phillip Effiong, who as previously shown had initially deposited his papers to run as UPN senatorial candidate for Ikot Ekpene, but subsequently opted to run as a PRP gubernatorial candidate for the Cross River State in 1979;[107] retired Col. Hassan Yakubu, from Ankpa in Benue State; who in late January 1979 withdrew from NPN to declare for the GNPP.[108]

By late 1982, the number of examples of retired military decampings had increased to include the ex-"Biafran" leader Ojukwu, who on being granted state pardon in 1982 found himself as an NPN stalwart, although in 1979 as we saw he had tried to contest for office under the GNPP platform;[109] retired Brig. Benjamin Adekunle who left the NPP, whose foundation and frontline member he had been since 1978, in order to join the NPN in 1982;[110] ex-Brig. U.J. Esuene, who on May 22, 1982 announced a change in his party of affiliation from NPN to UPN, and was thereupon admitted as a member of the National Executive Council of the latter party;[111] retired Col. A.P. Sawa, who crossed over from being an NPP gubernatorial candidate in 1979 to becoming NPN Senator-elect in 1983.[112] But there were many more cases of retired military-political decampings.

Meanwhile, of the phenomenon just described, one writer has observed generally thus: "these decampings from one political party to the other gave an opportunistic coloration to the politics of some of these retired military officers"[113] Who said retired military persons were unused to the political game, including "jockeying for position," "political bickerings," and "cross carpetings."? And who said " soldiers were never good politicians"?[114] Who said ex-military officers lacked the capacity for political oratory, together with "rambling discourses," "circumlocutions", "sterile excitations", and "rhetoric"? Who said members were not gifted for "electoral politics", including in the Nigerian case "thuggery and hooliganism", "crass materialism"" and "electoral chicanery"? The involvement of a number of them in the partian events leading to as well as in the 1983 controversial elections themselves belied all this, or rather confirmed that the ex-officers in politics at the time were as good a bunch of politicians as their civilian counterparts. To those controversial elections of 1983 and the involvement of retired military we must now turn, in order to conclude the discussions of the chapter.

4. Ex-Officers in the Controversial Election of 1983

The beginning of the Elections year 1983 saw the trickling stream of ex-officers in politics developed into an even larger cascade. Apart from the already known faces, that had previously participated in the various party political as well as electoral struggles between 1976 and 1979 detailed above, there were others more and mostly newer entrants. Top on the list of the newer entrants, as already indicated, was Ojukwu the *Ikemba* of Nnewi who filed to contest into the upper house of the National Assembly as an NPN candidate from the Onitsha senatorial district of Anambra state. The ex-"Biafran" leader had earlier in October 1982 taken over as the NPN National Vice-Chairman for Anambra State, following the resignation of the incumbent Chief C.C. Onoh who had vacated the post in order to become the NPN gubernatorial flag-bearer in Anambra State.[115]

Another distinguished contestant was the former military governor of the defunct South-Eastern (later Cross River) State, ex-Brig. U.J. Esuene, who became the UPN gubernatorial candidate for that State in the 1983 elections.[116] Chief Esuene had shortly before then been installed as the *Atta* of Eket, a traditional title. Yet a third was ex-Brig. Samuel Ogbemudia, former military governor of the Mid-West (later Bendel, now Edo) State, who was fielded as the NPN governorship candidate for Bendel State.[117] Other new names mentioned in connection with the 1983 elections included: retired Maj. Garba Mohammed, named as Chairman of UNP Sokoto State Executive, and by implication that party's gubernatorial candidate for Sokoto State,[118] retired Maj. Gen. Olu Bajowa, identified as the NPN Chairman in the Okitipupa division of Ondo State;[119] retired Col. Hassan Yakubu, named as leader of the GNPP from Ankpa, Benue State.[120]

Retired Maj. Gen. David Jemibewon did not openly contest for any political office, but was known to have been a partisan member of the ruling NPN.[121] Retired Maj.-Gen. Joseph Garba could have contested in the 1983 elections as we pointed out, but for what he called "one big constraint" which was lack of money.[122] In other words the latter retired general was, like the many others, also politically interested.

Of these, a number had been defeated at the various party primaries stage, and therefore hindered from pursuing their political ambition. For example, in the primary elections at the NPN Ondo State Secretariat in Akure in October 1982, retired Maj.-Gen Olu Bajowa, a gubernatorial aspirant, came second. He was defeated by a retired Police Officer Mr. Jacob Okunola Familoni who polled 1,266 votes, thus coming first. Mr. Jaye Faloye with 320 votes was third on the list.[123] The ex-Police Officer would probably have gone on to represent the NPN in the State governorship elections, but for the arrival of a political turn-coat, the UPN Ondo State Deputy-Governor Chief Akin Omoboriowo whom, for reasons of political strategy, the NPN preferred to field for the 1983 governorship elections in that State. Similarly in the NPN primary election in Imo State also held in October 1982, ex-Col. Hillary M. Njoku, a former member of the Constituent Assembly, had failed in his bid to contest for the governorship seat in the state by coming third with 152 votes. Chief Collins Obih with 1,402 votes and Dr. B.U.

Nzeribe with 261 votes came first and second respectively.[124] But there were many who sailed through the primaries to contest in the General Elections of 1983.

By the end of those General Elections, FEDECO had announced a number of retired military and police officers among others as elected into important executive and legislative offices. Easily the most notable of these successful cases was that of Chief Samuel Ogbemudia, who became Nigeria's first ex-military officer turned quasi-civilian State governor. But also the most notable among the crashed cases was that of Ojukwu the *Ikemba* who was apparently used to "capture" Anambra State from the NPP stronghold for the NPN, but could not be helped by the latter party to realise his political hopes for a senatorial seat.[125] Other unsuccessful cases included those of ex-Brigadier U.J. Esuene, the first military governor of the Cross River State, who failed in his bid to regain that state governorship under the UPN platform;[126] retired Col. Dan Suleiman, who failed in his bid to represent the Kano Central senatorial district of Kano State under the NPN in the Second Senate;[127] retired Maj. Garba Mohammed, of the UPN Sokoto State Executive, who lost to an opponent in the contest for Senate seat from the Sokoto North senatorial district;[128] retired Maj. Olu Fasewa, of the NPN, who lost the Ijebu-East Constituency (Ogun State), elections into the Second House of Representatives;[129] retired Col. Joseph Azhuzie, UPN, who lost in his bid to represent the Oshimili Constituency, Bendel State, in the lower house.[130]

The list of successful cases contained a number of those who had been previously elected in 1979 and succeeded in getting themselves re-elected. Among these were retired Col. Ahmadu Ali, NPN, still representing the Benue West senatorial district of Benue State in the Second Senate;[131] retired Lt. Col. Patrick C. Amadi, re-elected from the same Owerri North Constituency of Imo State in the Second House of Representatives.[132] The newly elected among the retired military and police contestants in the 1983 political struggles included retired Col. A.P. Sawa of the NPN, who won a seat from Gongola State into the new Senate.[133] It will be recalled that retired Col. Sawa had previously been a member of the NPP, and had actually contested but lost as the latter party's governorship candidate for Gongola State in the 1979 Elections. Obviously, retired Col. Sawa must have decamped, before he could be registered, fielded, and allowed to contest and go on to win his new senatorial post as an NPN member. Also, newly elected was retired Maj. Babatunde Osiemojie of the UPN, who won the election from the Owan constituency of Bendel State into the Second House of Representatives.[134]

Others among the successful cases were the ex-air force Capt. Andrew Ogbonnia Nwankwo, an NPP Member from Abakaliki North-West constituency of Anambra State into the Second House;[135] and former Commissioner of Police Edet Asuquo Ekpo, elected NPN Member of House of Representatives, from Uyo III constituency, Cross River State.[136]

However, only few numbers were discovered to have won their electoral contests at the state level. In fact, apart from Ogbemudia's gubernatorial come-back in Bendel State already remarked, the only other success case of note at the state level from the 1983

Elections results, that we were able to find, was that of Godwin N.C. Onyefuru, an NPP member representing Oji River constituency in the Anambra State House of Assembly. Mr. Onyefuru's biographical sketch has it that he had been commissioned in the Nigerian Army in 1964, detained in 1970 after the civil war, but released in 1974 and subsequently demobilised.[137] Perhaps there are more elected representatives at the state level, but we simply do not know.

All the 1983 Elections, meaning into the Presidency (August 6), State Governorships (August 13), Senate (August 20), House of Representatives (August 27), and State Houses of Assembly (September 2), were held amidst allegations and counter-allegations of large scale rigging and other electoral malpractices, including outright falsification of results. Apparently, all the six registered parties were guilty of these, but the greatest culprit was the NPN-controlled Federal government, if only because the latter also controlled the most political resources. Such resources included control of the Federal Electoral Commission (FEDECO), as well as the Nigeria Police Force (NPF) together with its Inspector-General Mr. Sunday Adewusi (now retired). These the incumbent party had no hesitation in using to realise its electoral game plan for being returned to power. The bogus so-called "band-wagon" factor, rationalised to explain the "landslides" achieved in the Senate, House of Representatives, and State Houses of Assembly elections results subsequent to those of the Presidency and State Governorships, was part of that electoral game plan.

We have just implied FEDECO to have been partially responsible for some of the controversial results of the 1983 Elections and the immediate aftermath. Actually, politicisation of FEDECO had for some time now been hampering the operations of the commission's work, creating inter-personal conflict among and between its officers, and this had been evident even before the elections. For example, the Resident Electoral Commissioner for Ondo State, retired Lt. Col. Ayo Ariyo (now deceased), had had a running conflict with the Executive Secretary of FEDECO, Alhaji Saidu Barda, literally calling the latter as tail wagging the whole of the FEDECO leadership.[138] Although its chairman, Mr. Justice Victor Ovie-Whiskey, subsequently denied being dictated to by the Executive Secretary, this internal struggle must have prompted the decision to have retired Lt. Col. Ariyo transferred from Ondo to Bendel State just before the 1983 Elections; even as another Residential Electoral Commissioner and former top army officer, retired Brig. Ignatius Obeya, was also moved from Cross River to Anambra State. But some of the civilian electoral commissioners were moved around as well.

Yet another issue that attracted considerable public interest or concern arose when Mrs Helen Esuene was appointed as one of the electoral officers in the Cross River State. Mrs. Helen Esuene is the wife of ex-Brigadier U.J. Esuene who was contesting in the 1983 Elections as the UPN gubernatorial candidate in the state. There certainly was some conflict of interest involved in Mrs. Esuene's appointment as an officer of FEDECO in the state. Besides, for other gubernatorial aspirants competing with the ex-brigadier, Mrs. Esuene's position as an electoral officer pointed to a potentially partisan role for FEDECO in the impending elections in the State. The ex-brigadier's political opponents loudly said so. They demanded that she be removed or re-assigned outside the state because of this. And removed she was in early January 1983 together with other electoral officers.

What role did the two retired military electoral commissioners play in the 1983 Elections? Retired Brig. Ignatius Obeya supervised the organisation and conduct of the elections in Anambra State. There is no way of showing whether or not the retired brigadier was partial towards the NPN in his handling of any of the elections in the state, although he was long known to have pro-NPN sympathies. But the NPP leader and Presidential candidate Dr. Nnamdi Azikwe, the *Owelle* of Onitsha, accused the FEDECO and the Federal government of rigging the presidential election by printing ballot papers which bore indistinct NPP symbols. There was some truth in that allegation. Also, we know that the electoral commissioner of Anambra State, retired Brig. Obeya, had to cancel the election results of three constituencies in the State on the grounds that those results had been delayed for four days, making their authenticity very doubtful.[139] By the time the remaining elections were completed not only was a new aspirant and NPN gubernatorial candidate Chief Christian C. Onoh elected, defeating the incumbent NPP Governor Chief Jim Nwobodo.[140] But a number of NPP legislators at Federal and State levels also failed to be re-elected, losing their seats mostly to NPN rivals. That the Vice-President of the Federation, Dr. Alex Ekwueme, an NPN, hailed from the state was advanced as another major reason for these NPN successes there.

Where the resident electoral officer for Anambra State, retired Brig. Obeya, was suspected of NPN leaning, that for Bendel State retired Lt. Col. Ariyo had pro-UPN sympathies. Yet retired Lt. Col. Ariyo could not (or rather did not) prevent the incumbent UPN Governor of Bendel State since 1979, Professor Ambrose Folorunso Alli, from losing to an NPN challenger and a one-time military governor of the state, ex-Brig. Samuel Ogbemudia, in the gubernatorial elections of August 13, 1983. Neither could a number of the UPN Bendel legislators contesting for re-election into the Senate, House of Representatives, and State House of Assembly be saved from defeat in the hands of NPN opponents. Admittedly, the FEDECO command in the state faced its own problems which affected the conduct and administration of the elections there. On the whole, however, retired Lt. Col. Ariyo's handling of the 1983 Elections in the state would seem to have been relatively free and fair. It showed the retired colonel's commitment to the best traditions of military professionalism and political impartiality carried over from active service.

But it was in Ondo and parts of Oyo, both of them until now strong UPN-controlled states, where the disparity between voting pattern and elections results became the acutest. Here NPN attempt aided and abetted by FEDECO and Police commands to dislodge the incumbent state governors Chiefs Michael Adekunle Ajasin and Bola Ige, and to have them replaced by Chief Akin Omoboriowo and Dr. Omololu Olunloyo respectively, provoked violent reactions. The news of Dr. Olunloyo's election as the winner of the August 13 governorship election was greeted with spontaneous violence in many parts of Oyo State, particularly in the Odo-Ona and Oke-Ado district of Ibadan the state capital, Osogbo, Ilesha, and Ife/Modakeke, resulting in dusk-to-dawn curfews being imposed by the State Police command in those affected parts. But this did not prevent Dr. Olunloyo being sworn-in as the new Governor of Oyo State, since his opponent Chief Bola Ige was unable to convince the electoral petition court sitting in Ibadan of the latter's greater claims to electoral legitimacy. Nor could Chief Bola Ige succeed in his subsequent appeals up to the Supreme Court. With the governorship tussle thus settled, the rest of the election in Oyo State marked by a poor turn-out of voters came to be dominated by the NPN, recording "landslides" in the Senatorial, House of Representatives, and State House of Assembly elections. For example, in the last elections, the NPN "won" as many as 112 (or 88.9%) out of the 126 seats at stake.[141]

Voters' reaction to the election of Chief Omoboriowo as the new Governor of Ondo proved more catastrophic, as it resulted in state-wide protests manifested in violence, destruction of lives and property, attacks on and looting of Federal establishments in the State, including FEDECO and Police posts. Obviously, the Ondo State electorate had returned the incumbent UPN Governor Chief Ajasin to power, and were determined to resist any imposition of Chief Omoboriowo from outside their own verdict. Faced with this recalcitrant situation, the near break-down of law and order in Ondo state, the prospects of a spill-over into other states, and the danger of this finally engulfing the whole Federation, the Federal government had to step into the matter. It got FEDECO national headquarters to "overturn" the results of the Ondo State gubernatorial election, meaning to restore UPN Governor Ajasin as duly re-elected, while at the same time suspending the rest of the election in that state until peace and calm was restored.

The resident electoral commissioners for Oyo and Ondo State at the time of the 1983 Elections were not retired military persons, but civilians by name Dr. Lateef O Aremu and Mr. O.I. Afe respectively. To that extent, none of the retired military connected with FEDECO could be said to have contributed to the controversial Elections of 1983 and their aftermath. If anything, one of the ex-officers, retired Lt. Col. Ayo Ariyo, after successfully seeing the Bendel State through its own electoral struggles as remarked earlier, had to be re-deployed to Ondo State to help restore the people's confidence in the electoral process. Retired Lt. Col. Ariyo it was who supervised the conduct of the remaining Senate, House of Representatives, and House of Assembly elections in the state, which subsequently held on September 21 23, and 25, 1983 respectively. These he conducted with a measure of objectivity, political impartiality, and fair play, traits that distinguished Ariyo as an officer and a gentleman. The retired Colonel's admirers would easily explain his success in Ondo State in those terms. For his opponents, though, retired Lt. Col. Ariyo's tasks in the state were made easy by the fact that, being the more UPN-inclined resident electoral commissioner and operating in a predominantly UPN territory, he had no problem harmonising FEDECO results with actual voting figures.

Retired Maj. Gen. Adebayo's role was the most controversial, judging by his own subsequent self-assertion. We refer to his personal letter of November 29, 1983 sent to President Shehu Shagari just before the fall of the Second Republic and apparently leaked to the press.[142] Since the retired general has up to-date never publicly denied the authenticity of that letter, we assume its contents to be true. And in evaluating it as an "inside" documentary material, we apply to the letter the same critical test that professional historians, including military historians, would apply to any such "inside" accounts: namely, of accepting the reliability of admissions, while treating assertions with critical doubt or healthy skepticism.[143]

This was a letter supplicating President Shehu Shagari then in his second term of office for some "patronage". In making his humble petition, retired Maj. Gen. Adebayo thought it necessary to recount his contributions to the ruling NPN from its formative stage as a party up to the 1983 Elections. Perhaps, much more revealing was retired Maj. Gen. Adebayo's assertion regarding his contribution to the growth of the NPN in Ondo State generally and the party's successes in the 1983 Elections in particular.

Apparently, the understanding in the NPN circles both before and after the 1983 election was that the share of spoils was to be commensurate with a person's contribution to NPN victory. It was an understanding that applied to all the states, and Ondo was no exception. Hence the need for retired Maj.-Gen. Adebayo having to itemise those contributions of his to the NPN 1983 electoral successes in Ondo State formally in his letter. But there were also the costs, and these the General considered necessary to set out.

We have no way of knowing whether President Shehu Shagari replied the letter, much less acceded to retired Maj. Gen. Adebayo's supplication, or not. The chances were that the president had no time. For within a month of the letter being written, a military coup occurred on December 31, 1983. It abruptly terminated the life of the Second Republic, commencing another era of military rule in Nigeria.

NOTES

1. For example, of the 59-member Constitution Drafting Committee (CDC) nominated in October 1975 to draw up a Constitution for the Second Republic, no retired military officer was included although there was one serving military officer involved, an army chaplain, by name Col. M. Pedro Martins

2. See Federal Republic of Nigeria, *Reports of the Constitution Drafting Committee,* Vol. II (Lagos: Federal Ministry of Information, 1976), pp. 10–26, for the list of memoranda submitted by members of the public.

3. *ibid.,* p.15

4. Cited in R.C. Ohale, "An Ex-Army Officer Turned Politician: The Election of Col. Njoku (Owerri Local Government) to the Constituent Assembly", (Department of Political Science, University of Ibadan: B.Sc. Thesis, June 1978), p.46.

5. At least that is the general belief, as for example argued by Alfred Vagts, *A History of Militarism: Civilian and Military* (New York: Free Press, 1959), pp. 299ff.

6. In which the author happened also to have participated.

7. An information communicated by an anonymous student of mine and himself an indigene of the Rivers State, Januray 6, 1982.

8. *Daily Times* (Lagos), January 1, 1977, p.25.

9. *Daily Times* (Lagos), January 1, 1977, p.5.

10. Retired Lt. Col. Oyeleke was to resign his chairmanship of the Ifelodun (Ikirun) local government council in November 1978, however, in order to contest for higher office(s) at the State or Federal level, see *Nigerian Tribune* (Ibadan) December 1, 1978, p.16.

11. Though this one was not without some controversy. For retired Lt. Col. Ayo Ariyo was alleged to have been defeated at the polls by Mr. Akin Omoboriowo, a civilian legal practitioner and also an Ijero indigene, but helped to that council's chairmanship through the direct intervention of the State military governor, see James Olubunmi Orisameyiti, "Ijero Local Government: A Case Study of December 1976 Election into the Council" (Department of Political Science, University of Ibadan, B.Sc Thesis, 1978), pp. 43–4.

12. See Samuel Horace Owonte, "The New Local Government Reforms in Rivers State: Bonny Local Government Authority Council as a Case Study" (Department of Political Science, University of Ibadan: B.Sc. Thesis, June 1978) pp. 99ff.

13. As we gather from Federal Republic of Nigeria, *Proceedings of the Constituent Assembly Official Report,* 2 Vols. (Lagos: Federal Ministry of Information, 1978), Vol. II, comprising periods January 9 - March 21, 1978, p. 5893.

14. I first came across this name in N.J. Miners, *The Nigerian Army 1958–66* (London: Methuen, 1971), p.98.

15. Ohale, "An Ex-Army Officer Turned Politician...", *op. cit.*

16. *Ibid.,* pp. 21ff.

17. A discussion of these military-related issues was first done by the author in a 1978 paper on "Military Clauses of the New Nigerian Draft Constitution: A Critical Analysis", which was later enlarged and embodied as Chapter 2 of his first book *Nigeria in Search of a Stable Civil-Military System* (Aldershot, Engl.: Gower, & Boulder, Co,, U.S.A.: Westview, 1981).

18. Adekanye (Adekson), *Nigeria in Search of ...,* op. cit., pp. 119-29.

19. Quoted, *ibid.,* pp. 44-5.

20. *Ibid.,* p. 120.

21. Federal Republic of Nigeria, *Proceedings of the Constituent Assembly Official Report,* Vol. II comprising January 29 – March 21, 1978 (Lagos: Federal Ministry of Information, 1978), pp. 5647, 5666-8.

22. Federal Republic of Nigeria, *Proceedings of the Constituent Assembly Official Report,* Vol. I comprising October 6, November 1–30, December 1–16, 1977 (Lagos: Federal Ministry of Information, 1977), pp. 618.

23. I touched on this in my paper on "Dilemma of Military Disengagement", in Oye Oyediran (ed) *Nigerian Government and Politics under Military Rule 1966–79* (London: Macmillan, 1979), pp.221–2.

24. Perhaps, under pressure from the "Ali must go" campaign following the university students demonstrations of April 1978 that had resulted in a number of them being killed by the police across the country.

25. Adekanye, "Dilemma of Military Disengagement" in Oyediran (ed) *op. cit.,* p. 301n

26. Oye Oyediran (ed), *The Nigerian 1979 Elections* (London: Macmillan, 1981), passim.

27. A.D. Yahaya, "The Struggle for Power in Nigeria, 1966–79" in Oyediran (ed) *Nigerian Government and Politics under Military Rule...* op. cit. p. 271.

28. *Nigerian Observer* (Benin), December 29, 1978, back page.

29. Oyediran (ed) *Nigerian 1979 Elections ...,* op. cit., p. 55; *Sunday Times* (Lagos), November 12, 1978, p.1.

30. *New Nigerian,* February 6, 1979, p. 3.

31. And was to go on to compete under the same party platform for a senatorial seat from the Phalga district of the Rivers State in 1979, see fn. 39.

32. Retired Lt. Col. Orpin also went on in 1979 to compete for a seat into the Senate as the GNPP sponsored candidate, see 39.

33. After resigning as the Chairman of the Ikirun-based Ifelodun local government council on November 30, 1978, *Nigerian Tribune* (Ibadan), December 1, 1978, p. 16.

34. *Daily Times* (Lagos), December 30, 1978, p.17.

35. As we soon show in the text.

36. *Sunday Times* (Lagos) June 17, 1979, p.1

37. *Ibid.*

38. Daily Times, *Nigeria Year Book 1980* (Lagos: Daily Times Publication, 1980), pp. 107–8.

39. *Ibid.*, p. 109.

40. *Ibid.*, pp. 128–56.

41. *Daily Times* (Lagos) October 26, 1979, p. 17.

42. *Daily Times* (Lagos) July 18, 1979, p.5.

43. The list of the successful candidates elected from the 1979 Elections into the House of Representatives is provided in Daily Times *Nigeria Year Book 1980..,* op. cit., pp. 111–24

44. From the names of legislators voted into the House of Representatives extracted from *ibid.,* as indeed those of various State Houses of Assembly referred to in fn. 46 below, one observes many of these successful candidates listed by the simple titles of "Mr", "Alhaji", and "Malam", and others without any at all. It is possible that a number of the elected candidates so titled (or un-titled) might have been ex-military men, more so if they had held ranks lower than army captain, or been previously dismissed from the force. The example of P.C. Ojukwu, elected into the House of Representatives from the Idemili constituency of Anambra State is instructive. J.C. Ojukwu, a former Second Lieutenant, was one of the junior officers (31 in all) detained for their alleged involvement in the January 15, 1966 coup, and retired from the army in 1974. Note that in the publication referred to above, J.C. Ojukwu went by the simple title of "Mr". There could be more such cases, but we do not know.

45. *Ibid.*, pp. 161ff.

46. Reference is to the circumstances surrounding the accession to power of the NPN presidential candidate Alhaji Shehu Shagari, including the sudden constitutional issue of "what's 2/3 of 19 states?", and the role of the departing Obasanjo regime in them, *see* Adekanye, *Nigeria in Search of..* op. cit., p. 134.

47. Lt. Col. Ayo Ariyo (rtd.), "Ojukwu, Gowon and Other Ex-Soldiers in Politics", *Daily Sketch* (Ibadan), July 7, 1982, p. 5.

48. Retired Maj. Gen. Olu Bajowa wrote from his home town to the editor to say he disagreed with retired Lt. Col. Ayo Ariyo, *Daily Sketch* (Ibadan) July 10, 1982, p. 2.

49. See concluding part of the chapter.

50. Lt. Col. Ariyo (rtd), *op. cit.*

51. *Ibid.*

52. Daily Times, *Nigeria Year Book 1983* (Lagos: Daily Times Publications, 1983), p. 146.

53. Daily Times, *Nigeria Year Book 1982* (Lagos: Daily Times Publications, 1982), p. 265.

54. Daily Times, *Nigeria Year Book 1980* (Lagos: Daily Times Publications, 1980), p. 399.

55. Lt. Col Ariyo (rtd) "Ojukwu, Gowon and other Ex-Soldiers ...", op cit.,

56. *Ibid.*

57 *Ibid.*

58. *Nigerian Statesman* (Owerri), June 3, 1982, p. 1.

59. *Daily Times* (Lagos), June 2, 1982, p. 1

60. *Ibid.*

61. *New Nigerian* (Lagos), February 6, 1983, p. 16.

62. Judging from retired Maj. Gen. Bajowa's earlier quoted rejoinder to retired Lt. Col. Ariyo's piece, see fns. 48 & 49.

63. As a top-ranking member of the NPN National Executive, retired Maj.-Gen. Adebayo was likely to have been involved in the decision-making leading to the presidential pardon for Gowon and Ojukwu.

64. As he subsequently confided in an interview, *Newswatch* (Lagos), Vol. 5, No. 2, January 12, 1987, p. 40.

65. E.A. Aina, "The Role of Ex-Military Officers in the politics of Nigeria's Second Republic", (Department of Political Science, University of Ibadan: B.Sc. Thesis, June 1986), p. 79.

66. One only needs to read for example the long, serialised piece by Dr. Nabo S. Graham-Douglas (SAN), "Candidates for Nation's Gratitude", appearing in *Sunday Times* (Lagos), June 27, July 11, July 18, 1982 in order to appreciate this.

67. *Ibid.*, the July 11, 1982 issue, p. 17.

68. Cf.J. Isawa Elaigwu, *GOWON: The Biography of a Soldier-Statesman* (Ibadan: West Books, 1985), p. 291–2.

69. See fn. 125.

70. George Ernest Boulanger (1837–91), a French army general, inspired the wave of nationalist agitation termed "Boulangism" which swept over France from 1886 to 1889, endangering the existence of the Third Republic. As a minister of war, his republican utterances, the popularity of his army reforms and above all his heroic appearance made him the idol of Paris, the embodiment of the desire for revenge

for defeated France. He was the long-awaited "man on horseback" who would lead France out of parliamentary disorder and restore her political and military prestige, see *Encyclopaedia of the Social Sciences,* 16th Printing (New York: Macmillan, 1967) Vol. 2, p. 649.

71. For this useful analogy, see Vagts, *History of Militarism ...* op. cit., pp. 316–22.

72. Phrase also borrowed from *ibid.,* p. 356.

73. For composition of the latter Federal executive body and definition of its functions under the 1979 Constitution, see Federal Republic of Nigeria, *The Constitution of the Federal Republic of Nigeria 1979* (Lagos: Department of Information, 1979), Third Schedule, Part 1, pp. 103–104.

74. Aina, "Role of Ex-Military Officers in politics ...", *op. cit.,* pp. 74–5.

75. *Ibid.*

76. The foregoing information on retired military officers serving on the top hierachies of the major political party organisations of the Second Republic is gleaned from reports on various political events covered by the country's national daily newspapers published during the period 1978–1983.

77. Daily Times, *Nigeria Year Book 1982* (Lagos: Daily Times Publications, 1982), p. 65.

78. *Ibid.,* p. 66.

79. *Ibid.,* p. 74.

80. *Ibid.,* p. 84.

81. *Ibid.,* p. 74.

82. *Ibid.,* p. 45.

83. *Ibid.,* p. 46.

84. *Ibid.,* p. 44.

85. *Ibid.,* p. 43.

86. *Ibid.,* p. 45.

87. *Ibid.,* pp. 43–4.

88. In fact, one of my postgraduate students.

89. Daily Times, *Nigeria Year Book 1983* (Lagos Daily Times Publications, 1983), p. 28.

90. Daily Times, *Nigeria Year Book 1980* (Lagos Daily Times Publications, 1980), p. 251.

91. Daily Times, *Nigeria Year Book 1982* .. op. cit., p. 424.

92. Daily Times, *Nigeria Year Book 1980* ... op. cit., p. 339.

93. Daily Times, *Nigeria Year Book 1983* ... op. cit., p. 338.

94. Daily Times, *Nigeria Year Book 1980* .. op. cit., p. 343.

95. Daily Times, *Nigeria Year Book 1983* .. op. cit., p. 332.

96. See O.O. Bello, "Federal Use of Police Powers under the Shehu Shagari Presidency in Nigeria, 1979–83" (Department of Political Science, University of Ibadan: M.Sc. Thesis, October 1984), pp. 164–77.

97. Daily Times, *Nigeria Year Book 1982*... (Lagos: Daily Times Publications, 1982), p.247.

98. Aina, "Role of.Ex-Military Officers in Politics ...", op. cit., p. 91.

99. *Daily Times*, June 2, 1982, p. 1.

100. *Daily Times,* December 6, 1981, p. 1, also quoted in Aina, loc., cit., p. 105.

101. On the contrary, retired Lt.-Gen. Danjuma strikes one as one of the most financially successful class of retired generals as we showed earlier, see Chapter 3 on "The Military-Business Complex".

102. J. 'Bayo Adekanye, "Military Expenditure under a Civilian Presidency: Nigeria under Shehu Shagari, 1979–83", paper presented at the Twelfth Annual Conference of the Nigerian Political Science Association (NPSA), University of Ilorin, Kwara State, May 7–11, 1985, p.7.

103. *Ibid.,* p. 8.

104. As vividly demonstrated by the case of the National Youth Service Corps (or NYSC) boss Col. Kolawole Obassa, now dismissed. For an analysis of the latter in the comparative context of military decadence, see David A. Alabi, "The Phenomenon of Military Corruption in Nigeria: 1960–83" (Department of Political Science, University of Ibadan: B.Sc. Thesis, June 1985).

105. Among the first contemporary scholars of civil-military relations to lucidly analyse the ideals of military organisation juxtaposed against the perceived vices permeating civil society are Samuel P. Huntington, *The Soldier and the State* (Cambridge, Mass.: Harvard Unversity, 1957), chapter 3; Vagts, *History of Militarism* ... op. cit., chapter 9.

106. *Sunday Times* (Lagos), June 17, 1979, p. 1.

107. *Daily Tide,* January 28, 1979, p. 2.

108. See fns. 42 and 125.

109. Retired Brig. Adekunle's decamping from the NPP to NPN was reported on February 3, 1981, see Daily times, *Nigeria Year Book 1982* (Lagos: Daily Times Publications, 1982), p. 257.

110. *Sunday Sketch* (Ibadan), May 23, 1982, p. 1, & *Daily Times* (Lagos), May 25, 1982, pp. 2 & 5

111. See fn. 133.

112. Aina, "Role of Ex-Military Officer in Politics...," op. cit., p. 110.

113. In February 1979, a retired army officer Lt. Col S.D. Gumut, who was also the Plateau State gubernatorial candidate for the Unity Party of Nigeria (UPN) at the time, had taken pains to explain that "soldiers are good politicians". This was to counter the criticisms by his opponents that "soldiers are never good politicians". The UPN gubernatorial aspirant said that he was not only "abreast with Nigerian politics," but had an "effective grasp" of the basic factors involved. Responding to a question by a newspaper correspondent, retired Lt. Col. Gumut said: "I am a well-trained soldier; and infantry man; a military engineer; and a mechanical engineer. But I can assure you that, with my knowledge of world history, my analysis of political activities in other countries, and my understanding of the military profession, I stand a better chance as a leading politician and an administrator", *Daily Times* (Lagos), February 24, 1979, p. 11. Obviously, retired Lt. Col. Gumut was here defining politics in the more positive sense. For contrasting views of this justification for military involvement in active politics, however, see fns. 106 & 100.

114. *Daily Times* (Lagos), October 30, 1982, p. 24.

115. *Daily Times* (Lagos), November 13, 1982, p. 24.

116. *Daily Times* (Lagos), October 25, 1982, p. 1–2.

117. As was generally known.

118. Retired Maj. Gen. Olu Bajowa contested the primary election for the NPN governorship for Ondo State, *Daily Times* (Lagos), October 25, 1982, pp. 1–2.

119. *Daily Sketch* (Ibadan), January 16, 1983, p. 1.

120. Aina, "Role of Ex-Military Officers in Politics ...", op. cit., p. 105.

121. As quoted earlier, see fn. 101

122. Aina, loc. cit., p. 106

123. *Ibid.*, p. 107.

124. Chief Emeka Ojukwu, the ex-"Biafran" leader, had been defeated by an NPP candidate Dr. Edwin Onwidiwe in the Onitsha Senatorial district election of August 20, 1983, but filed a petition in an Anambra State High Court to get the latter result nullified, which he did. Ojukwu's opponent took the case to the Federal Court of Appeal to argue that the latter's election had been unimpeachable. Dr. Onwudiwe's appeal was also granted. Ojukwu took the case to the Supreme Court which, finally, sealed his fate and in a majority judgement of five against two declared Ojukwu's complaints to have been baseless, *ibid.*, pp. 108–9.

125. *Ibid.*

126. As we know.

127. Aina, "Role of Ex-Military Officers in Politics ... op. cit 109.

128. *Ibid.*

129. *Ibid.,* p. 110

130. As a list of Members of the Second Senate available before the December 31, 1983 coup shows.

131. *Ibid.*

132. Aina, loc. cit., p. 109.

133. *Ibid.,* p. 110.

134. Extracted from the list of Members of the Second House of Representatives available before the December 31, 1983 coup.

135. *Ibid.*

136. Going by the compilation of the various State Houses of Assembly Members done after the 1983 Elections.

137. Reference is to the televised statement in Ibadan on September 7, 1982 by the Resident Electoral Commissioner for Ondo State retired Lt. Col. John Ayo Ariyo to the effect that the FEDECO Executive Secretary Alhaji Salidu Barda was more powerful than all the 24 electoral commissioners combined, see Daily Times, *Nigeria Year Book 1983* (Lagos: Daily Times Publications, 1983), p. 155

138. Aina, "Role of Ex-Military Officers in Politics ...," op. cit., p. 99.

139. Though this had to be settled by the courts of law, beginning with the five-man election petition tribunal headed by Mr. Justice John Araka which had initially awarded the governorship to Nwobodo, followed by the Court of Appeal in Enugu and the Supreme Court in Lagos, both of which reversed the lower Court's decision, and considered Chief Onoh instead as the winner of the August 13, 1983 gubernatorial election in Anambra State.

140. Daily Times, *Nigeria Year Book 1984* (Lagos: Daily Times Publications, 1984), p. 161.

141. First published in the *Daily Sketch* (Ibadan), December 12, 1983, pp. 1 and 12, and later reproduced in *Sunday Sketch* (Ibadan), December 18, 1983, pp. 6–7. A photocopy of this is also reproduced in Aina, "Role of Ex-Military Politics ..," op. cit., pp. 128–9.

142. Military historians, who use official archives for their historical writings, find this strategy of data gathering, evaluation, and analysis most indispensable, see B.H. Liddell Hart, *Why Don't We Learn From History* (New York: Hawthorn Books, 1971), p. 22.

5

Re-Engagement in Public Service

The economic motive is implied by some of our discussions of the study as an important factor underlying most post-retirement pursuits of Nigerian soldiers out of uniform, including the initial decision about "going private" rather than remain in public employment. However, this is not to say that economic interests have been the sole considerations deciding the second-career choice of military retirees. Certainly, there are as many job interests or motives as there are retired military officers. Nor would it be correct to say that all military officers turn their back on any other government employment once they retire from their present service.

To be sure, some military retirees still have enough public-service orientation. or commitment in them to want to return to one form of government work or another other than military. Apparently, for retired officers so oriented, the deciding factor here is not economic, but whether or not they are physically strong (or medically fit) enough to be able to stand the rigours of another full-time government job. A few, who are unable to stand such rigours, but still committed to public service, limit themselves to part-time board appointments on public corporations or parastatals.*

A number of the physically able, public-service oriented military retirees find themselves returning to full-time government jobs, although their proportion to the entire military retiree population remains very small. They are confined mostly to the ranks of majors or their equivalent and below, except those re-engaged in the diplomatic field where the prestige of the office is such as to attract much senior retired officers, that is retired army colonels or their equivalent and above. The aim of the present chapter of the study is to outline the major areas of government service where retired military men seek re-employment. The chapter gives as many specific examples and details as our research findings were able to come up with.

But before we proceed, a few introductory remarks are called for regarding the subject of analysis of this particular chapter. Retired military men seeking a second-

---

* The kind detailed in the first part of Chapter 6 below. This suggests that not all retired military officers on board appointments go into these solely for reasons of monetary interest.

career public job face a central difficulty that relates to the uniqueness of their initial skill (meaning, the military profession) itself.[1] Soldiering *per se* is not an easily marketable skill. This is because there is only one agency authorised to hire and employ persons possessing such a skill, and that is the State itself, meaning in this case the Federation of Nigeria, by virtue of the near-monopoly of the coercive machinery which it exercises. Compare this with the situation of persons in other occupations, like medicine, law, engineering, accountancy and economics whose skills enjoy horizontal mobility and therefore an inelastic marketability.

To elaborate on the comparative point just made, a qualified medical doctor has many job opportunities open to him/her, ranging from going into the public service (the health ministry) to work as a government doctor; taking up a teaching or research job in a university teaching hospital or medical research institution;[2] being employed as a corporate company doctor; or setting up a private medical practice. A professor of engineering may, on retirement from his university appointment, take up teaching at some other university or college or engage in other academic pursuit, join an engineering cum construction firm in the private sector, or set up a private consultancy outfit of his own. A qualified accountant may be employed as an auditor in a government department, teacher in a school of accountancy, an accountant to a business corporation, sole or part owner of a firm of chartered accountants. In short, each of the professionals mentioned has many job opportunities open to him/her.

The avenues of employment open to persons with an essentially military skill, on the other hand, tend to be very limited indeed. Outside of the defence and security establishment of the State, there is no other agency or level of government that has need for the use and hire of the military man's special expertise. This is what one means when one asserts that soldier's skill *per se* is not an easily marketable skill.

This lack of opportunities of employment for the peculiarly military skill may be one important reason why not many retired military officers can be found re-engaged in the public service. This point, of course, does not apply to retired military officers with additional professional/academic qualifications acquired either while in the service or prior to joining the force, namely the military doctors, military dentists, military lawyers military engineers, military accountants, etc. often found in the more specialised cr service units of the armed forces. That the latter class of professional officers (military specialists) possess additional skills makes them very much mobile horizontally and vertically in the job market, just like their civilian counterparts earlier remarked. But retired military specialists possessing such qualifications tend to go into areas of employment where their skills can be both handsomely remunerated and maximally utilised, which means very often in the private sector (see Chapter 3).

Does it mean that there are not areas of government service other than military that are in need of the retired military man's special skill or expertise? What of the more obvious, admittedly semi-military areas like police, intelligence service, civil defence, security guards, aviation and telecommunications where the soldier's skill can be easily marketable as it is transferable? Perhaps, there are no barriers to the use of the retired soldier's expertise in these areas? What does the current pension law say about this? Does it not frown upon retired military men being re-engaged in government service? The law permits, rather than prohibits, re-engagement.

Admittedly, for the civilian public retirees, the pension law is specific regarding the conditions of their re-engagement in the public service of the Federation; any public servant who retires, or is required to retire, and qualifies for the award of pension can only be re-engaged in any public service on *contract* appointment or temporary basis.[3] But the Armed Forces Pensions Law of 1979[4] which is still in force is somehow silent on this matter as applied to the military The implication is that a retired soldier on pension can be re-engaged on a permanent basis in the public service without being deemed to contravene any "dual compensation" principle.[5]

The closest to such a dual office and dual compensation restriction in Nigeria is the injunction entrenched as part of the code of conduct for public officers under the Fifth Schedule, Part I, Section 4 of the Constitution of the Federal Republic of Nigeria 1979 which requires that: "A public officer shall not after his retirement from public service and while receiving from public funds, accept more than one remunerative position as chairman, director, or employee of a company owned or controlled by the government or public authority or any other remuneration from public funds in addition to his pension and the emolument of such one remunerative position."[6] But there is no evidence of the latter having been enforced, let alone applied to the retired military.

Although the terms and conditions of service approved for the Nigerian army officers in 1981 tried to correct this anomaly in the pension law as applied to army retirees, the thrust of government policy operates to a contrary effect. Thus, since an increasing number of officers retire when they can still be usefully engaged in other professions than the military, the army retirement and resettlement scheme currently operative includes plans for serving officers to be encouraged to read for professional qualifications or degree in disciplines or fields related to a given officer's corps, particularly those in the infantry.[7] And on receipt of notification of retirement, the army headquarters are expected to "initiate contact with civilian establishments in *public* sectors with a view to placing the officer", having regard to " the officer's qualifications, administrative capabilities, experiences and other qualities."[8]

In other words, for most members of the officer corps, there are no restrictions on re-engagement in the public service. Even a retired four-star general may decide to be re-engaged in the public service, and be paid full salary from public funds, provided, of course, he is ready to forfeit completely his pension entitlement as well as other retirement benefits, under the 1981 revised terms and conditions of service.[9] After all, most retired top military officers are automatically placed on the Reserved List, and therefore subject to recall to service by the Federal Government whether civil or military. With these brief introductory remarks, we can now proceed to examine the major areas of government service in which retired military men seek re-employment and the specific examples illustrating these.

Semi-Military Public Jobs

The largest proportion of military retirees re-engaged in full-time work are at the Federal level and can be found employed in semi-military related organs, particularly the Nigerian Police, Prisons Service, the Customs and Immigration Departments, and Federal Fire Service. Initially, however, ex-soldiers employed in these Federal agencies had sought re-engagement as transfer cases from the regular armed forces. It was only in later years that retired military personnel proper began to be re-employed in the agencies concerned.

To be sure, since the end of Civil War, it had been a goal of public policy to encourage the Nigerian Army, considered by this time as rather over-sized, to transfer some of its redundant personnel into these other security services badly in need of trained and increased manpower. This was, for example, one method, devised by the Gowon regime, of getting round the problem of demobilisation together with its attendant social costs.[10] All the national development plans introduced since 1970 up to-date also considered the transfer of army personnel a useful strategy of manpower development and utilisation for the police force and prisons service in particular.[11] Other relatively new agencies believed to have augmented their strength through attracting a sizeable number of transferees from the regular army were the former National Security Organisation (or N.S.O.)[12] and the National Youth Service Corps (N.Y.S.C.), and the more recently created (1988) Federal Road Safety Commission (FRSC).

Undoubtedly, from the nature of their functions, the government agencies named above belong to the same organisational type, often referred to in the discipline of Sociology as "coercive organisations", and are therefore closer to the regular armed forces as regards career orientation and organisational structure. Above all, they are characterised by common bureaucratic features such as unitary command, concentrated authority, hierarchical pattern, communications network, disciplined outlook and *esprit de corps*. This is in addition to the fact that the agencies involved share with the armed forces the management of the country's defence and security functions. As such, inter-service transfer is a common occurrence here.

There are other agencies known to prefer as job applicants, and to have in the past actually recruited, retired persons with previous military, including naval and air force experience. They are the Nigeria Airways, Airports Authority, coupled with other Civil Aviation Department facilities such as the Civil Aviation Training School at Zaria; Nigerian Ports Authority, Nigerian National Shipping Line (NNSL), and the Nautical College at Oron; certain departments under the Ministry of Communications, particularly the Posts and Telegraph Department and what used to be called the (Nigerian) External Telecommunications Department, both of them now broken up roughly into or reconstituted as liability companies called Nigerian Postal Service (NIPOST) and Nigerian

Telecommunications Company Limited (or NITEL).

A sprinkling of retired military personnel can be found re-engaged in the service of one or the other of these above-named agencies. The Nigerian Security Printing and Minting Company, statutorily charged with the printing of all government securities and the minting of money, is also known to have on its staff a number of ex-military (and police) personnel. One such retired army officer known to have been employed for some time as Assistant Security Controller (physical) in the latter agency was retired Lt.-Col. B.O. Akpokabayen,[13] after having studied for and been awarded a Bachelor of Science (B.Sc.) honours degree in political science from the University of Ibadan in 1983. He was re-engaged at the Security Printing and Minting Company while the late Brigadier Abba Abdulkadir was its Managing Director.[14]

It is significant that all the agencies or establishments identified thus far in this section to have employed some retired military personnel or another are Federal-owned or at least Federal-controlled. Equally significant is the observation that the agencies or establishments involved are of para-military or quasi-military type. These observations thus confirm the thesis suggested in the introduction of the chapter: namely, that the agencies which have the greatest need for the use and hire of the retired military man's special expertise are mostly under the Federal government, given the near-monopoly of the coercive machinery vested in the latter.

Admittedly, at the state cum local government levels can be found a few para-military bodies recruiting retired soldiers as personnel. The most obvious are the various State and/or City Fire Services as well as the Traffic Wardens. With the creation in December 1977 of the Oyo State Safety Corps by that State military government then under Brigadier David Jemibewon, yet another avenue opened for the recruitment of ex-officers and ex-soldiers into new semi-security and quasi-police roles at the State levels. Appointed to head the latter particular institution from its inception was one retired Major T. Salawu, assisted by a disciplined corps of staff consisting also of ex-junior officers. The success of the latter state organisation in road-accidents prevention, coupled with potential use of members as auxiliaries for political control, encouraged other state governments in Ogun, Lagos, Anambra and Imo later to follow the Oyo example by establishing road safety corps of their own under various civilian governorships sworn to office in 1979. Again, as in the case of Oyo State, the experience and skill of retired military officers were relied on to build up such para-military bodies which were operated up to the end of the Shagari presidency.[15] But the various states' road safety corps were scrapped and their staff retrenched soon after the December 31 1983 coup; although a Federal-wide organisation of the same name – Federal Road Safety Commissions – has since been established under the Babangida military presidency, pursuing recruitment policies not unlike those of its predecessors.

Diplomatic Postings Abroad

Appointments to diplomatic or foreign affairs posts abroad are the second major area that has attracted the interests of retired senior military officers seeking re-engagement in public service. In fact, for army colonels and above or their equivalents, diplomatic postings, if available, are considered the only government service jobs worth contemplating after retirement, given the prestige, privileges, and level of remuneration attached to such postings. Not surprisingly, diplomatic appointments have since 1983 become the most sought-after of public service jobs.

However, as with those semi-military public posts previously analysed, employment of senior military personnel in the diplomatic field began as a chance affair. It was initiated in the wake of the July 29, 1966 counter-coup which saw Brigadier B.A.O. Ogundipe in effect resigning from his army post as the next most senior officer after General Aguiyi-Ironsi by now presumed killed, and forced to take up a new appointment as Nigeria's High Commissioner to London, United Kingdom. Ogundipe thus became the first military non-career diplomat to be so appointed, followed shortly after by Brig. Duke Bassey appointed Consul to Santa Isabel (now Malabo) in November 1966. About a year later (September 19, 1967), Lt. Col. George T. Kurubo, until now the head of Nigerian Navy, was posted as Ambassador to Moscow, Soviet Union.

Brigadier Ogundipe stayed at his London post until his death in 1972,[16] while Lt. Col. Kurubo remained in the diplomatic service throughout the Gowon era, becoming later Nigeria's Ambassador to Turkey and Iran, from which posting he was finally retired as a brigadier in August 1975.[17] Since then, the practice of hustling military officers away to diplomatic and consular missions abroad, like that of being palmed off on quasi-governmental corporations with executive positions at home, has been a consequent feature of most military coups and counter-coups, with the officers involved in such posting being retired either a little before or soon after.

Simultaneous with the latter development, the armed forces had for about a decade and a half now been building up their own corps of defence *attaches*. These were military officers sent to function as aides to Nigerian High Commissioners/ Ambassadors abroad and as a link in the country's intelligence network. According to the Federal ministry of finance sources,[18] two military overseas posts began to be budgeted for as a far back as fiscal year 1969/70, with the posts involved being named as London and Bonn, followed by Washington, and New Delhi in that order. Obviously, the location of these initial defence *attache* posts reflected in part Nigeria's ex-colonial origins, inherited pattern of economic ties, including trade, as well as sources of external military supplies and training. By 1976/77, however, the disposition of things had slightly changed. Moscow not only came to be added to Nigeria's list of military overseas posts, but was in ,fact placed third, coming only next after London and Washington in that order, with New Delhi, and Bonn following.

Marking a new dynamic phase in the conduct of Nigeria's foreign policy under the

Murtala/Obasanjo regime, the year 1976/77 also saw the government attempts at charting a genuinely "nonaligned" political and military course. By the fiscal year 1978/ 79, Tanzania (Dar es Salaam) had been added to the list of military overseas posts budgeted for, and this in response no doubt to the rising interests of Nigeria politically and militarily in the national liberation struggles raging in Southern Africa. In a sense, for a number of serving officers whose tour of duty had once or twice taken them through such military overseas posts, the subsequent choice of diplomatic service as a post-retirement engagement was simply a logical continuation of experience and interest gathered from the system of defence *attaches.*

Moreover, with the many commitments political, economic and military increasingly shouldered by post-Civil War Nigeria as a regional power on the African continent,[19] "security" has come to be emphasised as a basic criterion of "diplomacy"; and this consideration has further encouraged the phenomenon of high-ranking military officers whether in or out of uniform being appointed to ambassadorial posts. Nowhere has the phenomenon been more glaring than in Nigeria's mission in East and Southern Africa, particularly Addis Ababa (Ethiopia), Harare (Zimbabwe), Dar es Salaam (Tanzania), and Maputo (Mozambique), the so-called front-line states adjoining *Apartheid* South Africa. As we shall soon see, majority of the initial batch of retired military officers appointed ambassadors or high commissioners came to be located in that sub-region of Africa, where Nigeria's declared security-cum-diplomatic interests have to-date been the most concentrated

There are three other diplomatic posts which now and then attract military personnel either serving or retired, and these are located in countries sharing common land and/ or sea borders with Nigeria. The posts concerned are also of considerable geo-strategic interest to Nigeria. These are Malabo (Equatorial Guinea, including the Island of Fernando Po), given the problems of naval security associated with the area; Cotonou (Republic of Benin, formerly Dahomey), with whom we have signed a defence pact; and Ndjamena (Chad), a strife-torn neighbouring state to the north, whose security problems constantly spill over into the Nigerian territory.

The largest number of retired military officers to be appointed to-date to Nigerian diplomatic missions abroad took place under the Buhari/Idiagbon military regime in 1984. The list of diplomatic posting made by the latter regime included the appointments of retired Maj.-Gen. Joseph Garba, as Nigeria's Permanent Representative to the United Nations in New York; retired Col. Sani Bello, as High Commissioner to Harare, Zimbabwe; retired Rear Admiral Benson Okujagu, as High Commissioner, New Delhi, India.[20]

The list of those 1984 diplomatic appointments also contained a number of other serving military officers, Maj.-Gen. Tony Hannaniya, first as High Commissioner to London, United Kingdom, and later as Ambassador to Addis Ababa, Ethiopia; Maj.-Gen. Abdullahi Shelleng, Ambassador to Kinshasa, Zaire; Maj.-Gen. Zamani Lekwot, Ambassador to Dakar, Senegal; Brig. Harrison O.D. Eghagha, High commissioner to

Accra, Ghana; Commodore Raheem A.O. Adegbite, Ambasador to Maputo, Mozambique; Brig. Samuel A. Olajide, Ambassador to Ndjamena, Chad.[21] By December 31, 1985, however, these serving officers were to retire from *military* service,[22] while continuing on their diplomatic postings, thereby combining with the first group to form the largest batch of retired military officers to be (re-) engaged in government service, in this case the diplomatic.

A reshuffle took place in the staffing of Nigeria's envoys abroad three years later under the Babangida's military presidency, that involved the re-deployment of some retired military officers. Among the fifty-four (54) envoys approved by the government on June 1, 1987 were six (6) senior-ranking military officers – Maj. Gen. Joseph Garba, Navy Captain Porbeni, Commodore E.T. Okpo, Maj.-Gen. Solomon Omojokun, Brig. Samuel Olajide, and Maj. Gen. Tony Hannaniya.[23] Of these, three were re-appointments, i.e. those of Garba, Olajide, and Hannaniya who, it will be recalled, had been serving abroad since 1984. Retired Maj. Gen. Garba retained his posting as Nigeria's Permanent Representative at the UN, retired Brig. Olajide moved from Chad to Poland[24].

Completely new were the appointments of the three other military envoys Commodore Okpo, Navy Captain Porbeni, and retired Major-General Omojokun accredited to Sierra Leone, Equitorial Guinea, and Cuba respectively.[25]

We have been treating, in the foregoing section of the chapter, the examples of retired military personnel appointed to full-time ambassadorial posts. But there are occasions when retired senior military officers have also been employed on an *ad-hoc* basis and sent out as roving ambassadors to perform certain representational functions on behalf of the Nigerian government(s). Examples here are too numerous to recount. Suffice it to mention only a few of them.

Thus, General Murtala's regime in late 1975 despatched a special mission headed by Nigeria's battle-made "Black Scorpion" and hero of the civil war, retired Brigadier Benjamen Adekunle, to Angola to make an on-the-spot investigation and report on the situation in that country.[26] Clearance was given for the former head of state retired General Olusegun Obasanjo to serve as co-chairman of the special Commonwealth mission, the widely reported Eminent Persons Group (EPG), sent out in 1986 to South Africa to report on the escalating protests against, and avenues for peaceful change under, the *Apartheid* regime. Other retired military plenipotentiaries believed at various times to have been appointed to some special delegations to represent the Federal Government in certain external negotiations and at various times are retired Maj. Gen. I.B.M. Haruna, retired Maj. Gen. T.Y. Danjuma, retired Maj. Gen. Emmanuel Abisoye, and retired Maj. Gen. Shehu Musa Yar' Adua. Such delegations have to include top government functionaries, and leading businessmen, especially within the last four years when Nigeria's concern has been with negotiating debt-rescheduling terms with certain Western creditors. And more recently, there was the appointment of a former army brigadier Samuel Ogbemudia as a member of the special delegation sent by the

Armed Forces Ruling Council (AFRC) to represent the latter and help cheer the Nigerian team the Golden Eaglets at the finals of the Under-17 FIFA/JVC World Cup played in Toronto, Canada, on July 25, 1987.[27] No sooner did he come back from the latter trip than was Mr. Ogbemudia nominated *Chef de Mission* and Chairman of the National Sports Commission to the fourth All-African Games which held in Nairobi, Kenya, in August 1987.[28] These examples of senior military men both serving and retired branching out into international diplomacy we interpret as efforts to have military interests specially represented in a field hitherto reserved for civilians, particularly the career diplomats.

Employment in other Public Service Departments

In the home service, there are other administrative organisations or agencies where retired military officers can be found re-engaged. The judiciary is one of the agencies, that immediately comes to mind. To be re-engaged here, though, a retired military person need to have had the requisite qualifications for the practice of law. One of the first top retired military officers to have earned qualification of this kind is Maj.-Gen. E.O.E. Ekpo. A former Chief of Staff (Supreme Headquarters) at the time of the July 29, 1975 counter-coup, Maj.-Gen. Ekpo had been compulsorily retired with the overthrow of the Gowon regime, under which he had managed to read for a part-time Bachelor of Law (or LL.B) degree from the University of Lagos.[29] On retiring from the army in 1975, Maj-Gen E.O.E. Ekpo sought appointment in the Cross-River State judiciary. In 1982, he held the position of Magistrate Grade 1 at Calabar.[30] By 1985 he had risen to the position of Senior Magistrate Grade 1 in charge of Akamkpa station of that state judiciary,[31] becoming Chief Magistrate Grade II employed at the High Court Headquarters, Calabar, in the following year.[32]

We are dealing with appointment of retired military officers to higher judicial service at the state level. Other examples include the following names found on the list of magistrates of the Bendel State as at May 1, 1978: retired Maj. S.E. Aikhiobare, Magistrate Grade III, Magistrates' Courts, Benin City; retiree Capt. C. Isiakpona, Magistrate Grade III. Magistrates's Court, Benin City; retired Captain J. Omokaro, Magistrate Grade III, Magistrates' Courts, Benin City; retired Captain John J.O. Macdonald, Magistrate Grade III, Magistrates' Courts, Sapele; retired Major Peter A.E. Erakpofoke, Magistrate Grade III, Magistrates' Courts, Ughelli; and retired Maj. Michael O Edionseri, Magistrate Grade III, Magistraces' Courts, Abudu.[33] And assisting in the judicial department administration, in the Akure magisterial district, of the Ondo State in 1979 was one retired Maj. J.M. Adebusoye, holding the position of Magistrate Grade III. [34]

Apart from those quasi-civilianised officers acting as judges in the lowest courts just named, a score or more of such cases could have been ferreted out of the public services of the various states of the Federation if more intensive and cross-country researches had been directed at this level. A few retired military officers can be found serving in city administration and on local government management councils; although some of these officers tend to use such appointments to move up into higher public service at the state or Federal level, and others as a spring-board for seeking political office. Two examples readily come to mind: Brig. George Kurubo and the late Lt.-Col. Ayo Ariyo, both of whom sought their initial post-retirement jobs serving on some local government management councils, the former at Bonny local government authority area of the Rivers State in July 1977, and the later at Ijero in Ondo State in December 1976. But as we previously saw, retired Brig. Kurubo soon moved from here into seeking political office at the national level, while retired Lt.-Col. Ariyo got appointed to the Federal Electoral Commission (FEDECO), that Federal agency statutorily charged with the conduct of elections during the Second Republic 1979–83. (see Chapter 4).

The fact remains, as with other appointments discussed in the two previous sections, majority of the retired military officers re-engaged in the public bureaucracy are to be found at the Federal level, understandably, since the most vacancies obtain at this level, in part because the size of bureaucracy is the largest or administrative organisations the most proliferated at the Federal level. Space does not permit us to go into details of these other pubic service appointments. There are examples to be found in most of the government agencies scheduled under the Pensions Decree No. 102 of 1979.* Nor are the retired military personnel so re-engaged confined only to the executive cum management and administrative cadres of the public service. A number can be found employed also as professional heads of government departments, parastatals, or commissions. An example of the latter that we found in our research is retired Wing Commander Isaac Olupitan, employed by the National Sport Commission, as Chief Engineer at the National Stadium, Lagos.[35]

Teaching and Research as Second Career

The last but one major area of public service re-engagement for the retired military that the chapter identifies for analysis is teaching and/or research. Admittedly, not many retired military persons are to be found in the teaching cum research profession There are three major reasons for this. First, although many command and staff tasks involve teaching roles, there are few retiring military men who possess the formal educational credentials (e.g. certificates of education, bachelor's degrees, etc.) required for a career in teaching. Up to the early -1970s, the level of education within the Nigerian army in particular was very low.[36]

Of course, since then, many efforts have been made by the armed forces to raise the educational level of their personnel, as evident in the number of serving officers

---

*   Besides those agencies already mentioned above, the list includes the Federal Government itself with its multifarious Ministries and Departments, the Defence Industries Corporation (DIC) of Nigeria, Federal Capital Development Authority, various River Basin Authorities, Nigerian Television Authority. Recruitment into the various Universities and Research Institutes is treated in the next section of the chapter.

encouraged to take bachelor's degree, master's and even Ph.D. in a variety of fields.[37] However, not only are military men possessing such academic qualifications very few in number, but they also continue to be on the fringe of what most regard as normal military life.

Related to the latter, secondly, is what, for want of a better phrase, may be described as the antipathy of military men towards the academics. It stems, in part, from the inherent contradiction between military career and academic pursuit, between devotees to the military mind and those with intellectual orientation, between the "brawns" and the "brain". At the root of this is the fact that military organisations are differently organised and oriented from the universities. By definition, the former manifest attitudes that are conservative, authoritarian, apolitical, bureaucratic, and nationalistic – in short the very material or set of orientations supportive of an ideal military organisation; while the latter comprise men and women with invariably radical, populist, political, inquisitive, and individualistic views – views that would be regarded as essentially non-military.[38]

As if to top it all, finally, the teaching profession, though traditionally recognised as one of the noblest, has been treated as the cinderella among all the professions, one of the poorest rewarded. So that even among individuals with strong public-service motivation, teaching has always been a career of low priority. Not surprisingly, the few retired military men who branched into teaching or research and writing beginning from the late 1970s took to the latter more as a part-time than a full-time occupation. A number of examples are given later in the section to illustrate this point.

Meanwhile, there is one remarkable observation regarding the role of education and the retired military that is of relevance to our discussion here. I refer to the tendency of retired military officers to want to go back to school soon after leaving the force: some contemplating this as a way of improving themselves; others as a stop-gap measure, before deciding on their post-retirement pursuit; and others still, in order to convert to a completely new professional line, such as teaching or law. Thus, barely two months after being toppled as head of state, General Yakubu Gowon enrolled as freshman for a political studies and international affairs degree course at Warwick University, near Coventry, England, in October 1975. After obtaining his bachelor's degree, Gowon stayed through at Warwick to work on his Ph.D. which he received in 1987.

Similarly, retired Maj.-Gen. I.B.M Haruna had enrolled for and obtained a law degree from Ahmadu Bello University, Zaria. Soon after being retired, Maj. Gen. Joseph Garba took up a research position at the Centre for International Affairs (CFIA), Harvard University, Cambridge, Mass., in the U.S., although in this particular case there was no intention to work for a university degree. Retired Maj. Gen. David Jemibewon went back to school to take an LL.B. degree from the University of Lagos. On being retired, Lt. Col. B.O. Akpokabayen rushed to the University of Ibadan in 1980 to commence a bachelor's degree study in political science which he duly completed in 1983. After being retired from the department of armour at the Nigerian army headquarters, Bonny

Camp, Lagos, Brig. M.B. Mayaki registered to pursue a Ph.D. work in political science at the University of Sokoto. Brigadier Mayaki has had two previous university degrees, a Bachelor of science (B.Sc.) in political science and a Master of Literature (M.Litt), the former actually obtained from the University of Ibadan in 1975. While there are many more, the few examples just listed are easily the most memorable in part because they are the most distinguished.

Of these, the first to use his newly acquired university degree(s) to obtain a senior academic post was Dr. Gowon appointed Visiting Research Professor in the Department of Political Science, University of Jos, in 1986; while retired Brig. M.B. Mayaki, formerly of the department of armour was in early 1988 said to be doing some teaching stint at the University of Sokoto where he was also enrolled as a Postgraduate student. As Chairman of the Governing Council of the Nigerian Institute for International Affairs (NIIA), Lagos, for six years, retired Maj.-Gen. Haruna had been involved in the research activities of that Institute (1978-84). He was to move a couple of years later (1986) to the National Institute for Policy and Strategic Studies (NIPSS), Jos, to continue in a similar capacity.

On retiring from office both as head of state and commander-in-chief of the armed forces on October 1, 1979, General Olusegun Obasanjo accepted a Distinguished Fellowship at the Institute of African Studies, University of Ibadan in 1979/80, during which he wrote *My Command: An Account of the Nigerian Civil War 1967–70* (Ibadan: Heinemann, 1980). Retired General Obasanjo has since authored other books, his second and albeit the most controversial book being on *Nzeogwu* (Ibadan: Spectrum, 1987). He has also been writing for international journals, attending international conferences, on lecture tours literally of the whole globe, and addressing world bodies on major issues of international concern ranging from North/South dialogue, Third World Debt problems, South Africa, and conditions for world peace. Clearly, then, retired General Obasanjo combines sustained intellectual pursuits with private business interest,[39] and, at least for now, ranks first among Nigeria's new class of leisure writers comprising mostly of retired senior military officers.[40] Also, for now, retired General Obasanjo appears to have been contended with limiting himself to such public service-type engagements, particularly at the international level; although there are indications he would not mind taking a high-profile international job within the United Nations system, for example.

Nor is there a complete want of persons re-engaged as full-time university lecturers or/and administrators, college tutors, and school teachers from among the retired military. To be sure, there are some. An example most familiar to the present writer is that of Major F.A. Efunwoye who had been retired from the army since November 1975. With his B.Sc. (Agric. Eng.) (Tashkent) qualifications, retired Maj. Efunwoye came to be employed in 1976 in the Industrial Coordination Unit of the Faculty of Technology, University of Ibadan, on whose staff he was until 1980. He subsequently moved to a near-by institution, The Polytechnic, Ibadan, where he became Senior Lecturer and until very recently Head of the Department of Mechanical Engineering. Retired Maj. Efunwoye still lectures at same. Another officer similarly re-engaged is retired Maj. N. Dipeolu, who had for some time been Director of Works, in the Works, Maintenance, and Transport Department of Ogun State Polytechnic.[41] Holding the post of Deputy Registrar at the Federal Polytechnic, Ilaro, Ogun State, can be found a retired military officer Maj. R.O. Egbeyemi, a 1972 graduate of education from Ife. Retired Maj. Egbeyemi left the army education corps in 1979 and joined the said Federal Polytechnic Ilaro, Ogun State in 1979, where he has remained up to date.[42]

Finally, of course, and under this section must also be mentioned those demobilised scientists and technologists of "Biafran" war experience, who had been responsible for the little but significant innovations in indigenous weapons production during the Civil War 1967–70. Comprising mostly of conscripts, these had since found themselves re-engaged in other related research and projects development tasks under the agency of various research institutes, of which the best known is the Project Development Institute (formerly PRODA) of Enugu.[43] Examples and names involved here are too legionary to catalogue. By the same token, the heartland of former "Biafra", with its fully mobilised but later disarmed citizenry, produced ex-officers without number who are to be found in the employment of the successive state and local governments or their agencies.

Administration of Sports

The last most important area of public service re-engagement for the retired military personnel which we will discuss is in the administration of sports. The reader may wonder why intermittent appointments of retired military officers to various sports councils at federal, state and local government levels should not be considered along with part-time "board appointments", and therefore treated in Chapter 6 of the study, rather than singled out for discussion here or grouped under full-time "public service re-engagement". The reason for this has something to do with the continuous and permanent interest that military men invariably have in all things related to sports. The latter, in turn, is due to close association between military organisation and sporting activities, or better still the utility of the latter for the former

Excellent physical condition has long been considered a *sine qua non* for good military service, while constant training as well as discipline is recognised as necessary for keeping an army in top state of preparedness. Besides, it helps to chase away boredom that arises from inactivity or idleness. That is why war-making and sporting activities have long been considered inter-connected. In fact, a founding father of political/military science like Machiavelli was wont to accept games generally, including hunting, athletics, and gymnastics particularly, as simply imitation of war, and vice versa;[44] while sports at the international arena have come to be seen by scholars and statesmen, even in contemporary times as one form of inter-state conflict short of warfare.[45]

Little wonder, then, that military men tend to be often attracted toward most activities in the domain, particularly athletics, wrestling, polo, boxing, football, and golf. By the same logic, military men come readily to mind when matters relating to sports are being discussed. Most Nigerian governments past and present have tended to make use of military personnel whether in or out of uniform for administering various sporting activities in the country. In short, re-engagement of retired military personnel in the administration of sports which we analyse in this concluding section of the chapter could well have been treated as part of those "semi-military jobs" discussed in the opening section of the chapter.

As with government boards, statutory corporations, and state-owned companies, various sports councils have always had military personnel appointed to administer them right from the first Nigerian coup of 1966. Since then, serving military officers have often been named as sports administrators at Federal as well as State levels. Inclusion of ex-military officer is simply an extension of this long-standing practice. Nor is this a phenomenon manifested only under military regimes: that is, the first thirteen and two years of military rule which ended on October 1, 1979, and the second period of military rule begun on December 31, 1983 and up to-date. Serving as well as retired military officers were also utilised for sports administration under the civilian interregnum of President Shehu Shagari.

To give some illustrations that are germane to our study, for examples, Col. Mike Nduka Okwechime, the first Nigerian army chief engineer and retired from service at the end of the "Biafran" war in 1970, was for many years involved in the administration of the National Sports Commission (N.S.C), Bendel Sports Council, Nigerian Referees Association, and Nigerian Football Association (NFA) albeit at various times.[46] Another military man long involved in the administration of sports in the country is Brigadier Damian Kehinde Sho-Silva, a former Chairman of the Lagos City Council under the Gowon regime, but now retired. Brigadier Sho-Silva was appointed Chairman of the National Sport Commission (N.S.C.) in March 1979.[47] Although removed from that post with the return to civil rule on October 1, 1979, retired Brig. Sho-Silva was to be re-instated after the December 31, 1983 coup,[48] and continued as the NSC Chairman up to the beginning of General Babangida's presidency.

When they were at different times the military governors of the Mid-West (later Bendel) and Western (and later Oyo) states respectively, Brigadiers Samuel Ogbemudia and David Jemibewon distinguished themselves as good friends and patrons of Nigerian sports. Both were to continue their involvement long after leaving the force, as we shall soon see. Former "No. 2 citizen" in the Obasanjo regime, retired Maj.-General Shehu Yar' Adua, retired Navy Commander Edwin Kentebbe, and former military governor of the Midwest, Mr. Samuel Ogbemudia, were three of the 18 national sports association chairmen named on March 14, 1981 by the N.S.C. under Shehu Shagari's civilian presidency.[49] Of these, retired Navy Commander Kentebbe, made chairman of the Nigerian Football Association (NFA) for two terms, remained associated with central organisation of football activities in the country until his death in a London hospital on

October 19, 1985.[50]

On retiring from the army, Maj-Gen. (former Brigadier) David Jemibewon became even more available for service towards improving the standards of sports in the country. In 1982, he was appointed alongside others to serve on a newly constituted Nigerian Olympic Committee (NOC).[51] A 19-member board of directors was approved for the National Sports Commission (NSC) in March 1985 that included as many as three retired senior military officers: Maj. Omagie; Col. Ukor, Chairman, Boxing; Brig. M.A.T. Ajao (Army).[52] And more recently an ex-army brigadier and twice governor of Bendel (formerly Mid-West) State, Samuel Ogbemudia was appointed the Chairman of the National Sport Council (NSC) in August,.1987,[53] apparently in recognition of his past record of sports achievements. He was among the newly appointed 19-member board of national sports adminstration chairmen that also included some serving military officers.

At the state level had been discernible a similar trend towards the appointment of retired military personnel to various state sports councils; although because of space most of such examples cannot be mentioned here. To mention just a few random ones: retired Maj. T.L.O. Laoye, made Chairman of the Oyo State Sports Council, under the short-lived civilian governorship of Dr. Omololu Olunloyo in 1983;[54] retired Maj. S. Addingi, made Director, Benue Sports Council in 1984,[55] and succeeded in 1986 by yet another retired officer Col. Chris. I. Ode.[56] These ex-military state sports administrators have had the responsibility of co-ordinating sports activities from the local governemnt levels up to the state capitals, with the view to improving the standards of sports within their areas of jurisdiction.

The foregoing trend towards *militarisation* of sports administration, although a concomitant of the larger process of militarisation of society, has come to be accepted by most Nigerians, rather fatuously, as a necessary trend if the country is to continue to win recognition and laurels in international competitions of the kind involved here. The tremendous strides made by Nigeria sine 1970 are generally mentioned in justification of this. Significantly, most of the successes in sports were recorded under periods of military rule; thereby lending credence to the contribution of the military to them.

As if to underline the retired military's own growing role here, Nigeria's retired Maj.-Gen Adefope was one of the five members elected to the International Olympic Committee (I.O.C) at the end of its 90th Session in June 1985.[57] A trained doctor and former director of medical services of the Nigerian army (1967–75), Maj.-Gen. Adefope had during the latter period also served as Chairman of the National Sports Commission (NSC), and at the same time doubled as President of the Nigerian Olympic Committee.[58] Under the Obasanjo regime, he held various ministerial appointments, including those of labour and external affairs. Within two years of leaving the army, retired Maj.-Gen. Adefope was appointed in June 1981 as Chairman of Watson and Sons (Electro-Medical) Nigeria Ltd., a subsidiary of G.E.C. Medical Equipment Ltd., of Wembly, United Kingdom, as we show in the next chapter of the study. And, now exactly four years later the retired army surgeon general became one of the five members elected to the International Olympic Committee (I.O.C), a position he holds to this day.[59] A more apt illustration could not have been found of the movement of generals from active military service, through participation in government, into the world of business; politics and international diplomacy of sports.

NOTES

1. This point was first made by me in the earlier article, "Pay and Rank Differentiation Between the Nigerian Army and Police Force: A Comparison", *Nigerian Journal of Economic and Social Studies*, Vol. 23, No. 1 March 1981, p. 95.

2. *ibid.*

3. Section 13 of the Pensions Law 1979 applicable to civilians stipulates that any public servant who retires, or is required to retire, and who qualifies for the award of pension, can only be re-engaged in any public service on *contract* or temporary basis, but not on new pensionable terms, see Federal Republic of Nigeria, "The Pensions Decree No. 102, 1979", *Official Gazette of the Federal Republic of Nigeria*, Vol. 66, No. 48, September 19, 1979, pp. 795–806.

4. Federal Republic of Nigeria, "Armed Forces Pensions Decree (now Act) No. 103, 1979" *Official Gazette of the Federal Republic of Nigeria*, Vol. 66, No. 48, September 19, 1979, pp. 795–806.

5. The kind that operates in the U.S., see Albert D. Biderman, "Sequels to a Military Career: The Retired Military Professional", in Morris Janowitz (ed), *The New Military: Changing Patterns of Organisation* (New York: Sage, 1964), pp. 304–5.

6. Federal Republic of Nigeria, *The Constitution of the Federal Republic of Nigeria 1979* (Lagos: Department of Information, 1980), p. 110.

7. I am grateful to Capt. O.P. Awodola-Peters, a former student of mine, for this information apparently quoting from "Terms and Conditions of Service, Nigeria Army officers 1981".

8. *ibid.*

9. See Chapter 2 above on "Economics of Military Retirement"

10. As identified in my previous book *Nigeria in Search of a Stable Civil-Military System ...* op. cit., pp. 10–12.

11. See Federal Republic of Nigeria, *Second National Development Plan 1970–74* (Lagos: Central Planning Office, 1970), pp. 90–92; *Third National Development Plan 1975–80* (Lagos: Central Planning Office, 1975), pp. 325–31; *Fourth National Development Plan 1981–85* (Lagos; National Planning Office, 1981), pp.367–8.

12. Now broken up into a number of separate bodies, with the old NSU corps being re-named as the State Security Service (or SSS).

13. As the Acting Head of Department of Political Science, University of Ibadan at the time, I happened to have written one of the letters of recommendations supporting the initial application of retired Lt.-Col. Akpokabayen for job in that Federal

agency.

14. Brig. A. Abdulkadir, who was later killed in a motor accident on his way to Minna, Niger State, in December 1985, was to be posthumously promoted to the rank of Major General with effect from May 1, 1984. Apparently the promotion assessment had been in process before his death.

15. See O.O. Bello, "Federal Use of Police Powers under the Shehu Shagari Presidency in Nigeria 1979–83", (Department of Political Science, University of Ibadan: M.Sc. Thesis, October 1984), pp. 164–77.

16. After serving for six years, that is, as Nigeria's first "diplomatic soldier".

17. Daily Times, *Nigeria Year Book 1976–77* (Lagos: Daily Times Publications, 1976), p. 104.

18. We refer to the *Recurrent and Capital Estimates of the Federal Republic of Nigeria,* yearly issued from that ministry.

19. Adekanye, *Nigeria in Search of a Stable Civil-Military System ...,* op. cit., pp 105–9

20. These particular military ambassadorial appointments were made in the early months of the Buhari/Idiagbon regime.

21. First reported, by way of scoop, in *The Guardian* (Lagos), April 1, 1984, p. 1. For this news scoop, however, the two senior reporters Tunde Thompson and Nduka Irabor involved were to be tried and sentenced to a year's jail each. This was in spite of the fact that the news report was proved to be true; and that almost all the "eight military chiefs" reported as "tipped for ambassadorial postings" ended up being so appointed, even if not to the same countries as originally planned.

22. *The Guardian* (Lagos), January 11, 1986, pp. 1–2.

23. *The Guardian,* June 2, 1987, p. 5.

24. From Ministry of External Affairs (Marina, Lagos) sources.

25. *ibid.*

26. Adekanye, *Nigeria in Search of a Stable Civil-Military System ...,* op. cit., p 106

27. Almost all the Nigerian national dailies reported on this.

28. For ex-Brigadier Ogbemudia, this was the second diplomatic sporting experience and a rapid one at that since being appointed formally as Chairman of the NSC in 1987, see concluding section of chapter.

29. David M. Jemibewon, *Combatant in Government* (Ibadan: Heinemann, 1978), p. 27.

30. Daily Times, *Nigeria Year Book 1982* (Lagos: Daily Times Publication 1982), p. 431.

31. Daily Times, *Nigeria Year Book 1985* (Lagos: Daily Times Publication 1985).

32. Daily Times, *Nigeria Year Book 1986* (Lagos: Daily Times Publication 1986), p. 255.

33. Daily Times, *Nigeria Year Book 1978–79* (Lagos: Daily Times Publication 1978), p. 556.

34. *ibid.,* p. 598.

35. *Sunday Times* (Lagos), May 31, 1987, p. 3.

36. Adekanye, *Nigeria in Search of a Stable Civil-Military System* ..., op. cit., pp 97–99.

37. Both at home and abroad.

38. An elaboration of this theme is discussed by the author in an article elsewhere, "The 'Brawn' versus 'Brain' Conflict in Contemporary African Civil-Military History and Thought", *Plural Societies* (The Hague), Vol. 10, Nos. 3 & 4, 1979, pp. 3–20.

39. See the sketch on "Obasanjo: Farmer, Leader Writer", *Newswatch* (Lagos), Vol. 5, No. 2, January 12, 1982.

40. Other writings under reference here include the following: Alexander Madiebo, *Nigerian Revolution and the Biafran Civil War* (Enugu: Fourth Dimension, 1980); Adewale Ademoyega, *Why We Struck: The Story of the First Nigerian Coup* (Ibadan: Evans, 1981); Ben Gbulie, *Nigeria's Five Majors* (Onitsha: Africana Educational Publishers, 1981); Joe Garba, *"Revolution" in Nigeria: Another View* (London: Africana Journal Ltd., 1982); James Oluleye, *Military Leadership in Nigeria, 1966–1979* (Ibadan: University Press Ltd., 1985); Joe Garba, *Diplomatic Soldering* (Ibadan: Spectrum, 1987). David Jemibewon's book *Combatant in Government* (Ibadan: Heinemann, 1978), the first in the series, was published while the author was a state military governor and, therefore, still in service. Jemibewon has of course since joined the retired military class. More of such "inside" accounts, or potentially fast-selling stories, and memoirs scripted by members are known to be under present assessment or/and preparation as book projects.

41. Information regarding the last example was kindly provided by retired Maj. Efunwoye, but we have not bothered to cross-check this, which we should have done.

42. I am grateful to Professor R.A. Akindele of the Nigerian Institute of International Affairs (NIIA), who provided this information through personal communication, February 4, 1989.

43. See J. 'Bayo Adekanye, "The Role of Private Sector and the Universities in the Development of Military Technology", *Nigerian Journal of Policy and Strategy* (NIPSS, Kuru, Jos), June 1986, pp. 52, 56.

44. Niccolo Machiavelli, *The Art of War,* revised edition of the Ellis Farneworth translation, with introduction by Neal Wood, (New York: Bobbs–Merill Co., 1965), pp. XLIX ff.

45. On the latter see the special issue on "Sports Relations & International Understanding", *Current Research on Peace and Violence* (Tampere), 2–3, 1982.

46. *The Guardian* (Lagos), December 22, 1985, p. 3.

47. Daily Times, *Nigeria Year Book 1980* (Lagos: Daily Times Publication 1980), p. 411.

48. Daily Times, *Nigeria Year Book 1985* (Lagos: Daily Times Publication 1985), p. 198.

49. Daily Times, *Nigeria Year Book 1982* (Lagos: Daily Times Publication 1982), p. 266.

50. Daily Times, *Nigeria Year Book 1986* (Lagos: Daily Times Publication 1986), p. 216.

51. An office he held up to September 1987, *The Guardian* (Lagos), September 11, 1987, p. 15.

52. *New Nigeria* (Lagos), March 26, 1985, p. 11.

53. A post the ex-army brigadier from Bendel State still holds as at the time of writing.

54. Oyo State Government, *A Decade of Oyo State 1976–1986* (Ibadan: Ministry of Information, 1986), p 100.

55. Daily Times, *Nigeria Year Book 1985* (Lagos: Daily Times Publication 1985), p. 243.

56. Daily Times, *Nigeria Year Book 1987* (Lagos: Daily Times Publication 1987), p. 260.

57. Daily Times, *Nigeria Year Book 1986* (Lagos: Daily Times Publication 1986), p. 197.

58. *The Guardian* (Lagos), September 16, 1987, p. 15.

59. *ibid.*

6

Retired Officers on Corporate Boards and Other Interlocking Directorships

Military-corporate links generally, and the placing of senior military officers in positions within key industrial companies and government-owned corporations particularly, can be very obvious when the military themselves constitute the government of a given political society. For example, during the first phase of military rule in Nigeria lasting from January 15, 1966 to October 1, 1979, military personnel could be found posted as general managers or executive directors of various strategic sectors of the nation's economy, statutory corporations, and state-owned companies. The latter included the ports authority, railways, the airways, shipping lines, posts and telecommunications, electric power, steel companies, the petroleum corporation, various investment companies, banks as well as insurance houses in which the government had controlling shares, and of course the defence industries.

The process can be traced to the military government's promulgation of February 1966 which not only laid down principles determining the appointments of chairmen and members of the Federal boards of statutory corporations, but stipulated that such boards should each have at least one military member appointed to them.[1] Many of the government agencies, public corporations, statutory companies or parastatals concerned had been in existence shortly before the country gained her independence in 1960; a number got established during the Third National Development Plan period 1975–80; while a few, among them those dealing with the "commanding heights" of the economy, became government-controlled under the so-called "indigenisation" decrees of 1972 and 1977. But almost all of them had senior military officers posted to them as corporate heads, managers, or directors under the first military rule.

Admittedly, such military-corporate links may not be so obvious when/where the military are not in government, that is when/where civilian politicians are in charge. They may seem even less obvious when/where the military involved are no longer in active service, but retired. Yet even in these other conditions, the phenomenon can be equally, if not in fact more, pervasive.

In this sixth chapter of the study, we examine:

    (a)   The extent to which key decision-making posts in the public sector, particularly the economic (and we have particularly in mind here the boards of directors of government-owned corporations, agro-industrial concerns, investment companies, including banks), have come to be manned by retired military personnel;

    (b)   the spill-over of these retired military appointments into the boards of directors of Nigerian subsidiaries of leading multi-national corporations (MNCs).

The consequences of both for our subject-matter will also be examined. In a sense, the military-corporate relations investigated here are a continuation, on a higher plane, of the emergent military-business complex whose activities we discussed in Chapter 3. Our analysis is carried out under the two major sub-headings that have just been listed. Although, from the objectives of the study, we are concerned predominantly with retired military officers, however, other examples abound from the public service generally, including most especially the post-service career of retired top civil servants as pointed out in our conclusion, adding significantly comparative dimensions to the phenomenon being investigated.

(a)   Appointment to Key Public Boards, Corporations and Agencies

An examination of Nigeria's military-corporate scene since 1975 shows a steady increase in the number of retired high-ranking military officers appointed as members, and sometimes even chairmen, of boards of directors of key governmental agencies, statutory corporations, public enterprises or companies, and parastatals vital to the Nigerian economy. By 1985, the list included the National Electric Power Authority (NEPA), at least three of the nation's vehicle assembly plants, the Osogbo Steel Rolling Company among others in the iron and steel sector, most of the nation's university teaching hospitals, some of the public manufacturing industries in the agro-allied fields, banks and insurance companies where the Federal government had major financial interest, and various River Basin and Rural Development Authorities.

Retired military officers are to be found employed also at other junctures of governmental-economic control, such as the Nigeria Airways Limited, the Nigerian Airports Authority, the Civil Aviation Department, Nigeria National Shipping Line, Nigerian Ports Authority, Nigerian National Petroleum Corporation, and the Nigerian Security Printing and Minting Company. Admittedly, most of the public enterprises or corporations just named operate in areas of the economy where certain military skills have long been considered transferable. Other Federal government-owned companies, like the Nigerian Supply Company, although apparently less quasi-military in nature than the immediately preceding ones, have also had ex-military officers appointed to them.

Before we proceed to substantiate all the points made with concrete examples, it is important to stress that appointments of retired military officers to the governing boards of public agencies, corporations and government-owned companies are not a recent phenomenon, but go back considerably in time. Thus, a person like retired General I.B.M. Haruna, recently made Chairman of re-constituted 10-member Governing Board of the National Institute for Policy and Strategic Studies (NIPSS) in December 1986, had featured the longest among such appointments. As far back as 1978, he had been on the board of the Nigerian Institute of International Affairs (NIIA), whose Chairman he was for six years and up to 1984. Preceding that, Brigadier G.G. Ally had scarcely retired from the army when he was appointed Board Member, Nigerian Railways Corporations in 1977. These took place under the regime of General Olusegun Obasanjo. They were among the earliest board appointments to be offered to retired military officers at the Federal level.

But the practice was not confined to the period of military rule. For example, it was under the Shehu Shagari civilian presidency, (in 1980 to be precise), that Colonel Mohammed Sani Bello, another long-circulating retired officer, was appointed to the Board chairmanship of the Law, Union and Rock.[2] Between 1979 and 1980, the same retired Col. Sani Bello had held office as Chairman of the Niger State N.Y.S.C. Board.[3] There was the related example of retired Inspector-General of Police, Alhaji Kam Salem, who in 1979 was made Chairman of the Nigerian National Shipping Line, a post he held until his death in July 1981.[4] One also recalls retired Maj.-Gen. Adebayo's November 1983 letter to President Shagari pleading to be offered some board chairmanship as a reward (patronage) for contributing to the National Party's success in the controversial elections of that year (on the latter, see Chapter 4). Retired Maj.-Gen. Adebayo's preference was for the chairmanship of any of the three big banks (United Bank of Africa, First Bank, Union Bank), any of the country's oldest-established statutory corporations (Nigeria Railway Corporation, Nigerian Ports Authority, National Electric Power Authority), any of the three Federal government-owned firms in the petroleum sector (African Petroleum, Unipetrol, National Oil Marketing Company), or the National Insurance Corporation of Nigeria (NICON).[5] But there was no evidence of retired Maj.-Gen Adebayo's request being acceded to by the time of the December 31, 1983 coup toppling Shehu Shagari's civilian administration.

There is also the case of retired Brig. Abbas Suleiman Wali who, since his retirement from the army on health grounds in 1979, has at various times chairmanned the boards of a number of government establishments/parastatals at both Federal and State levels. These include the Nigerian Paper Mill Jebba (1979–80); Steyr Nigerian Ltd., Bauchi; Electricity Meter Company of Nigeria, Zaria; National Truck Manufacturing Company, Kano; Water Resource, Engineering and Construction Agency or WRECA, Kano (Kano State-owned); and, more recently, the Assets Disposal Committee set up by General Babangida's administration to wind up the affairs of the Groundnut Board. These appointments have been apart from retired Brig. Wali's own private business interests, including an agricultural venture run under the name of Abba Wali Agriculture

(AWA).[6] It is significant that some of these board appointments were offered the retired brigadier.under the Shagari civilian rule.

The fact remains however that the largest numbers of retired military officers to be appointed to such posts took place after the December 1983 coup and beginning with the Buhari/Idiagbon military regime. The appointments were in two streams and announced at separate times, in October 1984 and March 1985. The October 1984 list dealt with the boards of parastatals, commissions, and companies mostly under the Federal ministries of commerce and industries, mines, power and steel development, and finance, including development corporations, banks and insurance companies; while the March 1985 list was to be concerned with Federal appointments to the boards (or governing councils) of rural basin and rural development authorities, university teaching hospitals, and some of the agencies under the ministry of mines, power and steel development. The latter were to include the electricity, power authority, and various steel companies.

To analyse the October 1984 list of board appointments, first: of the country's vehicles assembly plants with re-constituted boards of directors, Leyland Nigeria Ltd., based at Ibadan, Oyo State, had a retired military man, Lt.-Col. O. Anifowoshe, appointed to its Board.[7] Other Federal agencies in the manufacturing sector which had retired military personnel appointed to their directorships were Savannah Sugar Company Ltd., Numan, Gongola State, with retired Maj. Adukpo Egi, as Board Member; Nigerian Newsprint Manufacturing Company, Oku-Iboku, in Cross Rivers State, with retired Brig. G.G. Ally, as Board Chairman;[8] and Nigeria Export Promotion Council, with retired Maj.-Gen. Emmanuel Abisoye, as Board Chairman.[9]

Although the last two officers did not have the usual "rtd", being an abbreviated inscription standing for "retired", appearing in the publication concerned, we know them to have in fact long left the force – Brig. Ally in 1977 and Maj.-Gen. Abisoye in 1979.[10] We are, therefore, correct in considering them as material to our analysis. Others also wrongly designated in the October 1984 list, but known to have been out of service even by the time of their appointments, included: retired Brig. Usman Abubakar, Chairman, Nigeria Paper Mills, Jebba; Brig. A. Wali, Chairman, Electricity Meter Company Nigeria Ltd., Zaria; Capt. Ibrahim Abudulahi, Board Member, Volkswagen of Nigeria Ltd., (VON), Lagos.[11]

Of the fifteen (15) or so insurance companies in which the Federal government held financial interest, four (4) had retired senior military officers appointed to their directorships in October 1984: Nigeria Re-Insurance Company, with retired Col. Isa Ahmed, as one of its Directors; Guinea Insurance Company, with retired Maj. Ejiga Okwa, a Director; Mercury Insurance Company, with retired Lt.-Col. H. Abdulkadir, a Director; and America International Insurance Company (AIICO), with retired Maj.-Gen. G.A. Innih, as Board Chairman.[12] Nor were the banking institutions left out. The Allied Bank of Nigeria Ltd. had retired Air Commodore Dan Suleiman appointed to it as a Board Chairman, while the Federal Savings Bank had retired Col. J.J. Brown as one of its Directors.[13] Others included retired Col. Datti Abubakar, made Board Member, Nigeria Bank for Commerce and Industry (NBCI), although also incorrectly listed in the October 1984 publication as a serving officer;[14] retired Group Capt. Usman Jibrin, Chairman, Nigerian Agricultural and Cooperative Bank (NACB);[15] and retired Lt.-Col. Ahmadu Yakubu, appointed Director, Nigeria Securities and Exchange Commission,[16] the latter being the apex regulatory body for the Nigerian capital market.

In March 1985, retired Brig. P.A. Eromobor was appointed to the Board of Directors, National Electric Power Authority (NEPA).[17] The latter was among the second steam of appointments announced by the military regime of Generals Buhari and Idiagbon reconstituting the boards of the remaining statutory corporations, state-owned companies, and companies in which the Federal government had interest – meaning, specifically, those under the Federal ministries of agriculture, water resources, and rural development; mines, power and steel; and the national petroleum corporation. Another was that of retired Capt. Adekunle Adebiyi, a former military engineer, appointed to the Board of Directors, Osogbo Steel Rolling Company Ltd.[18]

At the same time, almost all the medical institutions in the public sector, including especially university teaching hospitals under the supervision of the Federal ministry of health, had serving military officers (or military commandants) appointed to them as Chairmen; while a number of these institutions also had retired military officers on the membership of their Boards. Among the latter were retired Lt.-Col. (Mrs) B.W. Roberts, Member of Board, Food and Drugs Advisory Council;[19] retired Group Capt. T.O. Pereira, Member, Psychiatric Hospitals Management Board; and retired Maj. Olu Awojuyigbe, Member of Board, University College Hospital (UCH).[20] We should point out the circumstances under which these particular appointments to public medical institutions were made. They were made against the background of a nation-wide strike embarked upon by medical doctors under the professional banner of the Nigerian Medical Association (NMA) protesting against their deteriorating service and other working conditions, the repression of the latter body by the Buhari/Idiagbon regime, and the move towards getting the armed forces medical service units and personnel to take over the running of those civilian public hospitals. Thus, one can assume most of the retired military officers appointed to the management boards of those medical institutions, as indeed their serving military chairmen, to have had professional medical qualifications.

Equally marked was the preponderance of military officers on the Boards of Directors of agencies under the Federal Ministry of Agriculture, Water Resources and Rural Development, particularly the boards of various river basing development authorities (or RBDAs). Of the eighteen (18) RBDAs then operating in the country, two had retired military officers appointed to their directorships: namely, retired Brig. Baba Usman, Board Chairman, Mada-Dep River Basin and Rural Development Authority;[21] and retired Lt.-Col. E. Fakunle, Board Member, Upper-Ogun/Oshun River Basin and Rural Development Authority.[22] These were in addition to the fact that all of the RBDAs were each required to have a representative of the armed forces on their directorships, understandably, perhaps, given the growing interests of both retired and serving military personnel in large-scale farming as a post-retirement venture (see Chapter 3).

In early January 1986, the new Babangida military presidency, which had taken over power from Buhari/Idiagbon in the August 27, 1985 counter-coup, issued a directive dissolving all boards of parastatals and statutory corporations, including banks, and asked the chief executives of those bodies to carry on the day-to-day operations of their organisations under the close monitoring of their supervising ministries, until the former could be re-constituted. For in the history of operations of Nigeria's statutory corporations and government-owned companies, any change of government tends to be followed by dissolution of the boards of such bodies. Opportunity for the reconstitution of the boards is an opportunity that all incoming governments invariably seize for rewarding political supporters, or ideological faithfuls, ethnic partisans, family relations, or personal favourites.[23] It has been the practice since Nigeria became independent in 1960. This time, however, the dissolution of the statutory boards by the new Babangida government took place against the background of acute national economic recession, and demands for "privatisation" of government-owned corporations and enterprises as part of a general "structural adjustment" package worked out with the support of the International Monetary Fund (IMF)/World Bank for the country's economic recovery.[24] Initially, it seemed as if a number of the parastatals and therefore their governing boards were going to be liquidated.

Yet not all the parastatals could be "privatised" (or denationalised). Nor would "privatisation" necessarily mean a reduction of the growing influence of the retired officer class over the country's governmental-economic affairs. Indications from very beginning of Babangida's presidency pointed to the contrary. For example, as we saw, the first retired senior-ranking army officer to hold a cabinet position in contemporary Nigeria, and a former chief of defence staff, Lt. Gen. J.A. Akinrinade, had been appointed Federal Minister of Agriculture in September , 1985. It was at the very onset of the Babangida rule. That same month also saw the appointment of retired Major Aminu Dahiru as General Manager of the Nigerian National Supply Company (NNSC), a Federal agency established since 1972 for the procurement and distribution of essential commodities, and one of the government-owned companies definitely scheduled for liquidation by the Babangida government. The latter appointment was made along with three other retired military officers whose appointments as chief executives of certain government agencies were approved by the new Armed Forces Ruling Council (AFRC) in September 1985: retired Wing Cdr. M.D. Ahmed, to head National Freight Company; retired Col. Tony Steduru, in charge of Onnei Port; and retired Maj. A. Doherty, to administer Calabar Port among other facilities under the agency of Nigerian Port Authority.[25]

By July 1986, the Babangida government was announcing the chairmen and members of Boards of Directors for sixteen (16) banks. As many as four (4) chairmanships of these went to retired senior military officers, namely Lt.-Col. Y.M. Anifowoshe,

Col. Sani Bello, Air Vice-Marshall A. D. Bello and Group Capt. Usman Jibrin, appointed to head the Federal Savings Bank, Continental Merchant Bank, NAL Merchant Bank, and Nigerian Agricultural and Cooperative Bank (NACB) respectively.[26]

Announcements of more appointments to corporate positions continued to trickle out of the Cabinet office. Retired Lt.-Gen. Danjuma was re-appointed as Board Chairman Defence Industries Corporation of Nigeria (DICON).[27] Retired Maj.-Gen. Haruna, who had been Chairman of the Governing Council, Nigerian Institute of International Affairs (NIIA) for six years 1978–84, as we have noted, got a re-posting to chairmanship of the Board of a related agency, the National Institute for Policy and Strategic Studies (NIPSS), Jos, with effect from December, 1986. Meanwhile, relieving the latter general of the NIIA board Chairmanship 1984–86 was retired Air Vice-Marshall J.N. Yisa-Doko, a former chief of air staff, appointed to serve under the Buhari/Idiagbon regime. Appointments to the new boards of various university teaching hospitals, orthopaedic hospitals, psychiatric hospitals, and other medical institutions under Federal control were announced on August 26, 1986; and, unlike in the March 1985 exercise, there were almost no military personnel whether serving or retired on that list.[28] Perhaps, the only exception to be discovered later was that of National Eye Centre, Kaduna, which had retired Group Capt. T.O. Pereira, included as a member of its Board.[29]

New appointments were made by the Babangida regime to the reconstituted board chairmanships and memberships of twenty-two (22) parastatals, including vehicle assembly plants, cement factories, and sugar companies in February 1987. Of the reconstituted boards, as many as six (6) had retired military officers appointed as their chairmen, while there was an additional one with a retired army brigadier as member, bringing the ratio of ex-military representation on those boards to approximately 31.8%. The names of the officers appointed and their respective parastatals were as follows: retired Major Bala Adamu, Chairman, Peugeot Authomobile Nigeria (PAN); retired Maj.-Gen. Olufemi Olutoye, chairman, Leyland Nigeria; retired Brig. A.S. Wali, Chairman, National Trucks, Kano; retired Brig. U.S. Yaro, Chairman, Cement Company of Northern Nigeria; retired Air Vice-Marshall Usman Muazu, Chairman, Benue Cement Company; retired Capt. Kuma Kentebe (ex-navy), Chairman, Central Packages. Limited; retired Col. C.O. Ekundayo, Member of Board, Steyr Nigeria Limited.[30] The parastatals named are under the Federal Ministry or Industries, itself controlled by another retired top officer Lt.-Gen. Alani Akinrinade (hitherto Minister of Agriculture). Of the retired senior officers just named, Col. Sani Bello has circulated the most on government boards; and before his appointment as Chairman of the Continental Merchant Bank (CMB), he had served for two years (1984–86) as a non-career envoy posted to Harare, Zimbabwe, by the Buhari/Idiagbon regime.

The Armed Forces Ruling Council (AFRC) under President Babangida in May 1987 approved the appointment of a new batch of persons to various boards of parastatals and government-owned companies under the supervision of the Federal Ministry of Agriculture, Water Resources and Rural Development. The list included six (6) retired senior military officers: retired Major M. Ideho, Board Member, Agriculture and Rural Management Training Institute (ARMTI), Ilorin; retired Lt.-Col Chris Ugokwe, Board Member, National Grains Production Company, Kaduna; retired Col. C.C. Ude, Chairman, Anambra-Imo RBDA, Owerri; retired Maj.-Gen. A. Waziri, Chairman, Chad RBDA, Maiduguri; retired Maj.-Gen. G. Innih, Chairman Niger Delta RBDA, Port Harcourt; and retired Capt. Abdullahi Abubakar, Board Member, Benin-Owena RBDA, Benin.[31]

The last of the major public board appointments to be made by the Babangida government by the time of completing this part of the study were announced on May 29, 1987. They were in respect of nine (9) of the fourteen (14) parastatals and companies operating under the Federal Ministry of Transport and Aviation. Two retired army generals, a vice-admiral, one air vice-marshal, and a group captain were among the new board chairmen. Specifically, retired Maj.-Gen. Muhammed Shuwa was to head the Nigerian Railway Corporation (NRC) which also had one serving army officer Brig. S.G. Ikya as a Member. The Nigerian Ports Authority (NPA) had retired Major-General Martin Adamu as Chairman, while the Nigerian National Shipping Line (NNSL) the retired Vice-Admiral M.A. Adelanwa also as Chairman, and both boards with a representative each from the Navy although not immediately named. Appointed to head the board of the Nigeria Airways Ltd. was retired Vice-Marshal Yisa Doko. Group Capt. Olumodeji, apparently still serving in the Air Force, was appointed as Board Chairman, Nigerian Civil Aviation Training Centre (NCAT), now rechristened Nigerian College of Aviation Technology, Zaria, while another representative of the Air Force was being expected in 1987 as a board member.[32]

There are a number of other government enterprises, parastatals, or agencies still operating without boards. In this category are some of the older-established public utilities, as well as newer established public enterprises dealing with mining, manufacturing, transportation, construction and engineering, and agricultural production. The Babangida regime had delayed the appointments of chairmen and members of boards for these other bodies, because in all probability many of the parastatals may be either liquidated (abolished) outright, privatised (denationalised), or turned into limited liability companies (commercialised). Government policy on this issue is being awaited; and until then, one will not be able to say which ones among these other government corporations or companies currently without boards are being headed/directed by what retired military officers, how many, and beginning when. But the rate of circulation by retired senior military officers in government is such that more of these appointments can be expected, in the absence of any new national policy limiting same. The incidence of full privatisation, if and when finally implemented, is also unlikely to be much different from what we now know to be the effects of policy in general, either from its partial execution in the country thus far, or from the experiences of other countries elsewhere, with the (new) holders of power being also the policy's greatest beneficiaries.

The discussions of the chapter thus far have been concerned with appointments of retired military officers to the boards of public corporations, parastatals, and government-owned companies primarily at the Federal level. But we should point out that similar appointments have been taking place at the state, if not also local, levels. After all, a number of such public companies, parastatals, and corporations – excepting, of course, those dealing with aspects of the national economy currently considered the exclusive jurisdiction of the Federal government[33] – can be found duplicated more or less at each state level. Consequently, examples abound of retired military officers being appointed to statutory corporations and boards, public-owned companies, and parastatals operating at the state levels. Although we have not been primarily concerned with them here, suffice it to cite a few of the examples from the states. Retired Maj. J.F. Kehinde has since May 1984 been Chairman, Trans Nigeria Motels Ltd[34] belonging to the Oyo Sate government. From the same state, there is also retired Col. David Laoye appointed Chairman, Oyo State Integrated Self-Employment Scheme (OSISES) newly launched to help in combating the problem of unemployed secondary-school leavers and university graduates. From Anambra state at various times between 1985 and 1986 come the examples of retired Squadron Leader C.F.M. Oputa, holding the position of Chief Executive of the Nigerian Mineral Water Industries Ltd, a state-owned company based in Onitsha; retired Col. C.C. Ude, Chairman, Anambra State Broadcasting Service;* retired Col. S.O. Uwakwa, Chairman, Ada Rice Production Company Ltd.; retired Col. Emma Nwobosi, Chairman, Anambra State Environmental Sanitation Authority.[35]

To add a few more examples from three more states: in 1986, retired Group Capt. (Dr.) Ode was made Chairman of the Benue State Health Management Services.[36] In April 1986, Mr. Kosoko Adeyosoye, a combatant soldier who had fought during the 1966–70 civil war, risen to the rank of Captain in the Nigerian army before pulling out to train abroad as a mechanical engineer, was appointed by the Ondo State government as Chairman of the Board of Directors, Okitipupa Oil Palm Company Ltd. owned by that state.[37] Also appointed to serve as a Director on the Board of the same company was retired Lt.-Col. Adejoro Ikupolati.[38] In August 1986, retired Maj.-Gen. Mohammed Jega became Chairman of Board of Directors, New Nigerian Development Company Ltd. (NNDC), a public company owned jointly by the ten former Northern states, and based at Kaduna.[39] There are many more examples of corporate links of retired military officers at the state level which space and time prevent us from pursuing. The trend points to even still more of such examples in the future.

By now, the foregoing discussion of the first section of the chapter would have demonstrated, hopefully, the extent to which the key decision-making posts in the public

---

*   Retired Col. C.C. Ude was to be given higher Federal appointment as Chairman of Anambra-Imo River Basin Development Authority (RBDA), Owerri, in May 1987 as we saw, and later the Chairman of the Anambra State Mass Mobilisation for Social Justice, Self-Reliance, and Economic Recovery (MAMSER) recently launched.

sector, particularly the economic, have come to be manned by retired military personnel. It centres on the increasingly large numbers of the latter who got appointed during the last decade or so as chairmen and/or to boards of directors or governing councils of government corporations and agencies.

(b)   On Boards of Multi-National Corporations

Partly because of the underdeveloped and dependent state of Nigeria's economy, such appointments of retired military officers to boards of government corporations and companies tend to spill over into multi-national corporate spheres. This should not be surprising. Afterall, many of the public companies, particularly those forced to be incorporated in Nigeria by the decrees of the 1970s promoting indigenous enterprises, became national only in name, but remained in fact the subsidiaries of some giant multi-national corporations headquartered in foreign lands.

Illustrating our thesis here on the "spill-over into multi-national corporate spheres" were, for example, in the banking industry, those appointments to the directorships of not only the so-called "Big Three" the Union Bank (formerly Barclays Bank of Nigeria Ltd.), First Bank (formerly Standard Bank of Nigeria Ltd.) and United Bank of Africa (formerly the British and French Bank Ltd.), but also other former expatriate banks in which the Federal government had acquired 60% share-holding, e.g. Allied Bank of Nigeria Ltd. (formerly the Bank of India Nigeria Ltd.), Continental Merchant Bank (until now called Chase Merchant Nigeria Ltd.), and NAL Merchant Bank (with Continental International Finance Corp. of Chicago, U.S., and Credit Lyonnais of France as the two major foreign shareholders).[40] So also were appointments to the boards of such insurance companies as the Law, Union, & Rock, and the American International Insurance Company (AIICO).

In which case, board appointments like those of retired Col. Mohammed Sani Bello to Law, Union, & Rock (1980–83), retired Maj.-Gen. Innih to AIICO (1984–85), retired Air Cmdr. Dan Suleiman to Allied Bank (1984–85), retired Col. Mohammed Sani Bello to Continental Merchant Bank (since July 1986), and retired Air Vice-Marshall A.D. Bello to NAL Merchant Bank (since July 1986), referred to in the previous section of the chapter, may be considered also as board appointments to the subsidiaries of multi-national companies.

The fact is that, as Teriba and others observed long ago in their case-study on ownership and control structure of business enterprise in the wake of the indigenisation policy, "control of a firm is ... possible" even "with minority shareholding". This is often the case where there exists " a proxy committee which serves the interests of the minority share holders". Besides, "the increasing technical nature of management" in modern business organisation does mean that, in the words of Teriba *et. al.,* "where a local firm forms part of an international business corporation, many vital strategic decisions tend to be influenced by the metropolitan office".[41] The authors apparently had particularly in mind here conglomerates, like the United Africa Company (UAC), Union Trading Company, (UTC), *Compagnie Francaise de L'Afrique Occidentale* (or CFAO Nigeria Ltd.), John Holt, A.G. Leventis, and *Societe Commerciale de l'Ouest Africain* (or SCOA Nigeria Ltd.). Most of these companies had started as trading and commercial enterprises, but have since come to acquire direct investment in transportation, manufacturing and processing, and more recently agriculture.

As for the vehicle-assembly plants like Leyland Nigeria, Volkswagen of Nigeria (VON), Steyr Nigeria Ltd., and Peugeot Automobile Nigeria Ltd. (PAN), as well as other joint-ventures in the heavy-industrial (e.g. iron and steel, machine tools) and/or agro-allied fields (e.g. pulp and paper industries), conceived *ab initio* as public-sector enterprises, their foreign technical partners (parent bodies) no doubt wield the controlling influence. This is made possible by the latter's access to immense capital, privileged information, superior know-how, and abundant experience.

Nor has the situation been helped by the requirement, under the "indigenisation" policy, that these multi-national corporations must appoint Nigerians to chairmanship or membership of their boards, and that their businesses be incorporated in Nigeria. The policy has tended to achieve only token results, as the (new) chairmen and board members so appointed, consisting mostly of retired military officers and retired top civil servants,[42] become in fact powerless. In spite, or even because, of the influence of this class of Nigerians upon the country's decision-making machinery, their appointments to such board positions have had the consequence whether intended or unintended of creating a revolving door for further penetration and control of the national economy by the foreign companies concerned or their subsidiaries.[43]

Besides, there is the conflict of private with national interests inherent in the position of retired high-ranking military officers serving on the boards of multi-national corporations and foreign-controlled companies, which has considerable consequence for the nation's economic and military security.[44] Unfortunately, as far as we know, there is no legislation to take care of such conflict of interests and its attendant problems. Although the Code of Conduct provision in the Fifth Schedule, Part 1, Section 5 paragraphs (1) and (2) of the 1979 Constitution prohibits "certain retired public officers" "from service or employment in foreign companies or foreign enterprises",[45] this applies only to the President of the Federal Republic, Vice-President, Chief Justice of Nigeria, Governor and Deputy Governor of a State, but not to retired Army Generals or their Navy and Air Force equivalents, much less military officers of subordinate ranks. The implication is that retired generals are free to take up board appointments in foreign-interests dominated companies, including those doing direct business with the Federal Government. This is something unthinkable (neither is it allowable) even in the industrialised nations of the West, including the US, though the citadel of free-entreprise.

Of appointments of retired military personnel to the boards of big foreign companies operating in Nigeria, there are generally four types. First, there are those appointments made by various governments of the Federation invoking their authority as majority shareholders of given companies. For example, the Federal government has the authority to appoint the Chairmen and the Chief Executive Officers of all banks in which it has equity participation. Such government appointees are supposed to defend, maintain, and nurture the national interests while serving on these boards. Examples described in the previous section of the chapter fall under this first category.

Then, there are those board appointments made by the multi-national companies themselves, and motivated largely by self-interests. Big corporations which appoint top retired public servants, particularly generals and permanent secretaries, are usually large trading/manufacturing companies either holding sizeable defence contracts or dependent heavily on government business. Such companies very much need the prestige of well-known retired generals and other top officers, their special skills or expertise, managerial and organisational abilities as well as network of connections or ties for doing business with either the MOD in particular, the government or the public in general. The name of the game here, of course, is the profit motive.

In Chapter 3 of the study, we examined some examples falling under the latter, while discussing the many *souffle* of interests linking retired military officers with the corporate world of private business. But to illustrate with one concrete example: in June 1981, a medical equipment company Watson and Sons (Electro-Medical) Nigeria Ltd. appointed as its Chairman retired Maj.-Gen Henry Adefope, a trained doctor and former director of Medical Services, Nigeria Army 1967–75, who had served as a Federal Commissioner under the Obasanjo regime. Watson and Sons (Electro-Medical) Nigeria Ltd. is a leading supplier of diagonistic medical equipment in Nigeria, and subsidiary of G.E.C. Medical Equipment Ltd. of Wembly, United Kingdom.[46] There could be more.

Thirdly, there are those appointments to the directorships of multinational companies earned through becoming major shareholders. Historically, the process as regards this particular phenomenon would seem to have begun during the indigenisation era of the early 1970s that saw Nigerian directors of multinational corporations become also important shareholders of such multi-national corporations operating in the country. Thus, among the names of persons and institutions listed to have bought 40% of the share capital in SCOA was Rear-Admiral Nelson Soroh/Gmele Estates and Investments Ltd.,[47] General Gowon's chief of naval staff and retired with the latter soon after the July 29, 1975 counter-coup. Another example is that of retired Maj.-Gen. M.I. Wushishi, appointed a member of the board of directors of UAC Nigeria Ltd. since his retirement and currently described as one of the company's biggest share-holders.[48] Yet another example is retired Maj.-Gen. J.J. Oluleye, currently one of the Directors of UTC which also has for its Chairman and Vice-Chairman two top retired civil servants, namely, Liman Ciroma and S.B. Awoniyi respectively.

Related to the latter, finally, are those relatively well-endowed private companies established or newly incorporated, under Schedule II of the indigenisation policy, with technical management agreement with certain foreign interests, and which have influential Nigerians as their Board Chairmen/Managing Directors. We saw a number of examples of this in Chapter 3. For further illustrations here, such companies include the following: Roads Nigeria Ltd., a civil engineering works and construction company currently with Alhaji Musa Yar' Adua as Chairman, incorporated in October 1974 with Volker Stevin Roads and a member of the Dutch-based Royal Volker Stevin and International Construction Company as foreign technical partners; Nigerian Swiss Construction and Quarrying Industries, a quarrying business established in partnership with Engin-Consult Limited of Switzerland in December 1976, and having retired Brig. E.E. Ikwue as chairman/managing director and one of its major shareholders; Universal Trust Bank of Nigeria, a private bank first incorporated on June 21, 1981 under the old name of *Credit Commercial de France Bank* (Nigeria) Ltd., and which began operations in April 1985, with retired Lt.-Gen. Danjuma as Chairman; Habib Bank (Nigeria) Ltd., also a private commercial bank, affiliated to the Habib Bank Limited (Pakistan) as main foreign shareholder, and with retired Maj.-Gen. Yar' Adua as Chairman as well as major Nigerian shareholder.[49] Two other examples are: the Nigerian Sewing Machine Manufacturing Co. Ltd., connected with the Singer Company, Singer Machine Co., Singer International Security in foreign ownership (40%), but having retired Maj.-Gen. R.A. Adebayo on its board of directors, and The Estate of the late Chief Henry Fajemirokun as one of its major Nigerian shareholders;[50] West African Provincial Insurance Company Limited, linked to the Provincial Insurance Co. Ltd. (U.K.), and having retired Maj.-Gen David A. Ejoor as its Board Chairman.[51] There are certain to be more.

In the meantime, an increasing number of retired senior military officers are emerging who combine chairmanship/managing directorship of their own private businesses with part-time appointment to key government posts and parastatals relating particularly to agriculture, commerce and industry, in addition to holding interlocking directorships of many foreign companies incorporated in Nigeria. For some illustrations of this, a retired high-ranking officer like Lt.-Gen. Danjuma, also successfully established in the private shipping industry as we saw in Chapter 3, combines the latter with multiple board memberships in the public corporate sector, while also serving on the directorships of a number of foreign-based companies. A recent (1985) issue of *WHO'S WHO IN NIGERIA* published by Bibliographical Centre of Nigeria Ltd., Lagos, lists retired Lt.-Gen. Danjuma's current positions to include the following: Chairman, Nigeria-American Line Ltd.; Director, Ideal Flour Mills Ltd.; Director, Eastern Bulkcem Co. Ltd.; Director, Motor Tyre Services Company of Nigeria Ltd.; and Director, S.C.O.A. (Nigeria) Ltd.[52] Two other companies on whose boards of directorship Lt.-Gen. Danjuma is known to be, as we saw from our discussions in Chapter 3, are the Medafrica Group Ltd. in the shipping trade, and Sea Trucks (Nigeria) Ltd., a marine oilfield service company where the general is among the three major shareholders.[53]

But Danjuma is neither the first nor the only retired general to combine private business activities, and public sector involvement with multinational corporate links. Actually, retired Maj.-Gen I.B.M. Haruna had circulated the longest in this respect. He has since his retirement in 1977 been esconced in a number of important government posts mostly of a "think-tank" nature. For six years Chairman of the Governing Council of the Nigerian Institute of International Affairs (NIIA) as we saw, and more recently appointed Chairman of the Governing Board of the National Institute for Policy and Strategic Studies (NIPSS), retired Maj.-Gen. Haruna had featured prominently more than any other retired senior officer in numerous policy review boards, workshops, and brain trusts organised either directly by the Federal government or indirectly under its agencies. At the same time, he is currently listed in *WHO'S WHO IN NIGERIA* (1985) to be a Director of Mobil Oil Nigeria Ltd., and a Director of Chemical & Allied Products (or CAPL) Nigeria Ltd.,[54] being the two known foreign-owned corporations on whose boards he serve. Mobil Oil is a trade name associated with Standard Oil of New York, while the Chemical & Allied Products Company, formerly called ICI (Nigeria) Ltd., is a company in the chemical and paints manufacture business and associated with the Imperial Chemical Industries Ltd. (ICI) of the United Kingdom. All this, in addition to his own private business activities, including the running of a law firm Haruna & Co. Solicitors & Advocates, in which he is independently engaged.

These are some of the examples obtained from public sources[55] of the kinds of corporate links and interlocking directorships conjoined with private business interests held by Nigeria's top retired military officers operating in the Nigerian economy and society.

Conclusion: Comparison with Role of Top Retired Public Servants

In the foregoing chapter of the study, we have been discussing the phenomenon of top retired military officers appointed to the boards of some of the country's most important public utilities, state-owned companies, and other parastatals, on the one hand, and the directorships of Nigerian subsidiaries of various multi-national corporations (or MNCs), on the other, and the linkage between the two. The phenomenon was studied as manifested predominantly at the Federal level, but we indicated that similar trend could be discerned within the states, although we did not concern ourselves with the latter. The objective of the chapter was to deduce from those board appointments an emergent system of inter-locking directorships involving top retired military officers in the economic process of corporate consolidation. It sees such top retired military officers, turned big company directors, acting as an intermediary between the nation and foreign capital.

However, the military would not be the only group among retired public servants to be found in this role. To be sure, the boards of the subsidiaries of multi-national corporations (MNCs), banks, and other well-endowed private companies attract many of Nigeria's retired top public servants. Nor have retired university professors (top academics) been left out of the trend, although to date only a very tiny number of them has so far been involved. But top retired civil servants, particularly former permanent secretaries, heads of service, and/or secretaries to government have gone farther than any other domestic social group, including even the retired military officers detailed above.

Among members of other group whose names ring a chain of bells in the boardrooms of Nigeria's corporate circles[56] are Godffrey Amachree, Phillip Asiodu, Allison Ayida, Liman Ciroma, Mamman Daura, Ibrahim Damcida, Silas Bandele Daniyan, Joe Iyalla, Ahmed Joda, Babatunde Jose, C.O. Lawson, Mahmud Tukur, Jerome Udoji, and Tukur Usman. Now active in the various fields of commerce, industry, mining, and agriculture, where they have successfully established and do currently operate their own lucrative private businesses often jointly with cetain foreign technical partners, these retired top public servants – the precursors of retired top military officers studied here – can be found holding multiple directorships on the boards of the subsidiaries of many of the big foreign companies. Some of the companies have already been referred to in our discussions above. Others include UAC/Unilever, Phillip Morris Ltd., Beecham Group, Dumez, Tate and Lyle, Boots Company, Hagemeyer, Cadbury, Van Leer, Julius Berger. See Table 6.1 for the names and particulars of the twenty top retired public servants with such multi-national corporate links.

Numbered among the public servants listed in Table 6.1 are some of the "super-permanent secretaries" of the Gowon era - others are I.J Ebong, A.E. Ekukinam, S.O. Asabia, and S.O. Wey - who had controlled some of the most strategic government ministries, departments, or agencies. Until about 1975, these top bureaucrats had also been the largest single domestic social group to be found on the boards of various public corporations, government-owned enterprises, and commissions, literally sharing among themselves the directorships of such bodies. It was not unusual at the time to find a permanent secretary of a critical federal ministry, like finance, being a member of as many as fifty (50) government boards.[57] By the time of their retirement from public service, these "super-permanent secretaries" as well as other top bureaucrats had built up enough contacts to make their transition from government work to directorships of foreign companies an easy one.

We have brought up these comparable examples of top retired civil servants in this concluding section of the chapter in order to make an important point. The phenomenon of retired officers on corporate boards and other interlocking directorships, which we have been analysing, is not unique to the military. Apparently, what retired military officers studied above have done is to replace top civil servants on government boards, while competing with the latter group for the directorships of the Nigerian subsidiaries of various multi-national companies. The process continues.

Table 6.1   The Public Service and the Subsidiaries of Multinational Corporations in Nigeria: Retirements into Directorships: 1970 – 1985

Name	Highest Position/s in the Public Service	The Nigerian Subsidiary	The Multinational Firm
1. Simeon Adebo	(i) Chief Secretary and Head of Civil Service of Western Nigeria 1957–62 (ii) Permanent Representative in the United Nations 1962–68	(i) Nigerian Tobacco Company (ii) U.A.C. (Nig.) Ltd. (iii) Palm Line Agency	(i) B.A.T. Industries Ltd. of U.K. (ii) Unilever of U.K. and Holland (iii) Unilever of U.K. and Holland
2. Godfrey Amachree	(i) Federal Permanent Secretary (Justice)	(i) Phillip Morriss (Nig) Ltd. (ii) Thomas Wyatt & Sons Ltd. (iii) Lion of Africa Insurance	(i) Phillip Morriss Inc. of U.S.A. (ii) Lonrho Group of U.K. (iii) The Guardian Royal Exchange of U.K.
3. Michael Ani	(i) Chairman of FEDECO 1977–79	(i) Flour Mills Ltd.	(i) Exclesior Shipping Company of U.S.A.
4. Phillip Asiodu	(i) Federal Permanent Secretary (Industries, Mines and Power, and Housing) 1960–75	(i) Beecham (Nig.) Ltd (ii) Dumez (Nig.) Ltd. (iii) G.T.E. (Nig.) Ltd.	(i) Beecham Group of U.K. (ii) Phillip Morriss Inc. of U.S.A. (iii) G.T.E. Inc. of U.S.A.
5. Allison Ayida	(i) Federal Permanent Secretary (Economic Planning and Finance) 1963–1975 (ii) Secretary to the Federal Military Government and Head of Service 1975–1977	(i) Lever Bros. (Nig.) Ltd. (ii) Phillip Morriss Ltd. (iii) Berger Paints (Nig.) Ltd. (iv) B.R.G.M. Ltd. (v) Bewac Ltd.	(i) Unilever of U.K. and Holland (ii) Phillip Morriss Inc. of U.S.A. (iii) Lewis Berger Holdings of U.K. (iv) Dumez Afrique of France (v) Inchape Properties of U.K.

Name	Highest Position/s in the Public Service	The Nigerian Subsidiary	The Multinational Firm
6. Musa Bello	(i) Federal Permanent Secretary (Finance) 1975–1978	(i) ICON Merchant Bank	(i) Morgan Guaranty Trust of U.S.A. (ii) Baring Brothers of U.K.
7. Liman Ciroma	(i) Federal Permanent Secretary (Industries) (ii) Secretary to the Federal Military Government and Head of Service 1977–79	(i) Tate & Lyle (Nig.) Ltd. (ii) U.T.C. (Nig.) Ltd. (iii) G.T.E. (Nig.) Ltd. (iv) First City Merchant Bank	(i) Tate & Lyle of U.K. (ii) U.T.C of Switzerland (iii) G.T.E. Inc. of U.S.A. (iv) City Bank of U.S.A.
8. Mamman Daura	(i) Managing Director of New Nigerian Newspapers 1974–78	(i) Dunlop (Nig.) Ltd. (ii) Boots (Nig.) Ltd. (iii) Blackwood Hodge (Nig.) Ltd. (iv) Hagemeyer (Nig.) Ltd. (v) Bank of Credit and Commerce International	(i) Dunlop of U.K. (ii) Boots Company of U.K. (iii) Blackwood Hodge of U.K. (iv) Hagemeyer N.V. of Holland (v) B.C.C.I. of Luxembourg
9. Ibrahim Damcida	(i) Federal Permanent Secretary (Trade and Defence) 1966–1975	(i) Glaxo (Nig.) Ltd (ii) Nigerian International Merchant Bank	(i) Glaxo of U.K. (ii) First National Bank of Boston, U.S.A.
10. Silas B. Daniya	(i) Managing Director of Nigerian Industrial Development Bank 1966–76	(i) Metal Box (Nig.) Ltd. (ii) International Paints Ltd. (iii) Palm Line Agency (iv) Phillip Morriss (Nig.) Ltd. (v) John Holt Investments	(i) Metal Box of U.K. (ii) Courtaulds of U.K. (iii) Unilever of U.K. & Holland (iv) Phillip Morriss of U.S.A. (v) Lonrho Group of U.K.
11. J.T.P. Iyalla	(i) Ambassador to the U.S.A. (ii) Federal Permanent Secretary (External Affairs)	(i) Associated Electronic Product Ltd. (ii) Merchant Bank of Africa (Nig.) Ltd.	(i) National Trust of Canada (ii) Bank of America of U.S.A.

Name	Highest Position/s in the Public Service	The Nigerian Subsidiary	The Multinational Firm
12. Ahmed Joda	(i) Federal Permanent Secretary (Information, Education, and Industries) 1966–75	(i) Flour Mills Ltd. (ii) S.C.O.A (Nig.) Ltd (iii) George Wimpey (Nig.) Ltd.	(i) Exclesior Shipping Company of U.S.A (ii) S.C.O.A. of France (iii) George Wimpey of U.K.
13. Babatunde Jose	(i) Managing Director of Daily Times of Nigeria 1962–1973	(i) Boots (Nig.) Ltd. (ii) Blackwood Hodge (Nig.) Ltd (iii) Hagemeyer (Nig.) Ltd.	(i) Boots of U.K. (ii) Blackwood Hodge of U.K. (iii) Hagemeyer N.U. Naarden of Holland
14. Christopher Kolade	(i) Director-General of Federal Radio Corporation of Nigeria 1972–78	(i) Cadbury (Nig.) Ltd.	(i) Cadbury of U.K.
15. C.O. Lawson	(i) Federal Permanent Secretary (Health, Communications, and Transport) 1961 – 1971) (ii) Secretary to the Federal Military Government and Head of Service 1971–1975	(i) Boots (Nig.) Ltd.	(i) Boots of U.K.
16. Edwin Ogbu	(i) Federal Permanent Secretary (External Affairs, Works, Finance) 1962–1968 (ii) Permanent Representative to the United Nations	(i) John Holt Ltd.	(i) Lonrho Group of U.K.
17. Pius Okigbo	(i) Ambassador to E.E.C. (ii) Economic Adviser to the Federal Government	(i) Nigerian Tobacco Company (ii) R.T. Briscoe	(i) B.A.T. Industries Ltd. of U.K. (ii) The East Asiatic Trading Company of U.K.

Name	Highest Position/s in the Public Service	The Nigerian Subsidiary	The Multinational Firm
18. Mahmud Tukur	(i) Director of Institute of Administration, A.B.U. 1970–75 (ii) Vice-Chancellor of Bayero University Kano 1975–77	(i) Cadbury (Nig.) Ltd. (ii) Alcan (Nig.) Ltd. (iii) Associated Electronic Products Ltd. (iv) Van Leer Containers (v) ICON, Merchant Bank (vi) Bank of Credit and Commerce International	(i) Cadbury of U.K. (ii) Alcan of Canada (iii) National Trust of Canada (iv) Van Leer of U.K. & Holland (v) Morgan Guaranty Trust of U.S.A. and Baring Brothers of U.K. (vi) B.C.C.I. of Luxembourg
19. Jerome Udoji	(i) Chief Secretary and Head of the Civil Service of Eastern Nigeria	(i) Nigerian Tobacco Company Ltd. (ii) Wiggins Teape (Nig.) Ltd. (iii) R.T. Briscoe (iv) Nigerian International Bank	(i) B.A.T. Industries of U.K. (ii) B.A.T. Industries of U.K. (iii) The East Asiatic Trading Company of U.K. (iv) City Bank of U.S.A.
20. Tukur Usman	(i) Federal Permanent Secretary (Works) 1970–1975	(i) Julius Berger (ii) Agip (Nig.) Ltd. (iii) International Beer and Beverages Ind. Ltd. (iv) National Cash Register (Nig.) Ltd. (v) National Cereals Productions Company Ltd.	(i) Bilfinpe and Berger Ban AG of W. Germany (ii) E.N.I of Italy (iii) Kronenbourg of France (iv) National Cash Register of U.S.A. (v) National Cash Register of U.S.A.

SOURCE: Yusuf Bala Usman et. al., *The Nigerian Economic Crisis: Cause and Solutions,* (Zaria: Academic Staff Union of Universities of Nigeria, 1985), Table 8.1, pp. 161–64

NOTES

1. See *Daily Times* (Lagos), Thursday February 17, 1966, pp. 4, 5.

2. The Nigerian subsidiary of a foreign-based insurance company, whose Board Chairman the Federal government has had the responsibility of appointing since the 1970s.

3. Biographical Centre of Nigeria Ltd., *WHO'S WHO IN NIGERIA.*, 3rd Edit. (Lagos, 1985), p. 35.

4. *Nigerian Herald* (Ilorin), December 4, 1982.

5. A copy of General Adebayo's supplicating letter, as leaked to the press, was reproduced in *Daily Sketch* (Ibadan), December 12, 1983, p. 1.

6. *The Guardian* (Lagos), June 1, 1987, p. 13

7. *New Nigerian* (Lagos), October 18, 1984, p. 3.

8. *Ibid.*

9. *New Nigerian* (Lagos), October 18, 1984, p. 8.

10. See Chapter 1.

11. Information obtained through cross-checking from other sources.

12. *Daily Times* (Lagos), October 17, 1984, pp. 13, 19.

13. *Ibid.*

14. Information correcting this was obtained from *Nigeria Banking Almanac 1985/86* (Lagos: Research & Data Services Limited, 1986), p. 217.

15. *Daily Times* (Lagos), October 18, 1984, p. 12.

16. *Daily Times* (Lagos), October 17, 1984, p. 13.

17. *Daily Sketch* (Ibadan), March 27, 1985, p. 3.

18. *Ibid.*

19. *Ibid.*

20. *Daily Sketch* (Ibadan), March 26, 1985, p. 3.

21. *Ibid.*

22. *Daily Sketch* (Ibadan), March 25, 1985, p. 3.

23. This has been recognised as a major cause of the inefficiency or non-performance characterising the operations of most public corporations.

24. *New Nigerian* (Lagos), June 19, 1986, pp. 1,3.

25. *The Guardian* (Lagos), September 28, 1985, p. 2.

26. *West Africa* (London) July 28, 1986, pp. 1600–1. Retired Group Capt. Usman Jibrin was apparently retained in the chairmanship of the NACB to which he had been appointed under the Buhari/Idiagbon government, see fn. 15 above.

27. As reported in *National Concord* (Lagos) September 1, 1986, p. 1.

28. See *The Guardian* (Lagos), Wednesday August 27, 1986, p. 17.

29. Private Communication from Professor (Mrs.) Nike Abiose, Acting Director, National Eye Centre, Kaduna.

30. *The Guardian* (Lagos), Thursday February 5, 1987, p. 2.

31. *Daily Times* (Lagos), May 23, 1987, p. 4. But as that list shows, for the first time, Federal board appointments also featured the names of other retired top public servants, including a retired justice and two retired ambassadors.

32. *The Guardian* (Lagos), May 30, 1987, p. 16.

33. Including defence and security, customs, currency, aviation, shipping, mines and minerals, posts and telecommunications, and railways. These are exclusive functions or powers that most Federations tend to reserve for their Central Governments.

34. Although one of the parastatals scheduled to be "privatised" by the Oyo State government, as announced by the military governor Col. Adetunji Idowu Olurin while presenting the state 1987 budget in early January 1987.

35. *Nigeria Year Book 1986* (Lagos: Daily Times Publication, 1986), pp. 228; *Nigeria Year Book 1987* (Lagos: Daily Times Publication, 1987), pp. 244–5

36. *Ibid.*

37. See *Daily Sketch* (Ibadan), Friday December 12, 1986, p.11.

38. *Ibid.*

39. *New Nigerian* (Lagos), August 12, 1986, p. 16.

40. Of the banking industry generally it has been written: "Foreign Shareholders in Nigerian banks are generally multinational banking institutions", *Nigeria Banking Almanac 1985/86* ... op. cit., p. 39.

41. O. Teriba *et. al.* "Some Aspects of Ownership and Control Structure of Nigerian Enterprise in a Development Economy" in O. Teriba and M.O. Kayode (eds), *Industrial Development in Nigeria: Patterns, Problems, and Prospects,* (Ibadan: The University Press, 1977), p. 92.

42. Bade Onimode *et.al., Multinational Corporations in Nigeria* (Ibadan: Les Shyraden Nigeria Ltd., 1983).

43. *Ibid.*

44. Cf. "Retired Generals in Big Business", *New Horizontal* (Lagos), Vol. 7, No. 8, August/September 1987, pp. 10–41.

45. Federal Republic of Nigeria, *The Constitution of Federal Republic of Nigeria 1979* (Lagos: Federal Ministry of Information, 1979), p. 110.

46. *National Concord* (Lagos), June 26, 1981, p. 6.

47. Information obtained from Yusuf Bala Usman *et.al.,* "Who Owns What? The Multinationals and Nigerian Subsidiaries", *The Analyst* (Jos), Vol. 1, No 1, June 1986, p. 6.

48. *Ibid.,* p. 9. Also see UAC of Nigeria Ltd, *Annual Report 1985* (Lagos), p. 32.

49. See Chapter 3 for the sources of data supporting the examples used in this paragraph.

50. ICON Limited (Merchant Bankers), *ICON Nigeria Company Handbook 1983* (Lagos), p. 242.

51. *Ibid.* p. 351.

52. Bibliographic Centre of Nigeria Ltd., *Who's Who in Nigeria,* 3rd Edition (Lagos, 1985), pp. 42–3.

53. *ICON Nigeria Company Handbook...,* op.cit., p. 300.

54. *Who's Who in Nigeria...,* loc. cit., pp, 61–2

55. Suggesting that were it to have been possible for us to supplement these with other, more privileged, and private sources of information, we could have come up with an even greater number of examples.

56. See Yusuf Bala Usman *et. al., The Nigerian Economic Crisis: Causes and Solutions* (Zaria: Academic Staff Union of Universities of Nigeria, 1985), pp. 159–167.

57. Mr. Allison Ayida, former permanent secretary, Federal Ministry of Finance, by his own testimony, was one such an official, as quoted in Stephen O. Olugbemi, "The Civil Service: An Outsider's View" in Oye Oyediran (ed) *Nigerian Government and Politics Under Military Rule 1966–1979* (London: Macmillan, 1979), p. 105.

7

Filling the new Political Vacuum Post — 1983

In Chapter 4 of the study, we analysed the involvement of retired military officers in the politics and government of Nigeria's second Republic under President Shehu Shagari (1979–83). Although the country is now back under military rule, a programme of transition had since been initiated to hand over political power to a new democratically elected government via competitive party politics. The present chapter follows up developments in the area up to the time of completing the research study (1988). It focuses, of course, on the retired military among other competing political groups, while discussing their relative chances as successor to leadership post-military.

Informing the discussions that follow is a central assumption. It is this. Since the December 31, 1983 coup toppling Shehu Shagari's civilian presidency, a vacuum has been emerging in the Nigerian political leadership situation, rasing the question as to which power group will fill it if and when the second military administration leaves office as currently planned. The background to the emergence of the political vacuum postulated here was popular disenchantment with the leadership style of the former political class generally, and anger at the brazen system of Kleptocracy which had characterised the Shagari civilian presidency particularly. The public mood at the time of the 1983 coup was in favour of keeping out of any future political competition all would-be aspirants who had their hands tainted with corruption from the past political practices. The succeeding regime of Major-Generals Buhari and Idiagbon took some draconian measures in that direction.

When General Babangida took over following a counter-military coup attack in August 1985, it seemed initially as if there was going to be some softening of, if not a going-back on, the previous military government's action against the toppled politicians. On June 28, 1986, however, a proclamation went out proscribing past politicians from seeking or holding any public offices for ten years and with effect from the date of lifting

---

*   Reference is to the arrest and detention of all available Second Republic politicians both high and low, the trial and sentencing of many of them to long terms of imprisonment, under certain specially promulgated decrees.

existing military restriction on active politics. The ban was to be part of the Babangida transitional programme of return to civil rule, the first stage of which had involved the setting-up of a Political Bureau to help draw up proposals for yet another constitution for post-coup Nigeria.[1]

When that proscription was initially announced, it was understood to apply to certain categories of public officers who had served in the government and politics of the Second Republic from October 1, 1979 to December 31, 1983, namely: the President, Vice-President, Ministers, Special Advisers, Presidential Liaison Officers, all Members of the National and State Assemblies, all State Governors and Deputy-Governors, State Special Advisers, Governor Liaison Officers, as well as all public officers of the Armed Forces and the Police who were convicted by various special tribunals set up since the December 31, 1983 coup.[2]

The categories of banned public officers were subsequently expanded to include other public holders not considered by the June 28, 1986 ban order. Lest the ban become too blanket a measure treating "sinners" and "saints" among the ex-politicians alike, the Babangida government also initially gave indications that it intended not only to graduate the duration of the ban as between the politicians, but if need be to exempt some, depending on their levels of individual responsibility or culpability. Thus it was that Alhaji Balarabe Musa, a prominent politician of the Second Republic and former civilian governor of Kaduna State, won an initial exemption from the general 10-year ban, and was declared free to contest future elections; while ex-president Shehu Shagari and his deputy Dr. Alex Ekwueme were banned from holding public office or taking part in any form of political activities for life.[3] Twelve (12) former state governors and forty (40) other politicians and public officer holders had earlier been similarly banned for life.[4] The government promised a comprehensive list of all former politicians and public office holders affected by the measure, and for how long they were to be banned from participation in politics.

In the interim, the Political Bureau, set up to conduct a national debate on a new constitution for post-military Nigeria, had in its report supported the principle of the ban on the politicians, and recommended that it be back-dated to the time of General Gowon's overthrow July 29, 1975, and extended to cover all former public office holders both military and civilian and at all levels of government Federal, state and local.[5] That the Armed Forces Ruling Council (AFRC) accepted this particular recommendation of the Political Bureau among others,[6] was another indication that still more people were going to be affected by the political ban, if and when finalised.

And when, on September 23, 1987, President Babangida announced the AFRC decision on the long-expected list of categories of Nigerians banned from political participation,[7] it went much further than anyone expected. Apart from reaching back to the date of the country's independence on October 1, 1960, the final political ban no longer exempted any of the politicians. It also included top retired military and police officers (among them retired service chiefs) who had held office between January 15,

1966 and October 1 1979. What was more, the out-going military and police chiefs presently presiding over the transitional programme, including Babangida himself and the service chiefs, were not left out. One major lacuna, in what no doubt appeared to be a comprehensive political ban, was the omission of those politicians who had held office during the brief period between October 1 and December 31, 1983. But this was to be corrected by the "participation in Politics and Elections (Prohibition) Decree No. 25 of 1987" subsequently promulgated to give effect to the measure.[8]

Major Contending Groups

The result was to create a big vacuum of power and political authority that has since begun to attract other interested elite groups and individuals. What persons or groups of persons are the most likely candidates for filling the new political vacuum? Let us briefly assess the relative chances of the various major contending groups seeking to replace the banned politicians as a power group.[9] The thrust of our argument here, as indeed throughout the rest of the chapter, is to show that the retired military and police officer (as a faction of the military-cum police) elite are one such interested political group, with greater chances than others.

These include the traditional-aristocratic elites, comprising the various *emirs, obas, obis,* and others of the chiefly estate. Although they have shot into a new prominence since the December 31, 1983 coup, and more so under the Babangida presidency, members cannot be considered a serious contender, as their role is not likely to exceed the ceremonial and advisory under the next civilian constitutional order.

Also, existing regulations restrict trade unions (labour elite) from organising politically for party and electoral purposes; and until those regulations are changed, not many of their members can be expected to compete, although the present regime may disregard these if it suits it. Besides, the relations between military regimes and trade unions generally are uneasy at best and conflictual at worst, for the reasons not the least of which centres on the consideration that the former are oriented towards the maintenance of a given socio-political "order", while the latter tend to function more or less through "agitation". Organised labour is unlikely, therefore, to be the kind of group which military regimes such as Babangida's will go out of their way to promote politically; unless organised labour is forced to denature itself and becomes purged of its radical leftist elements.

As for the rural mass, although their participation in the nation's political life is virtually unrestricted, the members actually have too little an access to the means of influence to become a significant power group.[10] This is the more so, since the group, although the most numerous, comprises elements that are mostly illiterates, live in isolation from one another, and are totally unorganised.

Unlike either the chiefly estates or organised labour, however, the business elites are not restricted by any regulations from the participation in politics and electoral contests.

On the contrary, business and politics have long enjoyed a symbiotic relationship, with money providing the nexus. Consequently, one expects many businessmen to contest the power vacuum as a matter of course. For the same reason, a sizeable number of politically minded professionals in private or/and self employment, among them lawyers, can also be expected in large numbers to contest

Some intellectuals from the universities or polytechnics and various colleges of education, as well as other interested public servants may also be expected to join the new class of politicians-in-the-making. But the numbers from these particular elite groups – the intellectuals and bureaucrats – cannot be much, since public employees are not allowed to take part in active politics, let alone run for elective offices, unless they have first resigned their public posts.

With the exception of the business elites previously noted, then, the armed forces and police personnel currently ruling the country would have been the only major power group left in the vacuum-filling game, according to our scenario for Nigerian politics in the coming 1990s. However, under the liberal-democratic constitutional arrangement operated by Nigeria since independence, professional soldiers can only vote but cannot be voted for, as we saw in Chapter 4. Since the Babangida presidency has ruled out a "dyarchical", meaning military-turned-political, pattern of leadership succession, at least formally, if not also in reality, military officers and men still in the force are disallowed to engage in competition for political power hopefully, but can only do so if they resign to join the second and growing army of retired officers and men who are certainly known to be interested in the field.

Top retired military officers, combined with the politically minded among the business elite as well as some of the top retired public servants, are a potential power factor to watch in the emergent contest among elite groups on the Nigerian political scene. We saw in chapter 4 of the study how top retired military in good numbers debauched into politics during the Second Republic. An even larger number will be available for recruitment to various political roles under the next constitutional order.

Retired Military as the most visible Political Group

One unmistakable feature of Nigeria's recent political life has been the increasingly assertive role that top retired military officers had been playing in public affairs. This became the more marked during the last two years 1985-87 when the group shot into the most *visible* political role. For example, when the Political Bureau was set up and a call went out in early 1986 for a national debate on another new constitution for Nigeria, many of the top retired military officers played a prominent role, with retired Maj.-Gen. David Jemibewon, retired Maj.-Gen. I.B.M. Haruna, and retired Lt.-Gen. T.Y. Danjuma among others actually contributing written papers.

There are many more retired military officers to be found criss-crossing the country; meeting with people; presiding over various community fund-raising ceremonies; donating to charitable and other causes; taking chieftaincy and other honorific titles;

either writing books or launching their own newly established newspapers; participating in national symposia and seminars; addressing various gatherings, ranging from student groups to religious societies and business cum professional bodies; giving public lectures; talking to press; literally buying space or air-time on print or electronic media for self-advertisement; in short, building up broad coalitions supportive of their perceived political ambitions.

In particular, between 1986 and 1987 alone, the news was full of the activities of at least *four* such former military personalities. There was the former head of state Yakubu Gowon, and the news about the successful completion of his B.Sc. and Ph.D. political science degrees from Warwick in England; fanfare about his "second home-coming"; his attendance at an international conference on human rights organised at the University of Jos; followed almost immediately by the news of his appointment as Visiting Professor of Political Science in the same university; his distinguished presence at a ceremony at the Nigerian Institute of International Affairs (NIIA) launching a sympathetic biographical study on him. *GOWON: The Biography of a Soldier-Statesman* written by Professor J. Isawa Elaigwu; his restoration to full retired general's status together with all the attendant benefits and privileges.

There was also the ex-Biafran military leader Odumegwu Ojukwu, the *Ikemba* of Nnewi, throwing not only his charismatic self but also intellectual acumen all over the place. He was either being invited as a speaker to many student gatherings at university campuses, or featuring as a distinguished discussant on various television programmes across various state capitals in the federation. For some reason Ojukwu was, of all the ex-military class, the most sought-after by journalists, or rather he sought to make news-worthy events from his encounters with correspondents particularly at airports.

Besides, he it was who in his condolence on the death of Chief Obafemi Awolowo in May 1987, without necessarily claiming to be original here, described the latter veteran national leader as "the best President Nigeria never had," a statement that to some extent increased Ojukwu's standing among certain of late Awolowo's political aides from the Yoruba-speaking western parts. But it was on the people of Anambra and Imo states and other Igbo-speaking residents throughout the federation that the *Ikemba* appeared to be targeting the most, hoping to take over the mantle of leadership from the Octogenarian nationalist Dr. Nnamdi Azikiwe, the *Owelle* of Onitsha.

While Gowon and Ojukwu would seem to have been testing the ground for launching their respective political ambitions, another former military officer and chief of staff (supreme headquarters) in the Obasanjo administration, retired Maj.-Gen. Yar' Adua, engaged himself in a flurry of activities, also patently political in nature. This included holding meetings with various influentials across the country; coordinating along with others the so-called Northern Elders' Committee, formed in the wake of the Kaduna religious riots of 1987; taking a traditional chiefly title of *Tafidan* Katsina conferred with all the pomp and pageantry and under the blare of national publicity; founding a private newspaper *The Reporter*, which the retired general owns himself. It was during

1985-87 that were also publicised the new partnerships that retired Maj.-Gen. Yar' Adua had entered into with the Lagos-based business tycoon and ITT boss and publisher of the Concord group of newspapers Chief Moshood Abiola, himself newly conferred with two historic traditional titles the *Bashorun* of Ibadan and *Are Onakakanfo* of Yorubaland. The new partnerships ranged from joint ventures in banking and finance to shipping.

Yet another aspirant until now active on the military-political scene was Chief Samuel Ogbemudia, an ex-army brigadier. Chief Ogbemudia had been twice governor of Bendel (formerly Mid-West) State. Having served as a military governor under General Yakubu Gowon, he had staged a come-back to become one of the NPN State Governors under the Shagari presidency, and was among the public office holders actually sacked by the December 31, 1983 coup. Within the last two years 1986-87, the former brigadier-turned-politician was again back into prominence, featuring in many a public function. In the business sector, he was a regular participant in various workshops and seminars organised by National Association of Chambers of Commerce, Industries, Mines, and Agriculture (NACCIMA). But it was through his role in central organisation of sports that Chief Ogbemudia sought to impress his dynamic leadership on the nation, bringing memories of his previous contributions at the state level under his first governorship. For, in the ex-brigadier's view, as indeed the view of many within the military, sports was but an extension of the game of politics.

While these were going on, more and more members of the retired military elite were coming to accept and approach politics as "the art of possible" involving compromise and bargaining between groups, and (for the practitioners) the application of management skills to the multiple tasks of governing. This was a marked departure from the bellicose style of politics adopted by the soldiers when they were still in service. Obviously, retirement from service, meaning co-mingling with civilians in society, has contributed to the observed shift from "bellicose" to "managerial" skill[11] in the retired military officers' approach to politics and government. Coupled with the latter, of course, is the fact that retired military officers and soldiers now have enough stake in civil society to be materially interested in conflict-regulating strategies.

A noticeable phenomenon has also been the increasingly vocal identification by the retired military elite with popular political issues. Such issues in most recent times included demands for safeguards against arbitrary governmental power; restraint on the use of police force against unarmed university students demonstrations, as witnessed country-wide in mid-1986; security of life and property, against the menace of armed robbery; the need to keep defence spending to manageable level, and for the nation to invest more in the productive sectors of the economy; provision of jobs for the unemployed or relief against inflation, in the wake of massive recession in the nation's economy; rejection of the International Monetary Fund (or IMF) loan, as solution to the country's current foreign exchange and indeed national debt problems; the need for religious tolerance, made more urgent by the massive furore over Nigeria's application for membership of the Organisation of Islamic Countries (or OIC). Many retired military officers were heard in one forum or another to comment on these. The sometimes "soap-box" manner of their approach to these and other issues suggested that the top retired officers had been mastering the nature of power and the methods of achieving authority.

But, in courting popularity or talking as if unrestrainedly about politics, the top retired officers have occasionally also provoked controversies either among themselves, with the government of the day (in this case military), or with some segments of the civilian society. For example, retired Maj.-Gen. Jemibewon's statement of August 1986 confessing to insecurity of tenure (fear of death) as a motive for senior military retirement[12] was known to have provoked angry rejoinders from fellow retired generals, including I.B.M. Haruna and Joseph Garba.[13] Retired Brigadier Adekunle's recent criticism of the Nigerian army organisation as rather otiose in both structure and orientation and unprepared for serious war-making[14] must also have incurred the displeasure of the army chiefs.

In January 1987, a former chief of army staff and one time governor of Mid-West (later Bendel) state, retired Maj.-Gen David Ejoor, was quoted to have said: "Today, the North seems determined not only to dominate the Army but also the political and economic life of the nation. My contention is that any group that tries to dominate Nigeria to the detriment of the masses will ultimately fail."[15] The controversial statement immediately dragged not just Maj.-Gen. Ejoor himself but also other retired generals, as well as the whole of the army, into the latent north/south regional conflicts bedevilling Nigerian government and politics, and had the effect of causing reverberations everywhere.

About the same time, retired General Olusegun Obasanjo launched his second book *NZEOGWU,* a personal portrait on the leader of the first Nigerian army coup, that provoked some virulent reactions from a number of northern influentials, including Obasanjo's own one-time political deputy retired Maj.-Gen. Shehu Musa Yar' Adua.[16] Was one witnessing a kind of shadow-boxing against real or imaginary opponent in a projected future contest for gaining presidential political power? Things got so bad that on February 10, 1987, the Federal military government had to issue a statement advising retired military officers to refrain from making indiscreet and unguarded statement.[17] But that warning or advice could not completely put an end to the political interests and ambitions of the top retired military, as clear from the subsequent activities of many earlier described. So when the opportunity of extending the political ban came, the government though controlled by fellow military did not hesitate to include these top retired military personalities on the list of the banned. (See Appendices A & B for the listing).

But can the September 23, 1987 ban put an end to the political interest and ambitions of the retired military elite? And was it actually intended to achieve this? This related set of questions presupposes a third: What categories of retired military officers among others are actually excluded from direct participation in national politics?

The affected members fall under three categories. In the first category are those retired military and police officers classified in a sub-section of the political prohibition decree as follows: "All Military and Police personnel who held public offices during the period 15th January 1966 to the end of this transition period and who were or might be found guilty, and removed from office or dismissed from the services, or who were or are hereafter found guilty of corruption or other misdeeds or indicted by various Courts Martial, Tribunals, Special Investigation Panel, Judicial Commission, and Administrative Enquiries at both Federal and State levels".[18]

I guess under the category just mentioned may also be grouped all those military (and police) personnel retired for "fraud", "cheating", or "stealing", offences considered in military parlance as of scandalous nature, unbecoming the character of an officer and a gentleman. And there are quite a number of documented cases here.[19] Normally, as we had explained in Chapter 1 of the study, to be retired on this ground tends to earn one a dismissal, what in military legal parlance amounts to being sent out with ignominy.

Secondly, there were those retired military officers who had participated in the politics and government of the Second Republic (October 1, 1979 – December 31, 1983), and had held any of the following public or political party offices: State Governor; Presidential Liaison Officer; Chairmen of Committees or Selected Committee of the Senate, House of Representatives and State Houses of Assembly; Members of the National Executive Committees of all the Political Parties among others.[20] From our investigations in Chapter 4 of the study, some of the persons affected here would seem to include retired Col. (Dr.) Ahmadu Ali, retired Col. Garba Dada, retired Lt.-Col P.C. Amadi, retired Maj.-Gen. Olu Bajowa, retired Brig. Benjamin Adekunle, and retired Lt.-Col. Sati Gumut. They are among persons apparently disqualified from participation in politics and election and seeking or contesting any public or political party office during the on-going transition period.

The third category of retired military and police personnel proscribed from participation during the transition period were those officers who had before held any of the following high and essentially military public offices: (Military) Head of State/ President; Chief of Staff Supreme Headquarters; Chief of General Staff; Chairman of Joint Chiefs of Staff; Chief of Defence Staff; Deputy Chief of Defence Staff; Chief of Staff Army Headquarters/Chief of Army Staff; Head of Navy/Chief of Naval Staff; Head of the Air Force/Chief of Air Staff; Inspector-General of Police; Military Governors/Administrators; Members of the Supreme Military Council (SMC), or the Armed Forces Ruling Council (AFRC), between December 31, 1983 and the end of the transitional period.[21]

Thus, to specify some of the personalities involved in the latter category, this master-stroke would seem to have aborted at least for now the political ambitions of such former top military officers, as Gowon, Ojukwu, Yar' Adua, and Ogbemudia hitherto perceived as front-runners among the group. Other top retired military and police brass who could not contest, even if they wished, included Obasanjo and Buhari (as former Heads of State); Wey, Ekpo, Idiagbon and Ukiwe (as former Chief of Staff Supreme Headquarters); Soroh, Hasan Katsina (as former Deputy Chief of Staff Supreme Headquaters);

Akinrinade, Jalo (as former Chief of Defence Staff); Hussein Abdullahi (as former Deputy Chief of Defence Staff, Navy); Ejoor, Danjuma, Wushishi (as former Chief of Army Staff); Adewale, Aduwo (former Chief of Naval Staff); Kurubo, Ikwue, Yissa-Doko, A.D. Bello(former Chief of Air Staff); M.D. Yusuf, Adewusi, Inyang (former Inspector-General of Police).

The list of former state military and police governors, among them those who had served under Gowon, also disqualified from contesting for public office during the transition period, included retired Maj.-Gen. R.A. Adebayo, retired Brigadiers O. Rotimi and Mobolaji Johnson, as well as nine others actually dismissed from office after the July 29, 1975 counter-coup, namely, Audu Bako, A.P. Diete-Spiff, Abba-Kyari, Musa Usman, David Bamigboye, U.J. Esuene, Usman Farouk and of course Samuel Ogbemudia earlier mentioned.

Also banned from contesting electoral, public and political party offices in Nigeria's Third Republic were State Military Governors and Administrators, who had served under both the Murtala/Obasanjo and Buhari/Idiagbon regimes, and had since retired from the services: among them, retired Col. Anthony Ochefu, retired Maj.-Gens. David Jemibewon, Abdullahi Shelleng, Zamani Lekwot, Mohammed D. Jega, and George Innih, retired Grp.-Capt. Usman Jibrim, retired Col. Sani Bello, retired Grp.-Capt. Dan Suleiman, retired Grp. Capt. Ita David Ikpeme, retired Grp.-Capt. Salauden Latinwo, retired Commodore M.B. Otiko and perhaps retired Col. Yohanna Madaki.* There could be more.

Military and police personnel who might not have held any of the top military-political posts previously specified, or might not have served as regional/state military governors or administrators, but who belonged to the highest law-making body under the Supreme Military Council (SMC) between December 31, 1983 and August 27, 1985, and had since retired, also stood proscribed. Three examples quickly come to mind here: the retired director-general of the defunct National Security Organisation (N.S.O), Ambassador Mohammed Lawal Rafindadi; Minister of Internal Affairs under the Buhari/Idiagbon regime, retired Maj.-Gen. Mohammed Magoro; the former General Officer Commanding (GOC) 1 Mechanised Infantry Division, retired Brig. Joseph Olayeni Oni.

Drastic as the political prohibition measure looks, however, I dare-say it cannot possibly put an end to the interests and ambitions of the retired military elite as a political group. For one thing, the total number of retired military officers affected by the September 23, 1987 ban could not have exceeded 150–200, or at most 300, according to our own "guestimate". Yet Nigeria's military retiree population is much, much larger than this, as we tried to document in Chapter 1 of the study.

---

*   Although retired Col. Madaki was once a state military governor, he has since found himself back into the scheme of things as one of the few Federal Government appointees in the Constituent Assembly, thereby prompting speculations about his being exempted from the political ban.

Besides, the ban turns out in fact not to have been as comprehensive as it initially seemed. For example, the decree did not touch those who had served in the SMC under Ironsi, Gowon, and Murtala/Obasanjo. Top military and police officers from the Murtala/Obasanjo era concerned here included retired Maj.-Generals Martin Adamu, Mohammed Shuwa, E.O. Abisoye, John Obadan, A.O. Aduloju, Joe N. Garba, A. Mohammed, as well as the former N.S.O. director-general Umari Shinkafi. Perhaps, those are not disqualified. In fact, the current interpretation coming from sources close to the National Electoral Commission (NEC) headquarters is that retired military and police officers who had been members of the SMC between January 15, 1966 and October 1, 1979 are free to contest, provided only that they never served as military governors/administrators or held office as service heads.

Presumed free to run for political office, also, are top retired military and police who had held office as commissioners (ministers) whether Federal or State between January 1, 1966 and October 1, 1979, provided also of course that such officers had neither before been state governors/administrators nor served as service chiefs. One has particularly in mind here retired army generals like I.B.M. Haruna, Henry Adefope, James Oluleye and Olufemi Olutoye who were among the commissioners (ministers) in the federal executive council of the Murtala/Obasanjo government. They could also run, if they so wished.

Undoubtedly, most of the retired military officers affected by the ban are drawn from the upper-officer ranks, i.e. from Colonels and above or their equivalent, leaving the field quite open for their middle and lower-ranking colleagues. They are distributed among the various local government communities. Of course, as we have just shown, the number of top officers unaffected by the ban is still sizeable. Combined, all those unaffected by the ban, and therefore available for recruitment to various political roles, constitute a potentially powerful bloc.

Already, a number have begun to emerge politically. For example, among those who contested and won seats in the country-wide local government elections of December 12, 1987 were retired Capt. Samuel Gboyega Ige, elected councillor for Ikeretu II constituency in Abeokuta, retired Lt.-Col. (Mrs.) Veronica Oyefeso, elected unopposed councillor, Oke/Ere/Erunwa/Isienyon/Ilese constituency of Ijebu-Ode, both in Ogun State; retired Lt.-Col. E. Fakunle, Chairman, Lagelu local government in Ibadan area of Oyo State; retired Lt.-Col. Femi Ademulegun, Chairman, Owo local government, Ondo State.[22]

And more recently, retired Maj.-Gen. Olufemi Olutoye contested in the Constituency Assembly elections of April 23, 1988, and was elected to represent the Owo area of Ondo state in the nation's Constituent Assembly;[23] while two other retired top officers were to feature on the list of the special members appointed into the same body by the Federal government, namely retired Maj.-Gen I.B.M. Haruna and retired Col. Yohana Madaki.[24] Nor have many of the top retired generals who have been banned resigned themselves to the situation. On the contrary, a number of them, including retired Maj.-Gen. Yar'

Adua, continue with their "politicking," sometimes covertly and othertimes overtly, as if the ban does not exist, or as if the ban would not last. These and many, many more can almost be predicted to go into active politics if and when the time comes.*

In the meantime, for the retired military as a group and the society on the whole, the implication of the foregoing should be obvious. Were substantial members to join the political race and dominate much of the outcome, they would have moved towards adding political power to their existing concentration of wealth and erstwhile military influence. This, in turn, has certain consequences for the new democratisation process and transition-to-civil rule programme. Nor would the kind of legal cum administrative restrictions on retired military participation analysed above suffice as countervailing measures for dealing with what clearly is an emergent structural problem.

---

which was what happened three years after the Babangida regime lifted the ban on the various categories of persons, and by so doing gave a further flip to retired military participation in the politics of the Second Transition.

NOTES

1. *The Guardian* (Lagos), Saturday June 28, 1986, pp. 1, 2.
2. *ibid.*
3. *The Guardian* (Lagos), Saturday July 26, 1986, pp. 1, 2.
4. *Daily Times* (Lagos), Saturday August 2, 1986, pp. 1, 9.
5. The Political Bureau had recommended that all politicians and public office holders who held sway between August 1975 and August 1985 be banned from future politics. In the Bureau's recommendations, the categories of politicians and public office holders concerned were listed as follows:
    *   President, Vice President, Governors, Deputy Governors
    *   Ministers, Commissioners, Secretaries to Government
    *   Advisers, Special Assistants, Presidential Liaison Officers
    *   Legislators at Federal & State levels
    *   Political Party Officials at Federal, State, and Local Government levels, including Party Patrons & Matrons
    *   Chairmen of Boards of Parastatals at the Federal and State levels
    *   Head of the defunct National Security Organisation (NSO) and the Nigerian Police Force
    *   Judicial and other Public Officers removed for a cause
    *   Armed Forces Officers who held political offices.

    See Federal Republic of Nigeria, *Report of the Political Bureau* (Lagos: Federal Government Printer, 1987), p. 2, 8.
6. Federal Republic of Nigeria, *Government's Views and Comments on the Findings and Recommendations of the Political Bureau,* (Lagos: Federal Government Printer, 1987), pp. 76–77.
7. *The Guardian* (Lagos), September 24, 1987, pp. 12, 14.
8. Federal Republic of Nigeria, "Participation in Politics and Elections (Prohibition) Decree No. 25 of 1987", *Official Gazette* (Lagos), Vol. 74, No 57, October 9, 1987.
9. Most of the contending social forces identified here are similar to those pointed out in J. 'Bayo Adekanye, "Politics of Post-Military State in Africa", *Il Politico* (University of Pavia) Vol. XLIX, No. 1, 1984, pp. 32–42.
10. And this, despite recent attempts by the Babangida regime through the programmes of "directorate of food, roads and rural infrastructures" (DFRRI) and "Mass Mobilisation for Social Justice, Self-reliance and Economic Recovery" (MAMSER) aimed at reaching out towards and stimulating a broadening awareness in the rural areas.
11. This useful distribution is borrowed from Morris Janowitz, *The Professional Soldier: A Social and Political Portrait* (New York: Free Press, 1960), passim.

12. As subsequently quoted in *Newswatch* (Lagos), February 23, 1987, p. 27.

13. Retorted retired Maj.-Gen. Joseph Garba, for example: "to say that people run away from the army for fear of death is preposterous and very far from the truth. Many of us are very upset about Jemibewon's assertion, particularly since some of us did not retire voluntarily" see *ibid.*

14. Also alluded to in *ibid.*

15. *This Week,* Vol. 3, No. 3, January 1987, p. 16.

16. See the special issue "NZEOGWU": The Sound and the Fury", *Newswatch* (Lagos), Vol. 5, No. 10, March 1987, pp. 14ff

17. *New Nigerian* (Lagos), February 11, 1987, pp. 1, 3.

18. Federal Republic of Nigeria, "Participation in politics and Elections (Prohibition) Decree ...", op. cit., pp. 216–7.

19. One of the first detailed studies on military corruption that the present author knows is that by Dahunsi A. Alabi, "The Phenomenon of Military Corruption in Nigeria: 1960–1983, (Department of Political Science University of Ibadan: B.Sc. Thesis, June 1985.

20. Federal Republic of Nigeria, "Participation in politics and Elections (Prohibition) Decree ...", loc. cit., pp. 217–8.

21   *ibid.,* p. 218.

22. On the latter, see S.O. Adeleke "The Role of Retired Military Officers in the Local Government Elections of December 1987 (Department of Political Science, University of Ibadan. B.Sc Thesis, July 1988), pp 61–66. Adeleke's study was limited to the states in the Western part of the country. Of course on a country-wide basis, such a study would have revealed a much greater participation by the retired military.

23. *The Guardian* (Lagos), April 24, 1988, pp. 1, 11.

24. *The Guardian* (Lagos), April 27, 1988, pp. 1, 3.

8

An Elite of Power

We conclude this study, by distilling the major *working hypotheses* and generalisations on which the study was based, the central concepts underlying those hypotheses, and the implications of both the concepts and hypotheses for our subject of investigation. The hypotheses, that the study had set out to demonstrate empirically, were as follows:

1. That the traditional theory about civil-military relations in Nigeria, as one involving the separation between civil society and military organisation, has become outmoded, and must be replaced by a new one that views the lines between the two organs of state power as increasingly blurred.

2. That the growing size and role of Nigeria's military retiree population in society are a significant contributory factor to the latter observed trend.

3. That, beside their increasingly large size, retired military officers are fast assuming pivotal positions within the Nigerian society, particularly in government and politics, the public bureaucracy and corporations or companies (including the subsidiaries of large multi-national corporations), and even agriculture, where such retired officers develop interests or tentacles at once inter-locking and inter-changeable.

4. That many of the top retired military officers have available to them such resources as wealth, their ex-military connections, skill, prestige, and experience; and these they exploit to the maximum as bases of new influence.

5. That, even though as yet unorganised politically, pluralistic in their membership, and not that self-conscious as a group, Nigeria's class of retired military operating through a kind of "old boy" networks are fast emerging as a new elite of power, whose members considerably influence decision-making regarding major issues of "high politics".

We consider hypotheses (1), (2), (3) and part of (4) to have been hopefully successfully substantiated in the main-body of the study; although it was not possible to do so as rigorously and systematically as we would have liked to. As for hypothesis (5) and immediately preceding it part of (4), they raise some other pre-theoretical issues. These we must now analyse before considering their empirical substantiation.

There are two central organising concepts that orient each of the above Hypotheses, more so (4) and (5) particularly, and indeed the study as a whole. One is the concept of *elite* and the other that of *power*.

Although both are in fact related – our hypothesis (5) seeks to collapse the two, when it speaks of retired military officers as "a new elite of power" – the two concepts can be and are often differentiated in political analysis. We elaborate on each of the concepts briefly bringing out their relevance to our study in the process.

The Concept of Elite

The *elite* approach to political analysis postulates a number of generalisations that can be quickly summarised here. According to the founding fathers,[1] in every political society, there is and will always be a minority which rules over the majority of society. In the words of Robert Michels, "who says organisation, says oligarchy". However, elite theorists disagree on the source from which a given elite derives its power. For a number of them – particularly Mosca and Pareto – a given ruling elite derives almost invariably its original power from a combination of coercive, religious, and commercial sources. Wrote Pareto: "In the begining, military, religious, and commercial aristocracies and plutocracies – with a few exceptions not worth considering–must have constituted parts of the governing elite and sometimes have constituted the whole of it."[2] The coercive source relates to the monopoly of military function that the ruling elite initially enjoyed, although over time this source of power tends to be masked by myths, ideologies, and "political formulas", even as the erstwhile "warrior class" undergoes a metamorphosis into a political class or becomes subsequently "softened" by the leisure of political office.

But membership of this "governing elite" or "political class" – composed of those who occupy the posts of political command and more vaguely, those who can directly influence political decisions – is rarely fixed. Rather, according to the theorists, the governing elite tends to undergo changes in its membership over a period of time: ordinarily, by the recruitment of new individual members from the lower strata of society; sometimes, by the incorporation of new social groups thrown up by certain developments including economic and technological; and occasionally, by the complete replacement of the established elite by a "counter-elite" as occurs in a revolution. The latter phenomenon is what, following Pareto, elite theorists refer to either as "the circulation of elites," or "the circulation of individuals between the two strata (elite and non-elite)", or both. Such changes, however, affect merely the form, but not the structure, of society which remains at all times minority-dominated or "oligarchic".

In elite formulations, even avowedly socialist regimes, that have just had revolutionary change of governments, inevitably succumb to Michels' "iron law of oligarchy". This was what Pareto meant when he wrote: "History is the graveyard of aristocracies". In otherwords, elites come, and elites go, but society remains at all times structured into elites/non-elites, ruling class/the ruled, and dominant/dominated classes. That, in a nutshell, is the system of ideas general to elite theory.[3]

One of the major critical tests on which depends validity of the theory is the assumption of the qualities of *self-consciousness, coherence,* and *unity* predicated of an elite group in the society. To be of any relevance to a study of political influence, the group must first be organised as well as informed by some shared interests or *espirt de corps;* it must be cohesive; and it must act as a unified body. Otherwise, such a group does not qualified to be described as an elite.[4]

Interestingly enough, the above qualities of group consciousness, coherence, and common will to action assumed by proponents as defining an elite are among the properties known to characterise a typical military organisation. Others are unity of command, concentration of authority, hierarchy, discipline, network of communications, and of course monopoly of the coercive apparatus of state power.[5] Besides, there is the very dichotomous character of stratification internal to a typical military organisation, with its highly visible system of differential pay and priviledges for officers and ranks. It brings to mind not only "the minority that rules and the majority that is ruled" dichotomy, but also the ubiquity of inequality assumed by the elite theorists. It is not surprising, therefore, that one finds countless applications of the model of analysis extended to contemporary studies of the military.

One of the first contemporary social scientists to extend the analysis of the elite group to the military domain was Morris Janowitz, beginning with his seminal (1956) essay on "Social Stratification and the Comparative Analysis of Elites". Followed a year later with a piece specifically titled "Military Elites and the Study of War", both essays were to be synthesised into Janowitz's third piece of related interest, "Sociological Notes on the Analysis of Military Elites", appearing as an appendix to his 1964 book *The Military in the Political Development of New Nations: An Essay in Comparative Analysis.*[6] A variant of the same model of analysis underlies his U.S. case-study on *The Professional Soldier.* Janowitz argues here that the term "elite" in application to the military domain refers not to the total organisation, but "a small proportion of men within the military profession", in short the senior-officers nucleus, "those who have the greatest amount of actual and potential power, if power is defined as control over the behaviour of others."[7]

Related to this is what Janowitz has to say about the "post-retirement" occupations and activities of the military elite. An increasingly large number of retired military personnel in the U.S. have since the end of World War II sought employment with industrial corporations, followed by government service. According to Janowitz, the range of post-retirement employment of the officers included educational institutions; banking and finance; transportation and engineering concerns; defence contract industries, particularly aircraft missiles, ship-building, and defence related agencies; electronics; appointive federal government posts, especially in foreign affairs. However Janowitz sees the pattern of post-retirement roles of the military elite to be "one of extreme diversity", in short *pluralistic,* and by implications compatible with democracy.[8]

Yet another attempt to apply the concept of elite to the essentially military sphere, and no doubt from a radically different perspective, has been that of C. Wright Mills in his book *The Power Elite.* Like Janowitz, Mills has also been interested in the post-retirement careers of the military elite. From the long lists of retired generals and their positions in business and government, Mills has sought to demonstrate an interlink between the military, the big corporations and the political executives in the US. For Mills, however, the military chiefs, along with the corporation executives and political leaders, constitute in fact a *cohesive* group, otherwise called one giant military-industrial complex whose activities pose a threat to democratic government.[9]

Obviously, the latter view is in sharp contradistinction to that held by the pluralist school (as represented by Janowitz), who sees the military elite as but one out of many elite groups competing in society. The others include such ones as the political elite, business cum commercial elite, industrial elite, labour elite, religious cum cultural elite, intellectual elite, and bureaucratic elite (the last sometimes treated as part of military elite).[10]

Meanwhile, from the methodological stand-point, there is one implication to be drawn from the foregoing review of the concept of elite and its empirical applications to an analysis of the military. It is that contrary to the conservative bias which informs the approach, especially its "classical" from, the use of elite paradigm of political analysis can be from either *conventional* or *critical* perspective. References just made to Janowitz and Mills show this. I must admit that my own categorisation of Nigeria's growing retired military officers as "a new elite of power" partakes of these two contradictory-but, let me also quickly add, easily synthesisable-theoretical perspectives or insights.

The Concept of Power

The second major concept that informs our present study, and not unrelated to that of elite just treated, is the concept of *power.* To be sure, it inheres in the very title of the book, "The Retired Military as Emergent Power Factor in Nigeria". For political scientists, power holds a central place among the concepts of politics, and any basic text on scope and methods of political science will underline this.[11] The fact is that it is impossible to conceive of and write about any interaction involving political actors at any level whether domestic or external, which does not have latent to it or even manifest itself in some notion of power. And, of course, when it comes to conceptualising and writing about the State and its supportive agency the military, the phenomenon of power understandably looms even larger. For there is no state properly so called that does not possess a military organisation, a body of men (and women) charged with the management of the apparatus of coercion. And "coercion" is one of the oldest – and, undoubtedly, also crudest – forms of power. Some notion of power is also involved in the concept and definition of the military as an "elite", as we saw earlier. Thus, in whatever way one looks at it, the military, whether active, inactive, or retired, is more or less synonymous with not just "State power", but also "group power", that is in relation to other social groups competing on the political scene.

This is not to say that the question of what constitutes power is a settled issue. To be sure, even within an otherwise single discipline called political science, the concept can be problematic indeed, as there are as many definitions of and perspectives towards power as there are theorists or writers on the phenomenon. The best definitions and most useful to operationalise empirically, however, are definitions which approach power in relational and behavioural terms. Thus, military power exists only in relation to that of other states and regarding particular armed combat situations. A particular social group, such as the retired military elite studied here, can be said to have power either in relation to other competing social groups, or in terms of the influence that the said social group wields over the national decision-making process or rather its outcomes. These two examples are meant to illustrate what it means to conceptualise power as a relational phenomenon. Robert Dahl defines the behavioural aspects of power best when he writes, simply thus: "A has power over B to the extent that he can get B to do something that B would not otherwise do".[12]

The resources which an agent relies upon for exerting influence upon another agent subjected to that influence constitute what, in the literature, are variously referred to as the *bases*, elements, or factors of power. They consist of, in Dahl's phrase, "all the resources – opportunities, acts, objects, etc. – that the influencing agent can exploit in order to effect the behaviour of another."[13] Thus, in international relations, the list of elements that make up a nation's power is observed to include geography, national resources, industrial capacity, military preparedness, population, national character, national morale, quality of diplomacy, and quality of government.[14] And, in our own study on the Nigerian retired military elite here, we have listed elements of bases of power hypothesisedly possessed by members to include the latter's growing size, pivotal positions in society, wealth, ex-military connections, skill, prestige, experience, and "old-boy" networks (see Hypotheses 2, 3, 4 & 5).

But as often emphasised by political scientists, the sum of summation of elements or bases of power does not add up to power. At best, elements of power merely point to *potentiality* of power but not *power* itself. One of the logical traps into which most analysts fall is the equating of potentiality with power. For example, the creation or possession of military organisation by a state does not necessarily mean that such a state already has military power, although most writers tend to equate one with the other.[15]

By the same token, the bases of power, with which the Nigerian retired military personnel are credited, are in themselves, not an enough proof that the group already constitutes a "power factor". If those elements are to have any meaning, they must be empirically related to concrete actions of the group or its members: that is, to previously determined power acts or behaviours involving the retired military officers in their relations with other domestic social groups operating within Nigeria. The contention that a group, possessing such power bases as the retired military personnel, is powerful may be true, but only if it is established, through empirical research, that the group's rising influence over and ability to control (the outcomes of) the national decision-making process regarding "Who Gets What?" are related to the possession of wealth, ex-military connection, skill, prestige, experience, and "old-boy" networks among others. Fortunately, in this particular case, the study suggested the existence of linkage between the latter power resources and the activities of retired military officers in private business, corporate industry, politics and government described in Chapters 3-4.

Relationship With Other Elites

Let us now relate the preceding theoretical discussions on elite and power directly and empirically to the subject matter of our investigation. Judged from the methodological arguments of the first section, it can be asserted that Nigeria's retired military personnel (taken together with the active military) qualify indeed to be described as an "emergent elite", though not the sole elite in society, but one out of many competing elites. The other elites are:[16]

- Political elite, comprising the professional, meaning mostly ex-nationalist, politicians who until now had controlled the machinery of government, but whom the retired military personnel are slowly but steadily seeking to edge out of the country's rulership.

- Bureaucratic elite, comprising senior public employees cum technocrats working in various organs of government such as the civil service, public corporations and parastatals, whose members constitute the executors (and sometimes even initiators) of public policy

- Business elite, comprising the *nouveaux riches,* "Comprador" merchants and petty-traders in the import and export business, a few small-scale domestic manufacturers in clientelist links with some multi-national corporations, various "emergency" contractors, including market women-contractors, some retired military officers now in private procurement business links of all sorts with the military establishment.

- Intellectual elite, comprising university and college lecturers and students, writers, journalists, lawyers, and other professionals, as the purveyors of ideas and trained skills in society.

- Aristocratic elite, referring to members of the old aristocracy whether of birth, land, wealth and including the old propertied classes, old elite or feudal families, and the chiefly estates (i.e. of the *emirs, obas, & obis).*

- Religious elite, meaning those holding top positions in the country's religious system whether Christian, Islamic or traditional with all their various denominations or sects, and whose members include cardinals, bishops, chief *imams*, priests, pastors, prophets, *imams,* and *babalawos.*

- Labour elite, referring to the leadership of organised labour movement, at the top of which is the Nigerian Labour Congress or the NLC.

What has been the relationship of the military elite (including the retired ones) with these other elite groups? The relationship had been one of *interdependence,* with the military merely competing with those other elite groups for a share of allocatable resources or additional power bases. Since the beginning of the 1980s, however, and with the increased role of the retired military officers occupying various pivotal positions in the society as detailed in previous chapter, one observes the beginnings of a new trend of relationship. It can be described as one marked by *structural penetration* of other elite spheres by the military, meaning the retired military.

Thus, to draw some illustrations from our empirical study, we have had countless retired military officers transformed into businessmen, and a small number of them as captains of industry or entrepreneurs. Regular appointments to the boards of government-owned enterprises have made not only economic managers out of many retired military officers, but a new bureaucratic cum managerial elite competing with top civil servants, including retired ones, for influence over national economic decision-making. Some top retired military officers in large-scale farming are in the process of being transformed into a new landowning aristocracy. A number of retired military officers have had traditional aristocratic titles conferred on them by the chiefly estates;[17] while a few have crossed over to join the religious elite.[18] There are a number of retired military officers who have taken on the intellectual role, and would like to be considered in their own right as writers or even scholars, in addition to whatever post-retirement activities they may have engaged in. Between 1976 and 1983, we saw a sizeable number of retired military officers turned into active politicians, and many more are hoping to follow suit in the transition from the current military administration to another civil rule, inspite and even because of General Babangida's ban. These are examples illustrating considerable overlap between the military elite (including the retired members), on the one hand, and other occupants (elite) of high positions such as those in business and industry, government and bureaucracy, and politics, on the other.

But side by side with the second trend just summarised can be observed yet another trend: that of *coalescence* of the retired military elite with other elite groups. Coalescence refers to the coming together or combination of two elite groups in pursuit of common interests, while retaining their distinctive power bases or individual characteristics. What is involved here is the "pooling" of many but divergent resources so as to serve as a more effective instrument of power and influence. The most publicised example in early 1988 was that involving retired Maj.-Gen. Shehu Musa Yar' Adua and the civilian business magnate Chief M.K.O. Abiola, both of whom own major collective stakes in a number of joint business ventures, including banking, finance and shipping. There are joint undertakings of a similar kind involving some retired military elite members, ex-politicians and retired high officials among others.

It is possible that such new combinations, rather than break up and re-group in a flux of ceaseless alterations, may lead to the formation of a totally new elite group, larger and different from any of the component parts. Alternatively, one elite group may lose its identity through being incorporated into another elite group. If the latter should happen, one can almost predict that it is the weaker elite group – weaker that is, in terms of its power base – which is certain to be merged into the stronger one. The other possibility is to view the whole dynamics involved here as pointing to a completely new system of stratification and the makings of a new "ruling class". But these are conjectures on possible courses of future development about which nothing definitive can be written as yet.

Nigerian scholars of the radical left do not think so. They would argue that the process of re-constitution (or consolidation) of a new "ruling class", from the major elites of power, economic, military and political, had already begun.[19] In the view of such scholars, that process began with the consolidation of the ownership structure and control of property. Of course, the question of "who owns what property" and its implications for class relations in Nigeria has long been an issue of central concern to Nigeria scholars of radical ideological persuasion. Thus, in the maiden issue of a recently launched monthly *The Analyst* published by Bálarabe Musa (1986), retired Maj.-Gen. Shehu Musa Yar' Adua features prominently as one of contemporary "Nigeria's monied men". Described as "former No. 2 man in the Obasanjo regime, now a wealthy man, part owner of African Oceans Lines (a shipping line), part owner of Habib Bank, and a farmer", retired Maj.-Gen. Yar' Adua was ranked by the magazine among the "few Nigerian businessmen, retired military officers, civil servants and some professionals and chiefs" said to have such a "concentration of power and wealth".[20]

The others, according to the magazine, included: Alhaji Shehu Malami, "a Sokoto prince"; Chief M.K.O. Abiola, "Chairman I.T.T. Nigeria Ltd., publisher, shipping czar", and said to have "landed property around the country"; Alhaji Bamanga Turkur, "former Chief Executive of Nigerian Ports Authority (NPA), ex-Governor of Gongola State, and part owner of Africa Ocean Lines"; Mr. A.C.I. Mbanefo, "a chartered accountant and semi-partner in Akintola Williams and Co. (a firm of chartered accountants), and MD. of A.W. Consultant Ltd." and said to have "been a director of U.A.C. since 1978"; Alhaji Shehu Idris, "Emir of Zaria since 1975, a director of many companies since October, 1980 and a director of U.A.C."; Alhaji Ibrahim Dasuki, "a Sokoto chieftain, a leading figure in the Islamic Council of Nigeria, a director of many companies and part owner of fast growing Bank of Credit and Commerce International (B.C.C.I.)"; Alhaji Liman Ciroma, "former Secretary to the Federal Government, now a wealthy businessman with directorship of many companies. Also a Chairman of U.T.C. and a director of U.A.C"; and Chief E.A.O. Sonekan," a lawyer, now Chairman and M.D. of U.A.C. since 1980 and a director of other companies.

However, there are a number of things wrong with this radical thesis, most of them methodological. It assumes, erroneously, that the mere possession of economic wealth leads to political power. It also assumes, erroneously, that concentration of economic power automatically produces the consolidation of a ruling class. The thesis not only glosses over the important divergent interests of the individual personalities involved here as well as their respective "constituencies", but also the nature of the Nigerian political system which remains largely decentralised and still plagued by bad means of communication. Any suggestion of the existence of a cohesive ruling class arising from concentration of property is contradicted by these existing facts; namely, the as-yet incohoate state of Nigerian society and her decentralised system of political power.

The same critique would apply, were one to infer the existence of a cohesive "power elite" (a la C.W. Mills) from the acquisition by the military elite of positions of power and prestige in other facets of social life, economic, bureaucratic, intellectual cum cultural, and political. Nor, as regards the retired military personnel in particular, would it be enough to replace the criterion of economic concentration with that of geo-political concentration as a basis for demonstration of this other thesis. The "geo-political" concentration argument considers the centrality of Kaduna city in the study of post-retirement activities of the military elite. Kaduna city, being capital of former northern region, and for long the seat of the northern political elite, has long been considered Nigeria's *de facto* military power base.[22] The only northern city of note without an emir, and long considered a neutral (no man's) land as it were, Kaduna has become the mecca of top military generals; a number of whom have developed landed property there.[23]

The impression conveyed by this "geo-political" concentration thesis is that by living in the same city, and perhaps adjacent to one another within same residential area(s) or quarter(s), where they also share the same recreational facilities and clubs such retired military officers based in Kaduna are able to maintain a group spirit. This group spirit is conceded by the thesis as a *sine qua non* for the development of cohesiveness among members of and the elite of power. But, then, similar concentrations of retired military officers can be found spread throughout the Federation, and beginning with the other eighteen old state capitals: namely, Enugu, Bauchi, Benin, Markurdi, Maiduguri, Calabar, Yola, Owerri, Ilorin, Ikeja, Minna, Abeokuta, Akure, Ibadan, Jos, Port Harcourt, Sokoto, plus of course, the old Federal capital, Lagos (including Ikoyi & Victoria Island).* Nor is the new Federal capital currently under construction – Abuja – certain to escape this trend. Thus, the picture emerging from all this is that of a decentralised system of retired officer concentrations based in various state capitals of the Federation, but marked by considerable regional, ethnic, religious and linguistic differences. This decentralisation must be overcome before one can talk of the retired military elite as cohesive political power group.

---

* Katsina and Uyo, the capitals of the two recently (September 1987) created Katsina and Akwa Ibom states are too recent to experience this.

Besides, the military elite (including retired military) members have multiple economic interests, and possess divergent class affiliations. For example, as regard the latter, while many have had "lumpen militarist" backgrounds,[24] a number had been recruited into the army from "traditional aristocratic connections". A notable example of top retired military officers from the latter kind of social backgrounds is retired Maj.-Gen. Hassan Usman Katsina, son of the former Emir of Katsina. There are scores of such retired military officers with varying aristocratic (feudal) connections spread across the country.[25] Then, there are those retired officers from certain long established "middle-class" families[26] to be found in the cities and mostly in the southern part of the country. The effects of such divergent class affiliations might have been easy for military officers to resist while they were still in service. But those divergent affiliations do exert considerable political impact on military officers once they retire, making it more and more difficult for members to stick together as an "elite" group.

Measuring Retired Military Influence

If the descriptions of the last two paragraphs cast doubt about the retired military elite possessing a distinct group character, however, there are other tendencies that point in the opposite direction. Those are tendencies which seem to impart coherence and organisation to the role of retired military in contemporary Nigerian society. The core of the tendencies we tried to delineate in Chapters 3, 4, 5 & 6 of the study. There, we documented how an increasingly large number of top retired military officers had come to occupy certain pivotal positions in the structure of Nigerian society.

To recapitulate the structural trends concerned, an examination of Nigeria's military-corporate scene since 1975 shows a steady increase in the number of retired high-ranking officers appointed to the boards of directors of key governmental agencies, statutory corporations, public enterprises, and parastatals vital to the Nigerian economy. Admittedly, a number of the companies concerned, though "Nigerian" in name, are in fact the subsidiaries of some multi-national corporations headquartered in other lands. At the same time, a large proportion of top retired officers have set up heir own private businesses in large-scale farming and agro-allied ventures among others, where their influence has emerged dominant. Finally, in government and bureaucracy, including administration of external affairs and diplomacy, more and more military men in mufti have begun to occupy top decision-making posts, either as cabinet minister(s), diplomats, advisers, managers, or executives of various task-forces.

There are pieces of evidence to suggest that those appointments of top retired military officers to positions at the summit of key socio-economic structures are not a chance affair or haphazard development, but the result of deliberate and coordinated policy. For example, following the end of the Civil War in 1970, the government either established or began to support organisations and schemes like the Armed Forces Welfare Scheme, Directorate of Military Pensions, Nigerian Legion, National War Museum, Armed

Forces Resettlement and Rehabilitation. Run under the Ministry of Defence (MOD), most of these had been intended as welfare programmes for retired military personnel. These organisations in charge of veterans, together with their various welfare programmes came to be consolidated in 1986 into one, newly established central body called the Directorate of Veteran Affairs (DVA) which has one Major M. Ali, an expert in such matters, appointed as its first Director.[27]

It has been the official policy of the government that all military officers who retire "honourably" should be assisted to resettle in civilian life; and resettlement includes being helped with job placements in the public and private sectors. Thus, on receipt of notice of retirement from an officer, the Army Headquarters, taking the officer's qualifications, administrative capabilities, experiences and other qualities into consideration, are expected to initiate contact with civilian establishments in the public and private sectors with the view to placing the officer. The latter provision was specifically written into the revised Terms and Conditions of Service for Nigerian Army Officers in 1981. That was under the civilian presidency of Shehu Shagari; although provisions of this kind for the placement of retired military officers as well as ex-servicemen had long been in existence before then. The policy was to be reiterated in the Fourth National Development Plan 1981–85 where, as part of its armed forces rehabilitation and resettlement programme, the government had talked of plans to provide for the training, retraining, and deployment of retired officers in various productive sectors of the national economy, including agriculture, construction, commerce and industry.[28]

More recently, a new dimension has been added to the foregoing trend. It is a trend that can only be summarised as putting the whole machinery of The Nigerian State[29] *behind* the various "employment" campaigns, "welfare" schemes, and even "contracts" drive organised by the Ministry of Defence (MOD). A few illustrations are required here to clarify what we mean.

In July 1986, a widely publicised circular was despatched from the office of the Chief of Army Staff (COAS) requesting seven Federal Ministries as well as all State Governors under the Babangida military presidency to give consideration to retired military officers in the award of government contracts "so that they could earn a living in a respectable manner".[30] The aid was meant for honourably retired army officers from the rank of major and above either interested in or capable of post-retirement career in business. Seven specific Federal ministries believed to have been approached for this were those of internal affairs; communications; information; youth, sports and culture; transport and aviation; labour and productivity; and trade.[31]

Similar organised efforts were launched about the same time to help retired soldiers interested in farming. State military governors were directed by the Babangida regime to give land to individual ex-officers interested in undertaking large-scale farming as part of the Federal government's new programme of boosting national food production,[32] while the MOD announced plans to set up farm settlements in all the states of the Federation and Abuja territory, as part of the scheme of providing alternative source of employment for ex-servicemen, and encouraging retired and discharged soldiers to constitute themselves into cooperative farmers' associations.[33] It will be recalled that, under his first (1986) Budget, General Ibrahim Babangida had established a new Directorate of Food, Roads and Rural Infrastructures (DFRRI), and got ear-marked for the latter a huge financial allocation. It was the latest, and perhaps boldest, programme by the Federal authorities to tackle Nigeria's twin problem of food shortage and increasing marginalisation of the rural majority. The organised efforts on behalf of retired military officers in this area were apparently meant to get the members to benefit from this huge allocation. Along with other developments earlier highlighted, such measures can only add to the growing social differentiation of the retired military from the rest of society.

As if to counter anticipated criticisms from other public-sector interest groups,[34] supporters of these new campaigns or attractive and rewarding employment on behalf of retired military officers were quick to point out that there was nothing unusual about this pro-military welfare drive. It had always been part of the resettlement service package owed by any modern military establishment to its retiring members, the supporters rationalised. In the particular Nigerian case under present discussion, the drive for ex-servicemen's welfare was defended as being in consonance with the Ex-servicemen's Employment Ordinance of 1958 which makes it mandatory for all registered employers (Government and Private) to give employment to registered disabled or able-bodied ex-servicemen.[35]

Simultaneous with the foregoing trend has risen a number of new professional associations for the protection and promotion of military interests within the state. There is, for example, the new National Institute for Policy and Strategic Studies or (NIPSS) Alumni Association launched in 1984, and which includes in its membership retired officers, reservists, and officers on active duty among others. This is at the national level. At the state and local levels, similar associations have been formed to organise unity among retired military officers. For there is a growing realisation that the ability of retired military officers to act as a pressure group in the formulation of national, state, or local policies on important issues of common interest depends in part on members being able to organise themselves into effective purely military associations. Thus, a "committee of retired commissioned officers from the armed forces and police" was announced inaugurated on December 2, 1985 in Port Harcourt, River State.[36] It is one of the many and increasing examples of retired officers' groups seeking an institutional access (platform) for exerting pressure.

Let us move towards conclusion of our study by returning to the problem of power in politics, and the integrated social sciences way of determining the relative power of different actors. Of central interest to us is the question of measuring how much power the retired military members wield in relation to other social groups. According to Professor Robert A. Dahl, there are four major ways of detecting and weighing power among members of (or groups within) any political system:[37]

1. Which individuals or groups occupy what official or semi-official posts and how high within a political system?
2. What is the judgement of well-placed observers as to how power is distributed among members of the political system?
3. Which actors actually participate most often in making decision over how many issue-areas?
4. What weights does one assign to the activities of different participants in a set of decisions made over a period of time?

Of these methods of detecting and weighing power, we made use of the first in our study on the Retired Military Personnel as an Emergent Power Factor in Nigerian Society. This was in part because the method was the simplest to use. Official positions in key socio economic structures were easy to define, and their occupants easy to identify, as records on them were found extensive, and information readily obtainable. Thus, it was easy to obtain data on who the retired officers were, their rank at retirement, and from which of the services; who held what high positions in politics, government, bureaucracy, and private business, including agriculture, trade and finance, when, and how; and what relationships existed between retired military officers and the civilian elite groups also active in those sectors of the economy and society. Using the approach, not only were we able to establish the emergence of a new type of inter-locking directorate involving the government whether civilian or military controlled, the retired military, and private business cum industry. We also underlined the rising influence of retired military officers as one of the major elites of power in contemporary Nigeria.

Of course, the method relied upon to arrive at this conclusion has its own inherent weakness. I mean the method of detecting and measuring power through an examination of the occupants of top official and semi-official positions in society. It assumes that formal position is necessarily correlated with power, but this is not always the case. Professor Dahl points out the major weakness of the method when he observes: "This method would not necessarily uncover the *eminence grise,* the king-maker, the political boss, the confidants; nor would it record the power of a class or stratum that rules indirectly by allotting formal offices to other".[38] Putting the same point in slightly different language, Professor Roy C. Macridis writes thus: "We may well find, in other words, that the officials or the organs that are ostensibly responsible for the decision-making process are mere puppets manipulated by other groups. In such a case, the understanding of the location of political power involves the careful study of the relationship between the political elites and the *actual* wielders of power. The question of who makes the decisions cannot be resolved therefore by an examination of a system's constitution or formal legal structure. Very often we have to unearth the persons or groups of persons that control or influence directly the formally recognised officials who seem to make decisions."[39]

Power Behind The Throne: Civilian or/and Military

"The power behind the throne" syndrome has long been a problem of interest to political scientists theorising about or researching into power relations in society. Historical examples abound across time and space of governments manipulated by powerful individuals operating behind the scene. To pick three random ones, Ambrose Yankey, Snr., described elsewhere as "the rasputin of later-day Nkrumah's Ghana",[40] was one such an individual. Then, there was the real Gregory Efimotitch Raspotin himself who had been the power behind the throne of the Russian Tsar and Tsarina before world war 1. Yet another celebrated example was that of Cardinal de Richelieu, originally trained for the French army, who became private chaplain to Queen Anne, wife of Louis XIII, and an influential figure at the King's court. I am sure various Nigerian regimes to-date would have had their own powerful individuals or confidential agents exerting considerable influence upon incumbents of high political office behind the scene. But only "insiders" or privileged observers could help uncover who those individuals are.

Formal power holders can be dependent not only on powerful individuals, but also social groups or forces exercising power unofficially. References to such things as the "Kaduna Mafia", the "Offa connection", "Ikenne disciples", "the Ibo state union", "Ogboni confraternity", "Langtang group", "The kuru Syndicate" etc., etc. suggest that informed Nigerians are aware of the existence of the problem, meaning the disjunction between the formal and informal power holders, or between the formal and real elite of power. Those references aim at unmasking the men or groups of men who control, influence, as well as recruit new individuals into the ranks of the circulating political leadership that had been in charge of the country's public affairs since independence in 1960.

Such groups or forces exercising power unofficially can be internal or external. We touched on the external aspects of the problem in Chapter 5, where we talked of the deepening influence of multi-national corporations (MNCs) over the nation's governmental-economic affairs, despite efforts at "indigenisation". A corollary to the observation just made was the point that appointments of top retired public servants and top retired military officers to the boards of directors of the Nigerian subsidiaries of the MNCs tend to create revolving doors for increased penetration of the government's decision-making apparatus by the MNCs. Thus, within the emergent system of interlocking interests, these retired military and other public officers function as an extension of those multi-national corporate powers that control the national economy.

If we may now turn to the internal aspects of the phenomenon as related to our subject of investigation, how much of political power groups or bloc do retired military officers presently constitute? This question divides naturally into two interrelated parts. What has been the relationship of the retired military (taken together with the active military) to the political elite? What has been the relationship between the retired military members and actual wielders of power? In the last section of the chapter, we showed the military to be one of many competing domestic elite groups, including the traditional-aristocratic, intellectual, bureaucratic cum technocratic, as well as business; although the Marxist would consider all of them as but factions of the same "dominant class". In actual fact, some structural inter-penetration had been taking place among all the elites in various spheres. We saw this, for example, in the relationship between the military and business elites analysed in Chapter 3. Let us briefly examine that between the military and the ex-political elite.

Nigeria has had a little over twenty-six (26) years of independent existence. Of these, over fifteen (15) years had thus far been spent under (variants of) military rule lasting 1966–79 and from December 31, 1983 up to date. Even the short-lived civilian presidency of Shehu Shagari, as a typical "post-military" government[41] had owed its establishment and continued survival to the military presence. Strictly speaking, the only period the civilian political elite could be said to have clearly held power in Nigeria was during the first five and one quarter years following independence. Since January 15, 1966, the soldiers had been slowly but steadily edging the politicians formally from the country's rulership. Of course, the military rulers could not have been completely independent of the ex-political elite.

For one thing, the military leadership shared with many members of the latter group potentially the same political sympathies, social class backgrounds, and a combination of such other ties as regional, sub-regional, state, ethnic, linguistic, and religious; raising the possibility about the military leadership sometimes acting as a surrogate for certain faction(s) of the ex-political elite along with those other identifiable sectional interests. For another, the ex-politicians, though proscribed from active political activities, still possessed their old political networks as well as the channels of communication from the grassroots upward, which the military rulers as yet did not have. There is a third major reason why, in the past, it has been impossible for military ruler to be completely independent of the ex-political elite. When senior military officers retired from service to go into new civilian employments, politics and business were among the new employments they entered into. Thus, retired military officers came to be linked to the political as well as the business elites. In the last chapter of the study, we examined the emerging authority vacuum created by President Babangida's prohibition on the old political elite from contesting for power during the transition to civil rule recently announced, and the implications of this for the military (including the retired) among other interested domestic power groups.

On the relationship with governments of the day, a long-standing quip about the Latin America retired military general has it that "when officers retire, they conspire".[42] According to Professor John J. Johnson, the generalisation is especially true of those countries, including Argentina, "where officers are continually being retired for political reasons", and where the quip is meant "to emphasise the point that officers 'driven' into retirement, unless imprisoned and under guard, are a constant threat to political order."[43] That is Latin America, but there is no evidence the quip equally applies to the particular Nigerian case, although this country has also experienced its own periodic waves of military officers retired from the profession for political reasons (see Chapter 1). This is not to say that the generals in *agbada* have always gone along with, or given their unalloyed support to, all governments in power and on all issues of policy.

To be sure, there are instances where retired top officers stand up and are ready to be counted among opponents of an increasingly unpopular regime. Thus, retired Maj.-Gen Shehu Musa Yar' Adua came to join a disaffected northern group of so-called "Concerned Citizens", including intellectuals and retired public servants,[44] which combined with other social forces country-wide, though for divergent motives, to bring about the overthrow of President Shehu Shagari's weak and inept rule. Retired General Olusegun Obasanjo used the opportunity of a key-note address which he gave at the Annual Conference of Agricultural Society of Nigeria, Moor Plantation, Ibadan, on August 5, 1985 to make certain veiled, but damaging criticisms of the Buhari/Idiagbon military dictatorship.[44] The criticisms, which were widely reported in the print media, coincided with the latent views of politically relevant groups, including the intelligentsia, public servants, and organised labour. Within three weeks, the Buhari/Idiagbon regime had been toppled in a counter-military coup.

But there is no evidence that the generals just mentioned were personally involved whether directly or indirectly in the coup and counter-coup events of December 31, 1983 and August 27, 1985 under reference. Neither was there evidence to support the alleged involvement by retired officers of the Gowon administration about ten years earlier in the abortive counter-coup attempt of February 13, 1976[45] which had assassinated the then head of state General Murtala Mohammed. Although some retired military officers, including at least one of the generals, were said to have been mentioned in the mid-December 1985 counter-coup plot against the Babangida presidency,[46] again, this would appear to have been a mere speculation and without concrete proof, as no retired officer came to be included in the list of conspirators subsequently court-martialed for their involvement in that act, and for which some were ultimately executed.

The fact is that Nigeria's top retired military officers do not have to conspire – neither do they have to hold formal governmental power – before they can be adjudged politically influential. For one thing, by virtue of their high social status, they enjoy good *access* to the highest decision-making organs in government, including the top political leadership whether civilian or military, the highest law-making bodies, the upper levels of the executive and the bureaucracy, the top judiciary, and of course the top military establishment. Such an access to the high decision-making machinery can and tends to be utilised to obtain favourable policy decisions. Besides, with more and more of their members emerging as incumbents of some of these decision-making organs (as detailed in Chapter 5 & 6), top retired military officers are themselves fast becoming part of the structures of power; they influence (often make) policy on matters relating to various government-owned corporations on whose boards they sit. As we saw, a number of retired military generals have also been rising to high positions in the world of business, agriculture, defence procurement, banking and finance (see Chapter 3), where they are helping to shape policy. Above all, unlike their colleagues still in active service, retired military officers are not that inhibited from running for office through competing in party political elections (see Chapter 4 & 7).

Such is the structure of military organisation and its attendant socialisation that, long after leaving the force, typical retired top officers continue to wield an amazingly powerful hold over their colleagues, meaning most invariably erstwhile juniors, still in active service. The reason for this is simple: once a senior, always a senior, whom all must obey or defer to. Much of the patronage that the retired military have come to enjoy in contemporary Nigeria – appointment to public boards, offer of ambassadorial posts abroad, award of import licences, grant of soft agricultural loans, consideration for government contract, etc. – can be explained by this. For those senior officers still in service, there is of course some element of back-scratching here. Helping today's retired military with such goodies may well be one way of senior serving officers taking an insurance for their own future retirement.[48]

In conclusion, we must come to see the problem posed by the rise of the retired military as an institutional and structural problem. The fact is that Nigerian society now has operating within it this new group of men, most of them in their forties, differentiated from the rest of society not just by their new interests, new ambitions, and new energies, but also their new wealth, ex-military connections, skill, prestige, experience, and "old-boy" networks. These are elements of power and influence that would make any group possessing them restless for action. Their visibly prominent role in society within the last few years can be attributed to this. The retired military elite is a new social force to observe on the emergent political scene. But whether or not effective countervailing institutions can be devised to regulate its activities may well constitute the crux of the new civil-military relations, as indeed the democratisation project, for Nigeria in the coming 1990s and beyond.

NOTES

1. See T.B. Bottomore, *Elites and Society* (Baltimore: Penguin, 1966).

2. Quoted, *ibid.,* p.49

3. There are, of course, divergent schools of thought espoused by elite theorists, depending on the perspectives from which they wrote. There are those who belong to the "organisational" school (Mosca & Michels); others, the "psychological" school (e.g. Pareto); others, attempting a marriage of elitism and Marxism, through the "economic" approach (e.g. James Burnham and Raymond Aron); and others still, the "institutional" school (to which C.W. Mills belongs), See Geraint Parry, *Political Elites* (London: Allen & Unwin, 1969), for an elaboration on these.

4. For a parallel criticism of the theory, albeit from a methodological-pluralist viewpoint, see Robert A. Dahl, "A Critique of the Ruling Elite Model", *American Political Science Review,* Vol. 52 No.2, June 1958, pp. 463–69.

5. See, Kurt Lang, "Military Organisations," in James G. March (ed) *Handbook of Organisations,* (Chicago: Rand McNally & Co., 1965), Ch. 20.

6. Morris Janowitz, "Social Stratification and the Comparative Analysis of Elite", *Social Forces,* October, 1956, pp. 81–85; "Military Elites and the Study of War", *Conflict Resolution,* Vol. 1, March, 1957, pp. 9–18; "Sociological Notes on the Analysis of Military Elites," Appendix to *The Military in the Political Development of New Nations: An Essay in Comparative Analysis* (Chicago: The University Press, 1964), pp. 107–125.

7. Morris Janowitz, *The Professional Soldier: A Social and Political Portrait,* (New York: Free Press, 1960), pp. 6–7.

8. *ibid.,* pp. 374–82

9. C. Wright Mills, *The Power Elite* (New York: Oxford University Press, 1956), see especially chs, 6–10, & 12.

10. The kinds examined in Seymour Martin Lipset and Aldo Solari (eds), *Elites in Latin America* (New York: Oxford University Press, 1967).

11. For example, see Alan C. Isaak, *Scope and Methods of Political Science,* revised edition (Homewood, Illinois: Dorsey Press, 1975), ch. 16.

12. Robert A. Dahl, "The Concept of Power" *Behavioural Science,* Vol. 2, No. 3, July 1957, pp. 201–215.

13. *ibid.,* p 203.

14. Elements of national power popularised for the study of international politics by Hans J. Morgenthau, *Politics Among Nations.* Third Edition (New York: Knopf, 1961), ch. 9

15. Machiavelli also fell into this logical, trap, as shown in J. 'Bayo Adekanye, "Machiavelli and the Military: The Prince and the Psychology of Empty Power,"

Strategic Studies (Islamabad), Vol. VIII, No. 2., Winter 1985, pp. 26–27.

16.   Attempt at the following kind of categorisation was first advanced by the author, though in another context, in J. 'Bayo Adekanye, "Politics in a Post-Military State in Africa," *Il Politico* (Pavia), Vol. XLIX, No. 1, 1984, pp. 32–42.

17.   A former chief of army staff, Maj.-Gen. Hassan Usman Katsina was turbanned the new *Ciroma* of Katsina by his father, Sir Usman Nagogo, the Emir of Katsina, on November 22, 1974, and that was even before the former's retirement in 1975. He is a notable example of top retired military officers possessing "traditional aristocratic connections." Then, there are those retired officers who have simply taken Chieftancy titles from some communities or other. The examples here are legionary, and include the following: retired Brig. Benjamin Adekunle, *Ashipa* of Ogbomosho (in the early 1970's); the ex-"Biafran" leader Ojukwu, *Ikemba* of Nnewi (1982); ex-Brig. U.J. Esuene, *Atta* of Eket (1982); retired Maj.-Gen. A.O. Aduloju, *Jagunmolu* of Ikare Land (1985); retired Maj.-Gen. Yar' Adua, *Tafidan* Katsina (1987); retired Vice-Admiral A. Aduwo, *Taarelase* of Ife (1987).

18.   A noticeable example is that of retired Lt.-Col. Ogbonyomi, Bishop of the Kaduna Diocese, Anglican Church, Kaduna. But there could be more, including retired military *imams* now donning civilian cassock.

19.   On this viewpoint and other related issues, see for example, Bade Onimode, *Imperialism and Underdevelopment in Nigeria: The Dialectics of Mass Poverty* (London: Zed Press, 1982), & Claude Ake (ed), *Political Economy of Nigeria* (London: Longman, 1985) among others.

20.   See "Companies in Nigeria: Who Owns What" appearing in the maiden issue of *The Analyst,* Vol. 1, June 1986, pp. 2ff.

21.   *ibid.*

22.   Reference here is to the disproportionately large share of Nigeria's armed forces installations concentrated at Kaduna, within the city's environs, or in what until recently used to be considered the whole of Kaduna State.

23.   Along with others, of course, like University lecturers, managers in public enterprises, civil servants, political stalwarts, and petty contractors who combine to form either part or associates of the Kaduna power group, see Bala J. Takaya, & Sonni G. Tyoden (eds) *The Kaduna Mafia* (Jos: The University Press Ltd., 1987), p. 47.

24.   To use the term neatly coined by Professor Ali A. Mazrui, "The Lumpen Proletariat and Lumpen Militariat: African Solders as a New Political Class, *"Political Studies,* Vol. 2, No. 1, 1973, pp. 1–12; itself adapted from Karl Marx, *The Eighteenth Brumaire of Louis Bonaparte* (New York: International Publishers, 1963).

25. Also, see fn. 17 above.

26. Reference here is to the early Nigerian elite families, including the creole families, who as a group mediated between the European colonists and the traditional societies during the colonial times, and whose members tended to monopolise the local commercial and political offices, until the 1960s when mass education came to dilute their power. Some retired military officers had come from these old "middle class" families.

27. See *The Guardian* (Lagos), Saturday August 2, 1986, p. 3.

28. Federal Republic of Nigeria, *Fourth National Development Plan 1981–85* (Lagos: Federal Ministry of National Planning, 1981), pp. 367–8.

29. For useful ideas bearing generally on this point, see Bjorn Beckman, "Whose State? State and Capitalist Development in Nigeria," *Review of African Political Economy,* No. 23, January–April, 1982

30. As reported in "Contracts Drive for Ex-Officers, "*The Guardian* (Lagos), Wednesday July 16, 1986, pp. 1, 2.

31. *ibid.*

32. With Oyo State immediately taking the lead here under its rural and integrated self-employment scheme.

33. *Daily Sketch* (Ibadan), Saturday August 16, 1986, pp. 8–9

34. Particularly the universities, civil servants, and policemen, whose retired person-nel have not had the same organised support and welfare drive from any arm of government or the state. Very soon the civil servants in particular were to be pressuring the government for similar treatment as reported in "Welfare Drive for Civil Servants under Way," *The Guardian* (Lagos), Thursday July 24, 1986, pp. 1, 2.

35. See *Vanguard* (Lagos), Saturday July 19, 1986, p. 1.

36. *New Nigerian* (Lagos), December 6, 1985, p. 9.

37. Robert A. Dahl, *Modern Political Analysis* (Englewood Cliffs, New Jersey: Prentice-Hall, 1963), pp. 51–3.

38. *ibid*

39. Roy C. Macridis, *The Study of Comparative Government* (New York: Random House, 1955), p. 38, emphasis supplied.

40. J. 'Bayo Adekanye (Adekson), "Military Organisation in Multi-Ethnically Seg-mented Societies: A Theoretical Study with reference to Three Sub-Saharan African Cases," (Department of Politics, Brandeis University, Ph.D. Thesis 1976), p. 289.

41. For the sense in which this term is used, see Adekanye, "Politics in a Post-Military

State..," *op. cit.*

42. John J. Johnson, *The Military and Society in Latin America* (Stanford: The University Press, 1964) p. 127

43. *ibid*, p. 128.

44. Takaya & Tyoden (eds), *The Kaduna Mafia...* op. cit., pp. 78–80, 88–89, 141.

45. General Olusegun Obasanjo (rtd), "Nigeria Which Way Forward", Key-Note Address delivered at the 1985 Annual Conference of Agricultural Society of Nigeria, Moor Plantation, Ibadan, August 5 1985.

46. Although in a statement issued on February 18, 1976 the Federal Government said the previous head of state, retired General Yakubu Gowon, by now in self-exile in England, "knew of the abortive coup", (see *Nigeria Year Book 1977–78* (Lagos : Daily Times Publications, 1977), p.237, this has never been substantiated. In any case, Gowon has since been granted a state pardon, as we saw.

47. See *The Guardian* (Lagos), December 22, 1985, pp. 1, 12.

48. For a good magazine piece appearing about the time the last paragraph of our book was being written, and done within the framework of elite-theoretic construct similar to that advanced above, see *This Week* (Lagos), Vol. 8, No. 9, 1988, pp. 17–23. Cf &Ct. fn. 1 of our Introduction to the book.

APPENDIX A
Persons banned from Participation in Politics, Elections or holding any Public or Political Party Office, etc.

1. All persons including politicians who held political offices from 1st October, 1960 to 15th January, 1966, and from 1st October 1979 to 30th December, 1983 and who are subsequently indicted and found guilty of offences of misdeeds by any Tribunal, Special Investigation Panel, Judicial Commission or Administrative Enquiry;

2. All persons who served as Secretaries to Federal and Sate Governments, Permanent Secretaries, Judges, Chairmen and Members of Federal and State Boards of Statutory Corporations, and State-owned companies or on the Governing Boards of various institutions as well as all other pubic officers who had been found guilty of misdeeds by any Panel, Tribunal, Judicial Commission or Administrative Enquiry between 1st October, 1960 to the end of the transition period;

3. All Military and Police personnel who held public offices during the period 15th January, 1966 to the end of this transitional period and who were or might be found guilty, and removed from office or dismissed from the Services, or who were or are hereafter found guilty of corruption or other misdeeds or indicted by various Courts Martial, Tribunals, Special Investigation Panel, Judicia! Commission and Administrative Enquiries at both Federal and State levels;

4. All persons in both the public and private sectors who have been or will be dismissed from office or any employment during the period 1st October 1960 to the end of the transitional period;

5. All persons who may not have held any public office but who have been indicted and punished by various panels, Tribunals and Commissions of Enquiry for corrupting public office holders; and

6. All Legislators or persons including those elected into the Senate, House of Representative, Houses of Assembly of Regions or States from January 1960 to the end of transition period who either collectively or individually have been liable for or indicted and found guilty of acts of unjust enrichment, corruption, fraud, embezzlement of public funds, election malpractices or contributed in one way or the other to the economic adversity of the nation or such persons who exercised corrupt influences on public office holders.

Source: Federal Republic of Nigeria, "Participation in Politics and Elections (Prohibition) Decree No. 25 of 1987", *Official Gazette* (Lagos), Vol. 74, No 57, October 9, 1987, pp. A216–217.

APPENDIX B
Persons Disqualified from Participation in Politics and Elections or Seeking or Contesting any Public or Political Party Office During the Transition Period

PART 1 – OFFICE HOLDERS (CIVILIAN)

The holders of the following offices during the periods 1st October, 1960 to 15th January, 1966 and 1st October, 1979 to 30th December, 1983.

1. President
2. Prime Minister
3. Vice-President
4. Regional Premier
5. State Governor
6. State Administrator
7. Deputy State Governor
8. Minister, Presidential Adviser/Assistant
9. Commissioner
10. Parliamentary Secretary
11. Presidential Liaison Officer
12. National Assembly Liaison Officer
13. President of the Senate
14. Deputy President of the Senate
15. Speaker of the House of Representatives
16. Deputy Speaker of the House of Representatives
17. Speaker of the Regional House of Assembly
18. Speaker of the States House of Assembly
19. Deputy Speaker of the Regional/State House of Assembly
20. Chairmen of Committees or Selected Committees of the Senate, House of Representatives and Regional and State Houses of Assembly.
21. Members of the National Executive Committees of all Political Parties.
22. Members of Regional Working Parties/Committees or State Executive.

PART II – OFFICE HOLDERS (MILITARY AND POLICE)

All Military and Police personnel who held or are currently holding the underlisted public offices from 15th January, 1966 to the end of the transition period will not be allowed to contest any election into any elective office or hold any position in any political party in Nigeria during the transition period; the offices covered in this group include those of:

1. President
2. Head of State
3. Chief of Staff (Supreme Headquarters)
4. Deputy Chief of Staff (Supreme Headquarters)
5. Chief of General Staff
6. Chairman, Joint Chiefs of Staff
7. Chief of Defence Staff
8. Deputy Chief of Defence Staff
9. Chief of Staff (Army Headquarters)
10. Head of Navy
11. Head of Air Force
12. Chief of Army Staff
13. Chief of Naval Staff
14. Chief of Air Staff.
15. Inspector-General of Police
16. Military Governors/Administrators
17. Members of the Supreme Military Council and the Armed Forces Ruling Council between 31st December, 1983 and end of transitional period.

SOURCE: Federal Republic of Nigeria, "Participation in Politics and Elections (Prohibition) Decree No. 25 of 1987", *Official Gazette* (Lagos), Vol. 74, No 57, October 9, 1987, pp. A217–218.

Addendum

On February 15, 1999, retired General Obasanjo won his party's primaries to be its flag-bearer; and within the following two weeks he had also clinched the highest political office in the land by winning the presidential elections of February 27, 1999, though not without some controversy.[1] The People's Democratic Party (PDP) on whose platform he contested the civilian presidency, has come to be viewed by most informed Nigerians as "the party of retired generals", just to convey the tremendous power and influence which the men-in-mufti have come to command in Nigerian society.

The current transition-to-civil rule process also threw up its first ex-military officer turned quasi-civilian state governor, in the person of retired Rear Admiral Mohammed Lawal elected governor of Kwara State, albeit on the platform of one of the rival parties, the All People's Party (APP). The results of the national assembly elections held on February 20, 1999 saw another array of top retired military officers elected to serve as lawmakers in the next national assembly. Four top retired military officers who contested into the senate under the PDP banner won their seats: Maj.-Gen. Ike Nwachukwu (rtd), Brig. Jonathan Tunde Ogbeha (rtd), Brig. David Mark (rtd), and Nuhu Aliyu (a retired Deputy Inspector-General of Police);[2] although retired Brig.-Gen. Brimo Yusuf, campaigning on the platform of yet another rival party, the Alliance for Democracy (AD), also captured a senatorial seat.[3] Retired Maj.-Gen. Joseph Garba was another retired general seeking to get into the new Senate; he had run under the APP banner for a seat from the Plateau South senatorial district but lost. Retired generals dominated the list of PDP's most powerful financiers as well as presidential campaign. These include Lt.-Gen T.Y. Danjuma (rtd), Maj.-Gen. Ali Mohammed Gusau (rtd), Lt.-Gen. Wushishi (rtd), and Gen. I.B. Babangida (rtd).

All this is not a chance occurrence, but the result of certain factors and forces long at work and visible to the discerning eye. The author had predicted it all some ten years ago in his detailed, scholarly, and systematic study of the role and influence of retired military officers in contemporary Nigeria. With the clinching of the presidency by one of their own and the sole candidate for that matter, General Obasanjo, what the retired military brass have succeeded in doing is to add a new political power to their existing concentration of wealth, status, and influence. Retired General Obasanjo's election to the civilian presidency, and the crucial role played by other top retired generals in helping to achieve this outcome, may justifiably be viewed as the highest stage in the development of Nigeria's top retired generals as an "emergent power factor", the ultimate validation of the thesis about "The retired military".

Before now, top retired military officers had been found ensconced in all the major sectors of the Nigerian economy and society, including public bureaucracy and parastatals, the worlds of trade and commerce, banking and finance, subsidiaries of multi-national corporations, as well as agriculture. The name of somebody like retired

Lt.-Gen. Danjuma had long been known to ring a bell across the various corporate board rooms in the country. He it was in fact who coined the term "military-business complex" in January 1978, just before retiring as the Chief of Army Staff in the previous Obasanjo regime. Nor would 1998-99 be the first time to observe a sizeable number of top retired generals debouching into politics. To be sure, the foundation for the pattern of active political involvement by the retired military appeared to have been set during the Second Republic (1979-83). But there is a difference. Whereas in the past such an involvement was still viewed as an aberration and marked by considerable hesitation and doubt, today it shows a more determined and definite pattern.

Three reasons account for this. First, top retired military officers have come to acquire more political training and greater confidence and to see themselves as better equipped for the vocation of politics. Being better equipped includes having now also developed some capacity for political oratory, together with its rambling discourses, circumlocutions, and even double-talk. Second, there has been a change in the attitudes of military persons, both serving and retired, to the vocation of politics, including what role big money plays or ought to play in politics. Thus, whereas in 1981 retired Lt.-Gen. Danjuma said he had "neither the inclination nor the money to take part in politics" as we saw, by 1998/99 he had not only become actively involved but has been donating massive funds towards the PDP and Obasanjo's presidential campaign. In fact, retired Lt.-Gen. Danjuma had become so politically involved that on the occasion of one of the fund-raising events organised in support of retired Obasanjo's PDP presidential candidacy, he was reported to have threatened to go on self-exile if any other person than retired Gen. Obasanjo emerged as winner of the presidency.[4] Also, in 1992-93, when retired Gen. Yakubu Gowon was showing some inclination to run for higher political office, retired Gen. Obasanjo had himself asked of the latter "what Gowon has forgotten in the State House that makes him badly want to run for and regain that office". When reminded of this in 1998, retired Gen. Obasanjo had no problem rationalising his change of attitude, hinging his decision to now run, as it were, on some "call to duty".

But the third, and perhaps the most fundamental, reason accounting for the determined role that the ex-generals came to play in the transition politics of 1998-99 derives from the threats of imminent disintegration which Nigeria had been facing since the June 12, 1993 crisis. Should those threats be actualised, the top retired generals stood the most to lose, given the sheer size of their stakes in the state, the economy and its corporate existence. Such concerns awakened in the retired military class and its members, a yearning for an effective Bonaparte-like leader for stabilising the polity.[5] But the ex-generals were perspicacious enough to realise that the needed leader could not be the conventional "man on horseback" type.[6] An old-style military regime, however benevolent, would simply be unacceptable to the citizenry, given the recent experience with military rule and mood of the times. The Bonaparte-type ruler yearned for must therefore also combine the qualities as it were of the legendary Cincinnatus*** (From the mythology of classical Rome) called upon from the field to assume the leadership of the state and help stabilise things, but unambitious of power, and standing ready to relinquish the trappings of rule as soon as the mission was achieved. Retired General Obasanjo came to seen by the class as one such a leader.

But what is the consequence of all this for the traditional conception of civil-military relations in Nigeria as one involving the separation between civilian society and military organisation? Has the election of retired General Obasanjo not rendered that conception of civil-military relations outmoded? What major factors and forces had until now been at work in making the lines between the two organs of state power increasingly blurred? To what does one ascribe the new political influence that most Nigerians now see their retired military class as displaying and visibly enjoying?

The new political influence had long been predicted by me. Its source was seen to lie in the combination of *power, positions, new-found wealth, ex-military connections, "old-boy" networks, skills, prestige, and experiences* possessed by the group and its individual members. I had postulated these as potential resources waiting to be exploited to the maximum as bases of new influence. As far back as 1988, when the manuscript was completed, I had for example described "the problem posed by the rise of the retired military as an institutional and structural problem". I had also concluded the study with the following prescient words: "The retired military elite is a new social force to observe on the emergent political scene. But whether or not effective countervailing institutions can be devised to regulate its activities may well constitute the crux of the new civil-military relations, as indeed the democratisation project, for Nigeria in the coming 1990s and beyond". In the Inaugural Address on "Military Occupation and Social Stratification" which was delivered at the University of Ibadan in November 1993,[7] I had also talked about the phenomenon. How true all of this has proved to be!

Changes within the domain

Of course, there is no way that a research study completed some ten years ago and appearing in print for the first time today will not require some up-dating, even if merely to reflect the changes that have taken place within the domain and regarding the subject of investigation. This is what the addendum seeks to do. It is about the unfolding of "the retired military as power factor in Nigeria" both as a subject and thesis between then and now.

To move from the more obvious, though by no means necessarily also the more significant, changes: for example, some of the major *personae dramatis* earlier acting on the Nigerian scene both civil and military have since left the stage. I have in mind figures like Aminu Kano, Maj.-Gen Hassan Usman Katsina (rtd), Chief Obafemi Awolowo, Dr. Nnamdi Azikwe, Maj.-Gen. Shehu Musa Yar'Adua (rtd) Chief M.K.O. Abiola, General Sani Abacha. There are also the *changes of place names* that had occurred since, particularly the names of component states of the federation. Most of the state units referred to in the main-body of study, like Kaduna, Kano, Oyo, Ondo, Cross-River, Rivers, Kwara, Niger, and Sokoto, have since shrunk in both geographical size and population, even where they continue to go by the old names identified with their core areas. A few old names like Bendel and Gongola have simply disappeared, and new ones such as Bayelsa, Ebonyi, Jigawa, Kogi and Zamfara been born, invariably carved out of old ones.

The particular changes just talked about are linked to another set: namely *changes in the structure of the federation*. We refer to the periodic increase in the number of states making up the federation, from 21 (1987) and then 22 (1988), to 30 (1991), and now 36 (since 1996); even as the local government council areas have also multiplied, from the number of 304 inherited from the 1976 exercise to 453 in 1989, 589 in 1991, and 772 by 1996. At the same time, the Federal capital has moved from Lagos to Abuja, with the Presidential Villa at Aso Rock assuming the character of supposedly impregnable citadel of power. But those trends towards excessive centralisation of the federal government arrangement under the successive military regimes, coupled with glaring economic mismanagement, rising poverty for the majority, and the alienation of the rulers from the citizenry, have created their own inherent contradictions. By the time of Abacha's death, those contradictions had succeeded in reducing the Nigerian state to the conditions of "near collapsed state".

We might also point to some of the *changes in the format of military government,* the top personnel, and their names. By the latter we do not just refer to the changes in the succession of military-based regimes, from Babangida, through Shonekan, to Abacha and now to Abubakar, or the changes in the names of the highest ruling body from the Armed Forces Ruling Council (AFRC) through the Interim National Government (ING) to the Provisional Ruling Council (PRC). But, perhaps, much more fundamental, from the viewpoint of the study, had been the *quantum and rate of circulation of ranks within the officer corps* consequent upon the changes in government talked about. Since the latter particular kind of changes just remarked bears directly on the central subject of our investigations, it requires a much greater elaboration than the others.

Under the Babangida years (1985-93) alone, there were not less than five major reshuffles of military command posts and personnel.[8] With the removal of Commodore Ebitu Ukiwe (now retired) as Babangida's first Chief of General Staff (or CGS), Augustus Aikhomu was moved from his post as Chief of Naval Staff, to become the CGS. Rear-Admiral Patrick Koshoni became the new Chief of Army Staff. Shortly thereafter, Alhaji Muhammadu Gambo was appointed the new Inspector-General of Police, following the mandatory retirement of Etim Inyang. Thus, Aikhomu, Koshoni, and Gambo – in addition, of course, to Sani Abacha, who had been promoted to the rank of Major-General and made the new Chief of Army Staff soon after the 1985 coup - became among the first service chiefs to be elevated by the Babangida regime. Within one year, that is, as part of the celebrations marking the country's 27th independence anniversary on October 1, 1987, they were to be further elevated along with others.

The December 29, 1989 military reshuffle saw Babangida not just replacing but also retiring all but one of his service chiefs: Vice-Admiral Koshoni, Air Marshal Ibrahim

Alfa, Muhammadu Gambo the I.G. Named as their replacements respectively were Vice-Admiral Murtala Nyako, Air Marshal Nureni Yusuf, and Aliyu Attah as the new police boss, though made under circumstances that were to create rumblings of discontent both within the armed forces and civil society. Following Lt-Gen Domkat Bali's resignation from the government and retirement from service, Babangida took over the portfolio of defence minister, and allowed the Chief of Army Staff, Lt.-Gen. Abacha, to double as the new Chairman of the Joint Chiefs of Staff.

By September 1990, less than six months after the bloody counter-coup attempt of Maj. Orka and his co-conspirators that almost toppled the administration, Babangida was again reconstituting the country's military command structure, announcing a wave of retirements of top officers from all the services. Over 100 senior officers, mostly army generals, brigadiers and colonels and their equivalents in the air force and the navy were compulsorily retired. Many of the top officers retired, particularly the army generals such as Ike Nwachukwu, Yohanna Kure, Gado Nasco, Mamman Kontagora, continued holding ministerial appointments in the Babangida government. Also retired in this exercise were ten top air marshals and over thirty other senior and middle-ranking air force officers, including commanders. A number of senior navy officers (on a smaller scale) were also retired sometime thereafter. Under the military reorganisation, a number of new military appointments were also made, among them: the elevation of Maj.-Gen. Salihu Ibrahim as the new Chief of Army Staff and taking over from Lt.-Gen Abacha, and handing over to the latter the portfolio of defence minister as well as Chairman Joint Chiefs of Staff.

In 1992, both the air force and navy had their chiefs, Air Vice Marshal Nureni Yusuf and Vice Admiral Murtala Nyako, retired; and named as their replacements, respectively, were Air Marshal Akin Dada and Vice Admiral Dan Preston Omatsola. Babangida's last opportunity which he seized for reconstituting the officer corp was on the eve of his own departure from office and forced retirement in 1993. He thought he had the key command posts occupied and secured by his loyalists. But his forced resignation from office and compulsory retirement from the army on August 27, 1993 meant that power to decide and guarantee such things had passed on to others. General Abacha became immediately the *de facto* president and commander-in-chief, though *de jure* he was supposed to have been taking orders from Chief Ernest Shonekan the civilian head of the Interim National Government (ING). A major objective of Abacha's initial military policy after the take-over was aimed at flushing out the former military president's loyalists, the so-called "Babangida boys", from key command positions and replacing them with his own trusted men. Those considerations also exacted their own retirement toll from the military hierarchy.

Within the spate of the two-year period 1993-94, for example, the army alone had not less than four different generals occupying the office of the Chief of Army Staff. Replacing Maj.-Gen Salihu Ibrahim (rtd) as the Chief of Army Staff on the eve of Babangida's exit in 1993 was Maj.-Gen. Chris Ali who was himself to be retired within a year of Abacha's take-over. His replacement was Maj.-Gen. Anwali Kazir, who had been appointed by the Abacha government, but also retired by him after less than two years of tenure. Maj.-Gen Ishaya Bamaiyi took over thereupon and remains the current army boss to-date.

The two other armed services had experienced similarly a high turn-over rate at their top command level. Air Marshal Akin Dada was replaced as the Chief of Air Staff on September 16, 1993. The current Chief of Air Staff, Vice Marshal N.E. Eduok, has held the post twice. The first time was in 1993, and only for just 48 hours (September 16-17, 1993), when he was replaced with Air Vice Marshal John Femi. The latter's tenure lasted from September 1993 to March 1996. By March 30, 1996, Vice Marshal Eduok was back as the Chief of Air Staff, which post he still holds to-date. In the navy, Rear Admiral Suleiman Saidu succeeded Vice Admiral Omatsola as Chief of Naval Staff in 1993, but the former held the post for only 28 days (September-November, 1993). Rear Admiral Allison Madueke took over thereafter as the Chief of Naval Staff, and stayed on until 1994. The latter's replacement in the post, Vice Admiral Okhai Akhigbe, had since himself become the new Chief of General Staff, following General Abubakar's succession to the late Abacha as Head of State in June 1998. The current navy boss is Vice Admiral Jubril Ayinla.

Increased Circulation of ex-Officers in the National Economy

The high retirement rate of top military officers over the last ten years that we have just described has had obvious implications. To begin with, it could only have resulted in a further growth in the population of top military retirees, and a corresponding increase in military pension costs. But it does also mean that greater numbers of ex-soldiers are now available for various post-retirement pursuits whether directly in the national economy, society, or politics. There is another major implication of the increase in the membership of top military retiree population: many more, and in some cases even better, examples of retired military-business enterprises and interests covering all the business group categories studied above would have been available by now. But only a few and the most salient of the new examples can be added on here.

Thus, retired Col. Joseph Tardzua is said to have been Chairman and Managing Director Shingutar Group of Companies, since 1987; and retired Brig. Mobolaji Johnson, appointed Director, Julius Berger Nigeria Ltd., since October 1988.[10] During the period, retired Lt.-Gen. Alani Akinrinade came to broaden his business interests from agriculture to include investments in imports and exports trade. The information about the latter came from an indirect source, and even so this did not become available until most recently. Just this past February 1999, it was reported that the licence of the Inter-Global Shipping Company, a maritime outfit belonging to retired Lt.-Gen. Akinrinade, revoked by the previous regime, had been restored to him. The restoration order was reported to have been effected by the new Minister of Transport under General Abubakar's brief tenure, Rear Admiral F.B.I. Porbeni.[11] The shipping business concerned must have been established a little after retired Lt.-Gen Akinrinade was moved from his ministerial post in agriculture or in between the two other cabinet positions in industries and transport that he served under the Babangida regime.

Among *developments on the military-business* scene, those in *the private banking sector* provided the most abundant illustrations. Although the research study had remarked about the rash of new banks mushrooming all over the country, we could find only few examples of retired military generals with investments in the area, as the banking business was just opening up when the manuscript was completed. Since 1988, more information has become available regarding the activities in this particular military-business sector. Indeed, such had been the "money-spinning" opportunities offered by the banking sector under SAP that the boards of several hundred financial institutions, including the newly established ones, were found by two researchers in 1993 to have as many as 61 retired military officers with 105 affiliations in 95 of the firms; and by 1993, at least 17 of the post-1996 banks had former officers listed in their management.[12]

"From the barracks to banking halls" is the tag given by another and more recent work for describing this phenomenon of "retired soldiers in the banking business under SAP in Nigeria."[13] The examples listed by the source run into almost thirty and are worth being added here in the up-date: Maj.-Gen. Mohammed (rtd), Chairman, International Merchant Bank; Lt.-Col. P.Z. Wyom (rtd), Member, Rims Merchant Bank; Maj.-Gen. A. Rimi (rtd) Member, Royal Merchant Bank; Maj.-Gen. Zamani (rtd), Member, Prudent Merchant Bank; Maj.-Gen Hassan Katsina (rtd), Member, Prime Merchant Bank; Air Commodore Emeka Omeruah (rtd), Member, Nigeria Merchant Bank; Lt.-Col. Tunde Oyedele (rtd), Member, Nationwide Merchant Bank; Maj.-Gen. G.O. Ejiga (rtd), Member, Manufacturers Merchant Bank; Air Vice-Marshal Muktair Mohammed (rtd), Chairman, Group Merchant Bank; Maj.-Gen. David Jemibewon (rtd), Vice Chairman, Ivory Merchant Bank; Lt.-Gen. M.I Wushishi (rtd), Chairman, Chartered Bank; Col. Sanni Bello (rtd), Chairman, Broad Bank which also had both Maj.-Gen. George Innih (rtd) and Air Vice Marshal Usman Muazu (rtd) as Members of its Board of Directors; Col. C.O. Ekundayo (rtd), Member, Equatorial Trust Bank; Maj. M.H. Jokolo (rtd), Member, Gamji Bank; Maj.-Gen. J.J. Oluleye (rtd), Member, Gulf Bank; Air Vice Marshal Ibrahim Alfa (rtd), Chairman, Highland Bank.[14]

There were more examples cited. Air Vice Marshal Isa Doko (rtd) became Chairman, Intercity Bank whose Board of Directors also has one of the previously identified "retired officer-gentlemen bankers", Lt.-Gen. M.I. Wushishi (rtd), as Member. Air Commodore Dan Suleiman, Maj.-Gen. A. Mohammed, and Col. Sanni Bello, all of them retired, came to be named as Chairmen, North South Bank, Trade Bank, and Continental Merchant Bank respectively. Lt.-Col. P.O Ogbebor (rtd) was identified as Chairman, Great Merchant Bank on whose board Lt.-Col. D.E. Nehikhane (rtd) also sat as Member. Air Commodore Emeka Omeruah (rtd), earlier mentioned as share holder in Nigeria Merchant Bank, came to be known as being also Board Member of one of the country's first generation and "big three" banks, United Bank of Africa. Retired Maj.-Gen. Shehu Musa Yar'Adua (now deceased) was mentioned in the main study to have been a major share holder in and Chairman of Habib Bank Nigeria Ltd., which interests along with those in other businesses can now be assumed to have passed on to his legal survivors. Finally, the Universal Trust Bank, on whose Board as Chairman retired Lt.-Gen. T.Y. Danjuma was also shown to have long occupied, came to include Maj.-Gen. Paul Tarfa (rtd) as Member.[15]

As is to be expected, many more examples have been recorded of retired top-ranking military officers appointed to the *executive boards of public agencies, corporations and government-owned companies or industries* have been recorded since the main study was completed. This was in spite of the fact that, arising from the adoption of SAP as economic reform strategy, most of the statutory industries concerned were supposed to have been already scheduled for privatisation.[16]

Lt.-Gen T.Y. Danjuma had since 1984 been Chairman, Defence Industries Corporation of Nigeria (DICON), which he succeeded in taking into the lucrative salt importation trade. The incorporation of Dicon Salt Limited was effected by late 1984, with a joint-venture between the Defence Industries Corporation of Nigeria (DICON) and a new group of Technical Partners known for short simply as AIMS. Following an initially checkered experience, the company changed its name from Dicon Salt Limited to Union Dicon Salt in 1992, and became privatised shortly after. Today, Union Dicon Salt Plc is a blue chips company and reported to rank as the number two on the Nigerian Stock Exchange, with stock quoted at ₦42.00 per 50k share. The Defence Industries Corporation's stock in Union Dicon Salt Plc is also currently valued at N1,176,000,000. Of late, Union Dicon Salt Plc has been diversifying into other areas. It has only recently bought over Witt & Busch Limited, a company in the electric generators selling and maintenance business, and acquired substantial share of Access Bank Plc. Retired Lt.-Gen. Danjuma is the Chairman of both the Defence Industries Corporation of Nigeria (DICON) and the Union Dicon Salt Plc, in addition to having substantial interests in the Technical Partners, AIMS Limited, as well as in the various vessels used for the shipment of salt to Nigeria for Union Dicon Salt (UDS). DICON also has another top retired officer for its Managing Director in the person of Maj.-Gen. J.O Adeniyi (rtd).[17] Today, the DICON Chairman, retired Lt.-Gen Danjuma, ranks as one of the most economically successful and wealthiest of Nigeria's top retired generals, if not the most economically successful and the wealthiest.

Retired Lt.-Gen Danjuma came to add a few more to his multiple board directorships with top government appointments in the public sector. Between 1988 and 1992, he was made Chairman, National Revenue Mobilisation and Allocation Committee, as well as Chairman, National Science and Technology Fund. For other similar examples still, retired Brig. Samuel Ogbemudia was appointed Managing Director, and later Sole Administrator, Nigerian Railways Corporation, April 1989. Retired Maj.-Gen. Olu Bajowa is currently the Permanent Secretary (until recently Director-General), Federal

Ministries of Industry, and Science and Technology. He had previously been at the Ministry of Defence where he served in the same capacity. Preceding the latter still, retired Maj.-Gen. Bajowa had headed the task force on movement to the new Federal Capital. His first public appointment at the federal level since retiring from the army was that of Managing Director, Nigerian Airways, held between January 1988 and August 1989. Air Vice Marshal Larry Koinyan, who had been appointed as Executive Chairman, Directorate of Food, Roads and Infrastructures (DFRRI) from the very inception of the latter agency in 1986, continued for a long time on the post, even after he voluntarily retired from the Nigerian Air Force (December 21, 188).

Closely linked to these were the *appointments of retired military officers to cabinet posts and other top decision-making positions* in government. The examples here have increased in number since I wrote the book. Whereas Lt.-Gen. Alani Akinrinade was mentioned in the main-body of the study as the first retired general to be appointed to cabinet portfolio, namely that of agriculture, water resources and rural development, actually he held the latter post for only one year (1985 - 86), but was subsequently moved to other ministries, those of industries (1986-1989) and transport (1989-..). An increasingly common feature of the appointments of retired generals as cabinet ministers made in the post-1986 period was that of top retired generals being retired from service while still on their high political appointments, or rather being allowed to continue as ministers after being retired, and in some cases even promoted to higher military ranks while already retired.

For example, apart from the two bizarre cases subsequently involving Domkat Bali and Augustus Aikhomu, promoted after being retired, from Lt.-General (rtd) to General (rtd), and from Vice-Admiral (rtd) to Admiral (rtd) respectively, many of the top officers retired in the September 1990 exercise, particularly the army generals such as Ike Nwachukwu, Yohanna Kure, Gado Nasco, Mamman Kontagora, continued holding ministerial appointments in the Babangida government. Muhammadu Gambo was another example. A former Inspector-General of Police (October 1986 - September 1990), Gambo was made National Security Adviser to Babangida in 1990, and Administrator, Directorate of Social Mobilisation (1992-1995). Part of the latter tenure saw Alhaji Gambo serving the Abacha regime. His last appointment was that of minister of agriculture (1995-1998). Commodore Samson Omeruah, currently the minister for youth and sports, is yet another.

Of the officers mentioned in the last paragraph, Kotangora has over the last ten years stayed in political office the most as well as circulated the highest. He was appointed minister of works and housing in December 1987, and continued in that post after being retired from the army in September 1990. He served as Sole Administrator, Ahmadu Bello University, Zaria, for much of the Abacha years; and though he still doubles in the latter capacity, Maj.-Gen. Kontagora (rtd) has since August 23, 1998 been brought back by the Abubakar government into its cabinet where he currently holds the portfolio of minister of Federal Capital Territory (FCT). He took over from Abacha's *alter ego* Lt.-

Gen Jeremiah Useni (rtd). Finally, the late General Abacha's regime created a super-ministerial agency called the Petroleum Trust Fund (PTF) for executing programmes and projects being funded from the proceeds accruing from the removal of subsidies from petroleum products, vesting the agency's operation in one of the former military heads of states, Gen Mohammadu Buhari (rtd).

Participation in Politics, 1991-98

Until June 1998, when General Abdusalami Abubakar became Nigeria's new head of state following General Abacha's death, what progress in the transition programme from military to civilian rule had been about one scheme in self-succession or the other. Although the scheme became much more brazen under Abacha than Babangida, it was clear to most informed Nigerians that neither ruler had any intention of voluntarily relinquishing power. But this did not prevent a number of retired military officers along with many of the politicians from taking part in the politics of the *faked transition*, beginning with what a group of scholars have labelled as the "transition without end" of the Babangida years.[18] The top retired generals who sought to run for various offices between 1991 and 1998 included: Gen Yakubu Gowon (rtd), Maj.-Gen. Olufemi Olutoye (rtd), Maj.-Gen. I.B.M. Haruna (rtd), Col. Yohanna Madaki (rtd), Maj.-Gen. Shehu Musa Yar'Adua (rtd), Maj.-Gen. R.M. Dumuje (rtd), and Maj.-Gen Joseph Garba Of these, retired Maj.-Gen Yar'Adua had the longest and most sustained interests in things political, having been part of the disaffected northern group of "Concerned Citizens" organised to oppose the regime of the civilian President Shehu Shagari as far back as 1982-83. Nor did the retired general consider his political activities tameable by any government, however, awesome the power at its disposal. For example, when the Babangida regime appeared bent on proscribing the old-breed politicians and the top retired military officers from taking part in the future politics of the country as we saw, retired Maj.-Gen Yar'Adua refused to be bound by such a restrictive measure, and continued with his "politicking" as if the ban did not exist or as if the ban would not last. To be sure, even at the time, the ban placed on both the old-breed politicians and the top retired generals did not look like the kind of restriction that would be easy to enforce or sustain - indefinitely. On both counts, retired Maj.-Gen Yar'Adua was proved right. By December 1991, when the "participation in politics and election (prohibition) Decree No. 25 of 1987" was abrogated and the ban on former office holders both civilian and military cum police lifted, retired Maj.-Gen Yar'Adua had already built up a powerful political machine with grassroots all over the country, and got himself well-positioned as one of the leading contenders for the civilian presidency.

Between late 1994 and early 95, both Maj.-Gen Yar'Adua (rtd) and Gen. Obasanjo (rtd) found themselves criss-crossing the country and mobilising for one political project or another; either against Abacha's self-succession scheme; or continuing with their shadow-boxing of one another in preparation for a political race about to be declared open; or planning to team up again as they had done in 1976-79 in a project on dual rule.

o

Retired Maj.-Gen. Yar'Adua's political ambition was the more obvious and compelling. He it was who at the constitutional conference of 1995 moved a motion for General Abacha to hand over power to democratically elected civilians by January 1996. But the latter also proved his undoing: a few weeks after the motion, he was picked up by Abacha's security agents on one of those trumped-up charges of involvement in coup plotting, subsequently court-martialled, and jailed.[19] Retired Maj.-Gen. Yar'Adua was to die later in detention in December 1997. But the political machine he had built survived and was to be part of the organisational weapon later deployed by retired Gen. Obasanjo and his campaign team for capturing the presidency.

Role in the June 12 Crisis

The presidential elections of February 27, 1999 were conducted against the background of raging crisis and conflicts generated by the June 12 imbroglio. Similar elections had previously been organised on June 12, 1993, whose results were supposed to have brought to an end Babangida's rather tortuous, eight-year transition from authoritarian rule, and to have ushered in a new era of democratic rule. The June 12, 1993 elections had been freely and fairy won by Chief M.K.O. Abiola, a civilian business tycoon, from the Southern half of the country, and of Yoruba ethnic origins, though possessing multiple business links with the political and military elites past and present. The decision by the Babangida administration to annul the results of the 1993 presidential elections was the immediate cause of the problems that the successive military-based regimes of Babangida, Shonekan, and Abacha had with popular organisations over the June 12 confrontation around those presidential elections.[20]

While the crisis over the June 12 issue was not an ethnic affair, yet a general impression had been created from the very beginning that the only real reason for seeking to annul the results of what was otherwise an orderly, free and fair election, and aborting the democratic process, was that the winner Chief Abiola did not come from a preferred group or region. The question then arose whether a still badly divided and multi-ethnically conflictual society such as Nigeria could be governed, or even survive as one unit in the long run at all, where and when a segment was (perceived as) arrogating to itself a permanent control of Federal political power.[21] The coalition of pro-democracy forces and other organised social groups and interest from civil society were concerned about implications of the annulment event for Nigeria's democratic development. But those forces also rejected the arrogance of the military in substituting its corporate and individual members' interest for the sovereignty of the people. The struggles over June 12 were about those issues. The struggles had been as much an anti-military struggle, and a struggle for democracy, as it was also a struggle for the sharing and rotation of power.

Of course, members of the military profession, both serving and retired, came to be affected by the crisis. A number also stood up to declare their stand. For a serving officer to be stigmatised as a "NADECO" man or woman, belonging that is to the opposition

National Democratic Coalition, whether real or imaginary, for example, was one sure way to lose one's command position, if not one's entire commission. And quite a number of serving officers were retired on that basis. A number of retired military officers also joined the pro-democracy cause. For example, the Association for Democracy and Good Governance in Nigeria (ADGN) was one of the civic organisations thrown up by the June 12 crisis; and when it operated, the body could boast of containing a sizeable number of top retired generals in its membership. Among the founding members whose signatures appeared in the last pages of the ADGN constitution when it was adopted at Ota on July 12, 1993 were Gen. Olusegun Obasanjo (rtd), Maj.-Gen. Mohammadu Buhari (rtd), Col. E.N. Nwobosi (rtd), Lt.-Gen. Alani Akinrinade (rtd). Retired Gen. Obasanjo was the original convener. A couple of the ex-ADGN members were to turn pro-democratic activists, with links to the NADECO.

In the struggles against the Abacha regime and the enthronement of civilian democratic rule were top retired military officers like Lt.-Gen. Alani Akinrinade, Commodore Dan Suleiman, Col. Abubakar Umar, and Col. Yohanna Madaki. For this, the ex-officers concerned found themselves earmarked for physical elimination by agents of the regime. Most had sought to escape either by going underground or becoming political refugees abroad. A number lost their relations, houses and properties to organised arsonists, robbers or assassins, and their various businesses wrecked. Along with scores of other Nigerians drawn from the various organised groups and interests, including intellectuals, the press, lawyers' associations, human rights organisations, trade unions, civilian politicians, and of course, the military itself, retired Gen. Obasanjo was himself arrested and jailed after being tried on trumped-up charges of conspiracy and concealment in the 1995 phantom coup case. He was only lucky to have been freed after General Abacha's death in office. Retired Maj.-Gen Yar'Adua had not been as lucky, as we saw. But perhaps the greatest sacrifice of all was that paid by the jailed civilian opposition leader Chief Abiola who would rather die in prison, than agree to be pressured into renouncing his June 12 mandate to rule.[22]

The Retired Military as Campaign Issue in Presidential Elections
The heroic role played by some of these top retired generals in the struggle for democracy did not however prevent the retired military question from becoming a campaign issue in the 1999 presidential election. For one reason or another, the widespread suspicion had been created that the outgoing regime would be more comfortable having a retired general for successor than a "bloody civilian". In a sense, such a suspicion was unfortunate as the Abubakar regime, in particular, had tried to be fair and presented the semblance of being impartial between any of the individuals or parties contesting for the presidency; and in fact, one of the reasons for not voting in the February 27, 1999 elections was not to give any appearance of having a preferred candidate.

Yet on Saturday October 3, 1998 took place an event that later proved significant for the role the top-most retired generals came to play in the Abubakar transition programme. Although reported by a number of the national dailies, the event concerned was allowed to pass without its significance being appreciated at the time. The new military head of state, General Abubakar, had invited most of the country's most retired military generals for a special parley on his democratisation programme and how best to move Nigeria forward.[23]

The meeting was called against the background of certain key considerations affecting the military profession in particular: (1) the military's much-battered public image, arising from the June 12 annulment crisis, various human right abuses, and the phenomenal corruption experienced under military rule; (2) the fears about what the pro-democracy agenda on "federal restructuring" might do to the military's corporate existence; (3) the rising demands for restitution being made by various groups and important individuals from the civilian populace; (4) the need for some guarantees of indeminity; and finally (5) how to consign the military to the barracks, or prevent them from returning to power, after the hand-over of May 27, 1999. It is expected that the Head of State General Abubakar, assisted by his deputy Vice Admiral Mike Akhigbe (Chief of General Staff), Air Vice Marshal Al-Amin Daggash (Chief of Defence Staff), the three service chiefs Maj.-Gen. Ishaya Bamaiyi (Chief of Army Staff), Air Vice Marshal N.E. Eduok (Chief of Air Staff), and Vice Admiral Jubril Ayinla (Chief of Naval Staff), as well as the Inspector-General of Police Ibrahim Coomasie, would have used the opportunity of the five-hour long private luncheon parley with the ex-military heads of state, ex-generals and ex-police chiefs to articulate those fears and concerns of the departing military and seek advice about allaying them.

Present at the meeting were Gen. Yakubu Gowon (rtd), Gen. Ibrahim Babangida (rtd), Maj.-Gen. Tunde Idiagbon (rtd) (now deceased), Commodore Ebitu Ukiwe (rtd), and Admiral Augustus Aikhomu (rtd). Other retired generals who attended the parley included Gen Domkat Bali (rtd), Vice-Admiral Murtala Nyako (rtd), Lt.-Gen. Theophilus Danjuma (rtd), Lt.-Gen. G.S. Jalo (rtd), Lt.-Gen. Mohammadu Wushishi (rtd), Maj.-Gen Chris Ali (rtd), Maj.-Gen. Anwali Kazir (rtd), and Maj.-Gen. Salihu Ibrahim (rtd). Others still were Vice-Admiral Akin Aduwo (rtd), Vice-Admiral Adelanwa (rtd), Vice-Admiral Dan Preston Omatsola (rtd), Rear Admiral Suleiman Saidu (rtd), Rear Admiral Allison Madueke (rtd), and Vice-Admiral Patrick Koshoni (rtd). Also present were Brig-Gen. G.T. Kusobe (rtd), Brig.-Gen. E.E. Ikwue, Air Vice Marshal A.B. Bello (rtd), Air Marshal Akin Dada (rtd), Air Vice Marshal Nureni Yusuf (rtd), Alhaji M.D. Yusuf (rtd), Alhaji A. Suleiman (rtd), Mr. Sunday Adewusi (rtd), Alhaji Aliyu Attah (rtd), Muhammadu Gambo (rtd), and Mr. Etim Inyang (rtd). The only two ex-military heads of state conspicuously absent from the October 3, 1998 meeting were General Olusegun Obasanjo (rtd) and Gen. Muhammadu Buhari (rtd). No explanation was provided why the two did not attend.[24] Of course, by the time of the parley, Obasanjo had yielded to the pressure to run and declared an interest in the presidency, and the campaign for attracting wide support for his candidacy was already on.

That the military question came to dominate the presidential election campaign, then, was not surprising. It became an issue for campaigning for electoral support both within the dominant People's Democratic Party (PDP) at the level of primaries and between that front-line party and its rival political opponents in the Alliance for Democracy/All People's Party (AD/APP) coalition. Demands for "military restructuring", as part of the larger question of federal political restructuring, had until now been a major plank in the pro-democracy movement's anti-military struggles as previously suggested. But, surprisingly, that particular military issue fizzled out of the campaign debates, and came to be replaced by two other things, namely the phenomenon of military mis-governance and continuation of military rule under whatever guise, including that by the retired military. The civilian contestants made it a central campaign point to distance themselves from the military as a regime, stressing rather their own civilian backgrounds, and in sharp contrast to what they charged as the militarist outlook on and approach to politics of their opponents from the class of retired generals.

It was the strategy adopted by the Second Republic Vice-President now turned Presidential aspirant Dr. Alex Ekwueme, campaigning for the PDP ticket against retired Gen. Obasanjo, and by Chief Olu Falae, as the joint AD/APP presidential candidate vis-a-vis both retired Gen. Obasanjo and the PDP. The many newspaper advertisements, placed in support of the two principal civilian contestants by the respective campaign directors, supporters and apologists, harped on this theme, stressing the difference between them and their opponents by the use of such civil/military ideological polarities, as "a truly civilian rule" vs. "militarised democracy" "a true civilian president" vs. "civilianised general", "the generals versus the people", voting "a real democrat for president" as opposed to "the military in *babanriga*".[25]

But perhaps the most powerful imagery in the civilian campaign rhetoric was the advertorial placed by the Falae team titled "It's Time For Change" and run in a number of the national dailies for a couple of days each. The said advertisement depicted a circle with a military beret at its centre, in which ruling military generals were seen handing over the baton of power to one another in a "vicious cycle of militarism" from 1976 to 1998. The only exception was the brief inter-regnum of the Shagari era. Were retired Gen. Obasanjo to be voted into power in 1999, the country would have returned a full circle to where it started some twenty-three years ago. Rather than go back, what the voters needed was to "change course", the advertorial warned.[26] It was convenient, of course, for the two top civilian contestants to forget that they also had some retired generals, even if not as many, within their own political ranks. Also, the ADD/APP ticket in particular was far from what one might describe as "100 percent civilian": Chief Falae's running mate, Alhaji Umaru Ali Shinkafi, was himself a former top police officer and Director-General of the National Security Organisation (NSO), a successor organisation to what is now known as State Security Service (SSS).

Retired Gen. Obasanjo and his campaign organisation countered those arguments by presenting the vote for his presidency as a vote for "a strong bridge between the North and South, civilian and military". To a charge about his unsuitability for office because of his previous military backgrounds, the Obasanjo campaign group had a ready-made response, "it is not the hood that makes the monk", listing cases of successful retired generals in various walks: a retired General who "joined NADECO", "fought for justice and democracy, and was hailed by all"; a retired General who "set up several companies, providing jobs for thousands of Nigerians" and "boosting Nigeria's economic development"; a retired General who "heads a special trust fund", instilling in the process "discipline in the management of resources", and "upgrades the nation's infrastructure"; a retired General who has just been "elected as APP Governor in Kwara State in preference to a "pure/100 percent civilian".[27] These reference were obviously to Lt-Gen. Akinrinade (rtd), Lt-Gen. Danjuma (rtd), Gen. Buhari (rtd), and Rear-Admiral Mohammed Lawal respectively. There was nothing bad in having another competent retired General in the person of Olusegun Obasanjo as a civilian head of state for fixing the country's myriad of problems, the particular advertorial insisted.[28]

Another related campaign rebuttal placed by a certain committee of friends for and on behalf of retired Gen.; Obasanjo, titled "every man according to his deeds", began by admitting that: "In every society, there are good men and bad men. Good professionals and bad professionals. Good politicians and bad politicians. In Nigeria, we have had good civilian governments and bad civilian governments, good military governments and bad military governments Truly, we have had bad soldiers and good soldiers". The good soldiers were listed to include Admiral Akinwale Wey, late Gen Usman Katsina, late Maj.-Gen Shehu Musa Yar'Adua, Lt.-Gen T.Y. Danjuma, Lt.-Gen. Alani Akinrinade, Commodore Ebitu Ukiwe, Rear Admiral Ndubisi Kanu, Colonel Abubakar Dangiwa Umar, and late Gen. Murtala Mohammed. The committee presented retired Gen. Obasanjo as coming from that "stock of distinguished officers".[29]

Finally, by his nomination on February 15, 1999 as the PDP flag-bearer and his subsequent election on February 27, 1999, as the next civilian president for post-military Nigeria, retired Gen. Obasanjo hoped he had through that feat succeeded in laying to rest the old polarity between soldiers and civilians. The acceptance speech that he gave at Jos, following his nomination as PDP presidential candidate, summarised his feelings about this: " A lot of heat, but unfortunately little light, has been generated by the debate over my being a retired soldier, as if it were a crime to have chosen a profession with the potential for supreme sacrifice for one's nation. Much of the debate has sought, perhaps understandably, to feed on the feeling of frustration and despair experienced under recent military regimes. Nevertheless, I am happy that by nominating me today as the PDP flag-bearer, we will have buried the illogical polarisation of the nation into soldiers and non-soldiers. It would have been a great disservice to the cause of democracy to create the impression among serving officers and men that a future role in politics, as civilians, was foreclosed for them by an argument unsupported by the constitution".[30]

The import of that statement could not have been lost to anyone - a triumphalist statement made for and on behalf of the retired military elite announcing its arrival as a power factor on Nigeria's political scene. But a triumphalist statement is one thing, pronouncing "the end of history" to the military question is quite another. Perhaps, for those millions of Nigerian voters who expect, by the sheer fact of retired Gen. Obasanjo's victory at the presidential polls, to have succeeded in finally exorcising the spectre of the military problem from the body politic, it may be a bit too early to so pronounce. It is better to allow the future to be its own judge.

NOTES

1.   Reference is to the widespread irregularities, manipulations and fraud alleged to have been perpetrated in the conduct of the February 27, 1999 presidential elections and some of which came to be attested to by independent national bodies and international election monitoring groups. The defeated presidential candidate of the All People Party (APP), Chief Olu Falae, has since filed a petition at the Federal Appeal Court, Abuja; on March 15, 1999 contesting the election of retired General Obasanjo as president. The full text of the grounds of the petition can be found in *ThisDay* (Lagos), March 16, 1999, pp. 2, 3, & 28.

2.   Representing Abia North, Kogi West, Benue zone 'C', Niger North senatorial districts respectively.

3.   From Oyo North.

4.   See *The Punch* (Lagos), January 29, 1999, pp. 1–2.

5.   For the analogy, see Karl Marx, *The Eighteenth Brumaire of Louis Bonaparte*, Fourth Printing, New York: International Publishers, 1968.

6.   See Samuel E. Finer, *The Man on Horseback*, London: Pall Mall, 1962.

7.   J. 'Bayo Adekanye, *Military Occupation and Social Stratification: An Inaugural Lecture*, Ibadan: Vantage Publishers, for University of Ibadan.

8.   The analysis of the next few paragraphs of the Addendum is taken directly from J. Adekanye, "The Military in Transition", in Larry Diamond, A. Kirk-Greene and Oyeleye Oyediran (eds) *Transition Without End: Nigerian Politics and Civil Society Under Babangida*, Ibadan: Vantage Publishers, 1997, pp. 39-40.

9.   The circumstances referred to were part of the so-called "Bali affair" discussed in *ibid*, p. 49ff

10. See Nyaknno Osso (ed), *Who's Who*, Lagos: Newswatch Communications Limited, 1990, pp. 215, 408.

11. *Nigerian Tribune* (Ibadan), Thursday February 18, 1999, p.21.

12. P. Lewis, & H. Stein, "Shifting Fortunes: The Political Economy of Financial Liberalisation in Nigeria", *World Development*, Vol. 25, No. 1, January 1997.

13. Adejumo Said, "The Military as Economic Manager: The Babangida Regime and Structural Adjustment Programme, Department of Political Science, University of Ibadan, *Draft* Ph.D Thesis.

14. *ibid.*
15. *ibid.*
16. Or could it have been because of this? It is possible that a number of the appointments to government-owned companies, taking place just before or a little after their privatisation was about to start, could have facilitated the conversion or take-over of some of the nationalised sectors of the economy as private property.
17. For more details on the particular example and other related matters, see Ednut Egavas, "The Role of Union Dicon Salt Plc in Economic Development of Nigeria", *The Guardian,* Tuesday January 9, 1999, p.56
18. Larry Diamond, A. Kirk-Greene and Oyeleye Oyediran, eds., *Transition Without End..., op.cit.*
19. See Benjamin Adesina Bejide, "Fabrication of Phantom Coups as a Strategy of Eliminating Opposition Elements under the Abacha Military Regime in Nigeria", Department of Political Science, University of Ibadan: B.Sc Thesis, February 1999.
20. The brief analysis of the June 12 crisis and its underlying issues provided here is summarise from the author's larger study, see J. 'Bayo Adekanye, "Debt, Democratisation and Conflict: The Nigerian Case", in Patrik Eklof (ed.) *Africa Yearbook 1996/97 Theme: Debt, Structural Adjustment, and Conflict,* Oslo: Norwegian Council for Africa, 1996, pp. 147-170.
21. The fact of the matter is that, until the most recent election of General Obasanjo to the presidency, political and military figures from the North, particularly the Hausa-Fulani and Kanuri from the "Far" North, have dominated the government for much of the country's history since independence. Of the ten heads of government produced at the Federal level, eight have been Northerners, and only three Southerners; and of the eight from the North, as many as four have belonged to the Hausa-Fulani group (Balewa, Murtala, Shagari, Buhari), and three from groups with a long history of "super-tribalisation" with the Hausa-Fulani group and certainly all Hausa-speaking (Babangida, Abacha and most recently Abubakar), and only one (Gowon) from the minority-ethnic areas of the Middle-Belt and a Christian. All the three Southerners until now opportuned to rule (Ironsi, Obasanjo and Shonekan) were products of military circumstances, with one of them (Shonekan) generally perceived to have been planted as a tool of continuing the Hausa-Fulani scheme. June 12, 1993 presented the prospect of the first Southern civilian leader on his own making a bid for the presidency and, without being helped, taking control of government after winning a country-wide mandate; and apparently some powerful Hausa-Fulani interests were unhappy about that potential change in the locus of power and sought to use a segment of the military high command to block Abiola's accession to the presidency.
22. Held by the security since June 1994, Chief M.K.O. Abiola died in prison albeit under mysterious circumstances (June 15, 1998), and eight days after his chief

captor General Abacha had himself expired (June 8, 1998) and General Abubakar had taken over the mantle of headship.

23. It was reported under the caption, for example, of "Abubakar hosts ex-leaders, ex-military, police chiefs", in *The Guardian* (Lagos), Monday October 5, 1998, 4.

24. *ibid.*

25. For a few representative publications carrying advertorials along these lines, see *The Guardian* (Lagos), February 7, 1999, p.35; *The Guardian* (Lagos), February 7, 1999, p.10; *The Guardian* (Lagos), February 7, 1999, p.11; *Nigerian Tribune* (Ibadan), February, 1999, p.29; *Nigerian Tribune* 25, 1999, p.7.

26. *Nigerian Tribune* (Ibadan), February 25, 1999, p.10; *Nigerian Tribune* (Ibadan), February 26, 1999, p.9; *The Punch* (Lagos), February 26, 1999, p.11.

27. *The Guardian* (Lagos), February 12, 1999, p.38.

28. *ibid.*

29. *Vanguard* (Lagos), February 2, 1999, p.14. See also *The Guardian* (Lagos), February 7, 1999, p.7; *Nigerian Tribune* (Ibadan), February 25, 1999, p.6; *The Punch* (Lagos), February 26, 1999, p.30.

30. Text of full acceptance speech is published in *The Guardian* (Lagos), February 16, 1999, p.7.

Index

www.ingramcontent.com/pod-product-compliance
Lightning Source LLC
Chambersburg PA
CBHW081433270326
41932CB00019B/3191